TEST DRIVE THE MICROSOFT® PRIVATE CLOUD

RON CARSWELL

Cengage Learning PTR

CENGAGE
Learning®

Professional • Technical • Reference

Australia • Brazil • Japan • Korea • Mexico • Singapore • Spain • United Kingdom • United States

Professional • Technical • Reference

**Test Drive the Microsoft®
Private Cloud
Ron Carswell**

**Publisher and General Manager,
Cengage Learning PTR:** Stacy L. Hiquet

Associate Director of Marketing:
Sarah Panella

Manager of Editorial Services:
Heather Talbot

Product Manager: Heather Hurley

Project and Copy Editor: Marta Justak

Technical Reviewer: David Acosta

Interior Layout Tech: MPS Limited

Cover Designer: Luke Fletcher

Indexer: Valerie Haynes Perry

Proofreader: Sam Garvey

Library of Congress Control Number: 2014949528

ISBN-13: 978-1-285-87445-6

ISBN-10: 1-285-87445-5

Cengage Learning PTR

20 Channel Center Street

Boston, MA 02210

USA

Cengage Learning is a leading provider of customized learning solutions with office locations around the globe, including Singapore, the United Kingdom, Australia, Mexico, Brazil, and Japan. Locate your local office at: **international.cengage.com/region**.

Cengage Learning products are represented in Canada by Nelson Education, Ltd.

For your lifelong learning solutions, visit **cengageptr.com**.

Visit our corporate website at **cengage.com**.

Printed in the United States of America
1 2 3 4 5 6 7 16 15 14

ACKNOWLEDGMENTS

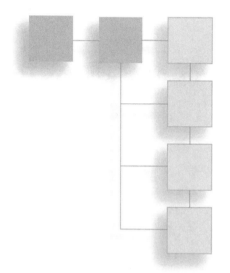

This book is a product of many talented people. First, I want to give a well-deserved pat on the back to the staff at Cengage Learning, especially my product manager, Heather Hurley, for her patience and help. And, of course, thanks to my editor, Marta Justak, for providing the inspiration to mold thoughts clearly and concisely. I also would like to thank my technical editor, David Acosta, for the numerous hours he devoted to proofing the text and testing each exercise. A special thanks to a cohort of Microsoft private cloud students at San Antonio College (Ann L. Acker, Michael Brisko, Jeffery Escobedo, Carl Faulkner, Carlos Fernandez, Regina Fonderburk, David Hastings, Keith Lyons, Mario J. Solivan, and Kristin Wilburn), who worked through the exercises in the initial drafts of this book and enhanced the quality of this book. And, last but not least, I thank my wife Coleen for the hours I spent away in the "man cave" with the private cloud.

About the Author

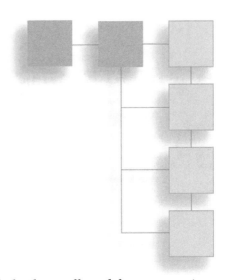

With more than 20 years of computer experience with both small and large organizations, **Ron Carswell** is a practically focused, proficient writer and successful instructor. Mr. Carswell is professor emeritus at San Antonio College, where he has instructed students in Microsoft Server Administration and other courses for numerous years. In addition to this book, Professor Carswell has authored or coauthored numerous successful books on Microsoft Windows and Microsoft Windows servers, Parallel Operating Systems with Windows and Linux, Virtual PC and Virtual Server, and C++ and other related computing topics. His previous book was *Guide to Supporting Microsoft Private Clouds*. Professor Carswell holds a BBA from the University of Texas and an MBA from Baylor University. He has also earned A+, Network+, CTT+, MCSA, MCSE, MCDST, and MCITP certifications.

Contents

Chapter 3

Chapter 4

INTRODUCTION

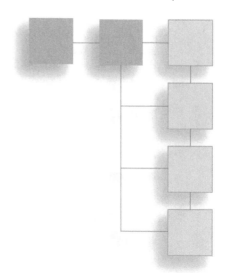

Welcome to *Test Drive the Microsoft Private Cloud*. This book prepares system administrators who want to explore Microsoft's private cloud technology. By following the detailed instructions, you will be able to implement and evaluate a Microsoft private cloud in a test environment.

An IDC study presented the first five-year forecast for the worldwide private cloud IT infrastructure market in April of 2013. It estimated that this market totaled $12.3 billion in 2012 and will increase to more than $22.2 billion by 2017.

"Demand for private cloud IT infrastructure continues to grow rapidly as enterprise customers increasingly see cloud as the next logical step beyond datacenter virtualization," explains Mary Johnston Turner, IDC research vice president, Enterprise Systems Management Software.

Readers of this book deploy Windows Server 2012 R2. In addition, readers will use Hyper-V Manager, System Center Virtual Machine Manager (SCVMM) 2012 R2, and System Center Application Controller (SCAC) 2012 R2 to implement a Microsoft private cloud. Readers will develop the skills to implement the following Microsoft private cloud technologies:

- **Hyper-V virtualization:** Creates and manages a virtualized server computing environment.

- **Virtual Machine Manager:** Manages a series of host computers and virtual machines from a central console.

- **Fabric resources:** Provides the building blocks for the provision of virtual machines' host groups, the VMM library, networking, and storage elements, which are all part of the fabric resources.

- **Virtual machine networks:** Provides network isolation, which restricts network access to the proper sets of virtual machines.

- **iSCSI Target server:** Supports a storage area network (SAN) to store virtual machines.

- **Hyper-V Cluster:** Provides high availability by creating failover clusters out of separate physical computers.

- **Self-Service User Roles:** Defines the scope of management operations for tenant and application user roles.

- **Application Controller:** Manages applications that are deployed in private clouds.

- **PowerShell:** Provides a new Windows command-line shell designed especially for server administrators to create scripts for administrative tasks.

HARDWARE OVERVIEW

Figure I.1 shows the network diagram for the private cloud pod implemented in this book. The private cloud implementation requires three servers. The cluster consists of two servers (COMPUTE1 and COMPUTE2) that provide fault tolerance for the virtual machines. A third server (MANAGE) manages the virtual machines in the private cloud. Around the periphery are network switches and routers that support the four required networks (Heartbeat, Storage, Management, and Service). For more detailed information see the "Hardware Components" section in Chapter 1, "Introduction to the Private Cloud."

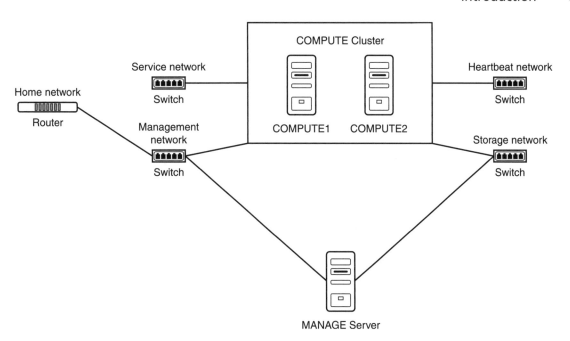

Figure I.1
Hardware diagram for the private cloud.
© 2014 Cengage Learning®.

OVERVIEW

Windows Server 2012 R2 Datacenter Edition will be installed on each of the three servers. On the MANAGE server, you will install Hyper-V, Active Directory Domain Services (AD DS), and Domain Name Service (DNS). On the COMPUTE1 and COMPUTE2 servers, you will install Hyper-V. Windows Server 2012 R2 will be installed in a virtual machine to provide access to virtual machines. Hyper-V and Windows Server Failover Clustering will be installed on the two cluster servers. Windows Server Failover is designed to allow servers to work together as a computer cluster, which provides failover and increased availability of applications. For more detailed information on these software components, see the "Software Components" section in Chapter 1, "Introduction to the Private Cloud."

INTENDED AUDIENCE

Test Drive the Microsoft Private Cloud is intended for administrators to develop the skills to implement the Microsoft private cloud. Think of this book as the tool to implement a "proof of concept" private cloud. By following the detailed instructions, you will learn the skills to implement and evaluate the Microsoft private cloud for your organization.

CHAPTER DESCRIPTIONS

The book contains the following 10 chapters:

- Chapter 1, "Introduction to the Private Cloud," defines the private cloud terminology including server virtualization. You will complete exercises to install Windows Server 2012 R2 and add Hyper-V virtualization for three servers.

- Chapter 2, "The Microsoft Private Cloud," describes Microsoft's private cloud strategy and the components for System Center Virtual Machine Manager (SCVMM) 2012 R2. You'll identify the requirements required by VMM and install the VMM prerequisites. The last step will be to install the VMM server.

- Chapter 3, "Configuring the Fabric Resources," describes fabric resources that you will use to build your private cloud. You will set up the COMPUTE1 and COMPUTE2 servers as the COMPUTE resource. The VMM Library holds resources that you can use to build virtual machines, so you will start to populate your library.

- Chapter 4, "Working with Networks Using VMM," shows how VMM maps logical networks to physical networks for host computers. Building on these concepts, you will learn how these logical networks will be extended as VM networks are made available for virtual machines. Then you can learn the steps to fine-tune your VM networks to provide optimal efficiency.

- Chapter 5, "Working with VMM Storage," describes how VMM implements storage. You'll install the Microsoft iSCSI target server to support a storage area network (SAN), which provides storage for the COMPUTE resource in your private cloud. You will learn to use VMM to manage the storage resource and provide storage for the COMPUTE host computers for your private cloud.

- Chapter 6, "Creating the Hyper-V Cluster," describes the concepts related to the Hyper-V cluster. One of the benefits of Hyper-V is the Hyper-V cluster, which supports high availability by creating failover clusters out of separate physical computers. First, you will learn to build the Hyper-V cluster. Then to test it, you'll perform a live migration and simulate a failover.

- Chapter 7, "Creating the Private Cloud," shows how to use the resources created in the previous chapters to create the private cloud. You will create User Roles that control the actions, such as create, start, or shutdown, which self-service users can take while working with their virtual machines in a private cloud.

- Chapter 8, "Working with Application Self-Service Users," continues with the actions of the tenant administrator and implements the application self-user role. A key component for the application self-service user to gain access to virtual machines is the App Controller. Microsoft provides App Controller as a product for managing applications that are deployed in private clouds. In this chapter, you will install and configure it.

- Chapter 9, "Introducing PowerShell," describes PowerShell, which is a new Windows command-line shell designed especially for server administrators. You have been using PowerShell scripts, starting with Chapter 2. VMM creates and executes PowerShell scripts for administrative tasks. In this chapter, you will increase your ability to simplify tasks using PowerShell 4.0.

- Chapter 10, "Working with PowerShell Scripts," you'll learn how to manage virtual machines, create user accounts, and deploy virtual machines with the PowerShell scripts for repetitive tasks. This is the second of two chapters on PowerShell.

SPECIAL FEATURES

Test Drive the Microsoft Private Cloud differs from other books on private clouds. The book provides the skills to create a working private cloud. Each chapter builds on the previous chapter in a linear fashion.

- **Chapter objectives:** Each chapter begins with a list of the concepts to be mastered. This list provides a quick reference to the chapter's contents.

- **Tutorials:** Tutorials are incorporated throughout the book to give you a strong foundation for carrying out tasks to build your private cloud. Because the tutorials build on each other, you should complete the tutorials in each chapter before moving on to the subsequent chapters.

- **Chapter summaries:** Each chapter ends with a summary of concepts introduced in the chapter. These summaries provide a helpful way to recap and revisit the chapter's ideas.

- **Case projects:** Each chapter closes with a section that asks you to explore real-world situations. These projects provide an opportunity to expand your knowledge beyond the contents of each chapter.

ERRATA AND BOOK SUPPORT

We have made every effort to ensure the accuracy of this textbook. Any errors reported since publication are listed on the Cengage Learning website at www.cengageptr.com. To find the list after accessing the site, enter "Test Drive the Microsoft Private Cloud" in the Go box.

THE AUTHOR WANTS TO HEAR FROM YOU

As you are working with this book and you need a tip or a question answered, you can send an email to the author at carswellprivatecloud@gmail.com.

COMPANION WEBSITE DOWNLOADS

For additional information about the private cloud, check out the author's website at carswellprivatecloud.org.

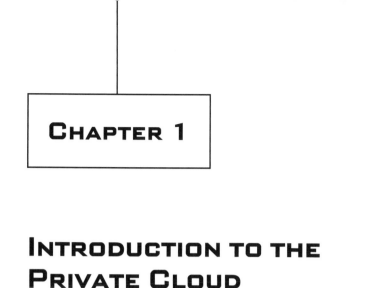

CHAPTER 1

INTRODUCTION TO THE PRIVATE CLOUD

After reading this chapter and completing the exercises, you will be able to do the following:

- Describe the transition to the private cloud.
- Describe the Hyper-V virtualization environment.
- Install the virtualization host servers.
- Install the Hyper-V Role.
- Create and configure a virtual machine.

This book explains how to implement a private cloud—a computing platform that operates behind a private organization's firewall under the control of the information technology (IT) department. Cloud computing is the use of multiple server computers on a digital network that work together as if they were one computer. Virtualization is the use of software to simulate a physical computing environment and the use of virtual hardware on which you can install a number of OSs and interact with them.

THE TRANSITION TO THE PRIVATE CLOUD

In this section, you will learn about the transition to the private cloud. Virtualization permits server consolidation, which allows the operating systems of multiple physical servers to be run as virtual machines. This consolidation initiates the transition to the private cloud within the data center. The user interface to applications transforms from client/ server computing to the client Web.

Making the Transition to Virtualization

In the past, a server application could not be created without purchasing server hardware, an operating system, and the application software, which is illustrated in Figure 1.1. This purchase of the hardware and software delayed the build out of the server. Depending on the vendor and server model, you might have experienced delays of up to 30–45 days. You needed to purchase a system license to install and activate the operating system. Likewise, you purchased a license for each application from a software vendor, which permitted the application to be installed on one server. A problem that you might have encountered was how to explain these delays to anxious future users of these servers.

Server

Figure 1.1
Server with installed software.
© 2014 Cengage Learning®.

As the organization expanded and new applications were required, additional servers were added to the data center. This extra equipment resulted in a phenomenon called *server sprawl* (see Figure 1.2). Another issue with server sprawl was the lack of efficient use of processor resources. The percentage of processor time and the percentage of time that the processor was executing non-idle threads could fall to 20 percent or less.

As the demand for data storage increased, storage devices were added. These storage devices permitted multiple servers to store massive amounts of data. Data packets flowed between the servers and the storage units. Each data volume residing on the storage units was identified by a logical unit number (LUN). The storage units deployed redundant array of independent disks (RAID) technologies to provide data redundancy and performance improvements.

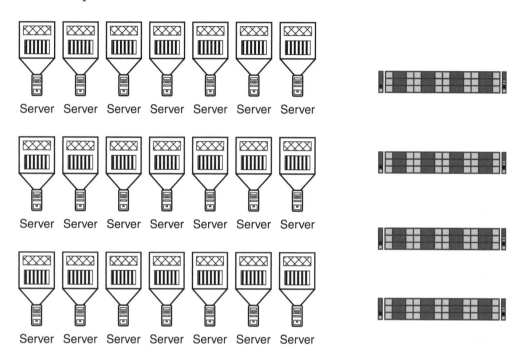

Figure 1.2
Server sprawl.
© 2014 Cengage Learning®.

Server Virtualization

Currently, server virtualization provides a way to reduce server sprawl while reducing the time to deploy a server with the required operating system (OS) and applications software. With virtualization technology, you can run a range of OSs on top of the host operating system.

Figure 1.3 provides a high-level overview of how server virtualization is used to deploy a hypervisor. The hypervisor allows multiple operating systems, called *guests*, (or guest operating systems) to run concurrently on a host computer. In the figure, the base layer represents the hardware within the physical computer, including the system board, memory, disk, network, and other hardware components. The hypervisor is so named because it is conceptually one level higher than a supervisory program. The hypervisor presents a virtual operating platform for the guest operating systems, and it manages their execution. Multiple instances of different operating systems can share the virtualized hardware resources. Hypervisors are installed on dedicated server hardware that exists only to run guest operating systems. Hyper-V is the Microsoft hypervisor.

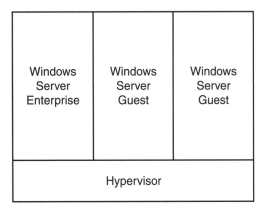

Figure 1.3
Overview of server virtualization.
© 2014 Cengage Learning®.

A standard hardware system environment, which imitates the function of a computer system, is provided within each virtual machine for each guest OS. The OS and software within each virtual machine are unaware of the other virtual machines and have full access to the virtual platform.

If you need to install a new OS in a traditional system, you must purchase a new computer, install an additional hard drive, create a partition on the existing hard drive, or remove and replace your existing OS. Virtualization permits the installation of a new OS on an existing computer system without disrupting the previous OS. Because each virtual machine uses the same standard hardware, you can save time by copying a standard system image for use by this virtual machine. The system image contains the operating system and related files, installed applications, and configuration preferences. This standard image would be available in a library of previously installed virtual machines.

Making the Transition to Private Cloud

In the past, a document could not be created without application software installed on the user's computer. A license for each application was purchased from a software vendor, which permitted the application to be installed on one computer system. The introduction of local area networks (LANs), which connect computers in close proximity, led to the creation of the client/server model. In this model, server computers with enhanced capabilities and large storage devices could be used to store data for multiple users.

To enable the client to access data stored on the server, a network-aware version of the application was installed on client computers, and the application used the client system's memory and CPU for processing. Rather than storing documents and other data files on the clients, the files were stored on data servers. This model also required the purchase of multi-user licenses.

The basic concept of cloud computing represents a major transition from the client/server model. Cloud computing provides applications from a server that are executed and managed by a client's Web browser. No applications are required on the client computer. Cloud service providers have complete control over the browser-based applications, eliminating the need for version upgrades or license management on client computers. The term *Software as a Service* (SaaS) is sometimes used to describe the application programs offered through cloud computing services. These services, or the aggregation of all existing cloud services, are sometimes simply called the *cloud*.

Any computer or Web-friendly device connected to the Internet can access the same pool of computing power, applications, and files in a cloud computing environment, as shown in Figure 1.4. You can remotely store and access personal files that contain music, pictures, videos, and documents. You can also perform word-processing tasks on a remote server. Data is centrally stored, so you do not need to use a storage medium such as a thumb drive. As an employee of a private company, you can also use the company's customized cloud email servers, such as Microsoft Exchange.

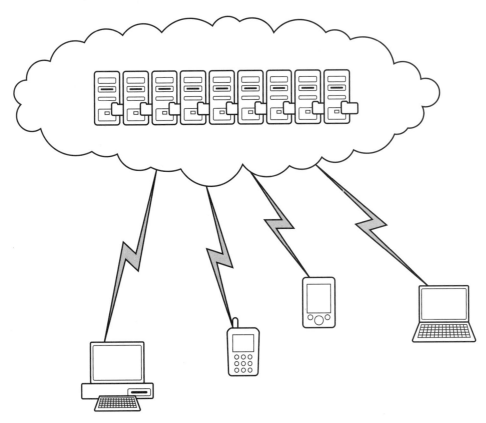

Figure 1.4
Cloud computing using Web devices.
© 2014 Cengage Learning®.

A traditional Web application runs on a single computer or a group of privately owned computers. Such computers are powerful enough to serve a certain number of requests per minute and can provide an acceptable response time for Web requests. If a website or Web application suddenly becomes more popular, the increased traffic can overwhelm the Web server, and the response time of the requested pages will increase from the overload. On the other hand, much of the server's capacity is unused when demand is low.

By contrast, if the website or Web application is hosted in a public cloud, additional processing and computing power is available within the cloud. If a website suddenly becomes more popular, the cloud can automatically direct more individual computers to serve pages for the site. If the site loses popularity, the cloud will scale down the number of servers to reduce the cost of service. The website might share the cloud servers with thousands of other websites of varying sizes and memory. Cloud computing is also popular for its "pay-as-you-go" pricing model.

A private cloud is designed to offer the same features and benefits of public cloud systems, and it removes a number of objections to the cloud computing model, including control over enterprise and customer data, worries about security, and issues of regulatory compliance.

Figure 1.5 shows a hybrid cloud in which the public cloud supplements the power of the private cloud. The hybrid cloud approach is effective when the private cloud is not capable of scaling to meet the needs of an infrequent event, such as increased online sales on "Black Friday," the day after Thanksgiving in the United States. In such cases, the private cloud will offload sales transactions for the peak sales period to a public cloud.

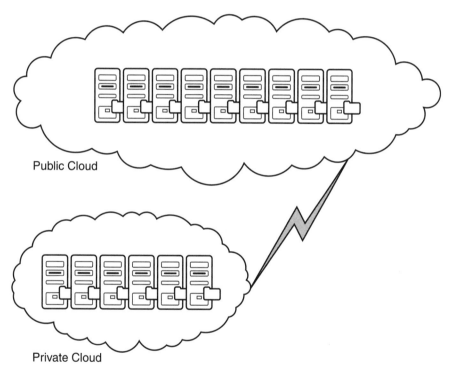

Figure 1.5
Hybrid cloud.
© 2014 Cengage Learning®.

Storage Virtualization

Within a network, a file server is a computer that has the primary purpose of providing a location for shared disk access. The term *server* highlights its role in the client/server scheme, in which clients are workstations accessing the shared storage. A file server is not intended to run applications for its clients.

Network-attached storage (NAS) is file-level data storage on a computer network that provides data access to clients. Unlike a general-purpose file server, a NAS is a specialized computer built specifically for serving files. NAS systems usually contain two or more hard drives that are combined and arranged in RAID arrays.

Multiple disk drives can work together as a team to form a disk array (see Figure 1.6). Data that is frequently needed is retrieved from a cache. The temporary memory of the cache is faster than the magnetic disks. Redundant components such as RAID, processing modules, and power supplies increase availability.

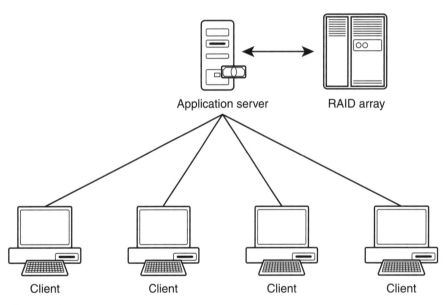

Figure 1.6
Disk array.
© 2014 Cengage Learning®.

Disk arrays also can be consolidated into a storage area network (SAN). A SAN, as shown in Figure 1.7, connects RAID arrays so that all data appears to be stored in a single source. This approach is much easier than managing individual disks on multiple servers. Using a SAN, system administration tasks such as disk replacement and routine backups are easier to manage and schedule. In some SANs, disk arrays can be automated to copy data to other disks for backup without requiring processing at the servers.

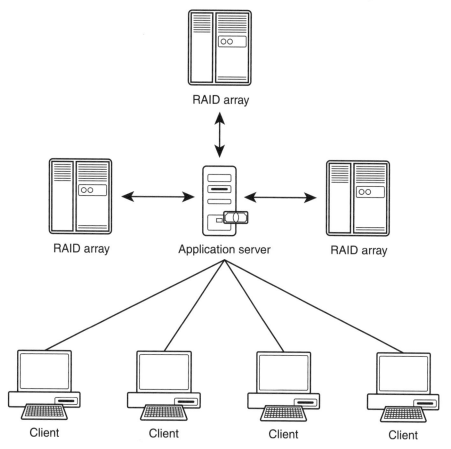

Figure 1.7
SAN.

A SAN uses the principle of storage virtualization, which handles storage as a unified whole. In this system, the locations of available physical media are not important. Storage virtualization enables virtual machines to use data from a unified storage entity rather than individual disks, which permits more flexibility in the management of storage. A logical unit number (LUN) is a unique identifier used to designate a unit of storage. Although a LUN represents a single client connection, the connection can be made to part of a hard disk, a whole hard drive, or even multiple hard drives. As storage requirements change, LUNs can be adjusted in size, which makes storage easier to manage.

Storage virtualization works well for migrating LUNs from one disk array to another without downtime (see Figure 1.8).

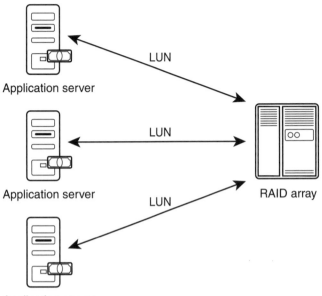

Application server

LUN

Application server

LUN

RAID array

LUN

Application server

Figure 1.8
Virtualized storage.
© 2014 Cengage Learning®.

The Internet Small Computer System Interface (iSCSI) is an IP-based storage networking standard for linking host computers to data storage facilities. The protocol allows clients, called *initiators*, to send SCSI commands to SCSI storage arrays. Fibre Channel provides connectivity similar to iSCSI but uses fiber optic or copper cables.

You can use thin provisioning with storage virtualization. In this approach, you can create LUNs for new servers in the system but assign more disk space on those servers than the actual amount of space configured for the SAN. For instance, a Windows 2012 R2 Server that hosts your database may appear to have 100GB allocated for data storage when only a small percentage of that capacity is actually allocated. Over time, up to 10GB might be used as the database file is populated. If so, you can save up to 90GB of disk space but still be able to store more data on the LUN without taking further action.

Network Virtualization

A virtual LAN (VLAN) is a group of PCs, servers, and switches that appear to be connected to a single, logical network segment, even though they may not be. The resources and servers of other users on the physical network are invisible to other VLAN members. However, there is much more to network virtualization than just VLANs.

In network virtualization, a computer network's resources and client/server system are combined and put on a virtual network. This network treats all hardware and software as a single collection of resources that can be accessed regardless of physical boundaries. This globalized approach requires using routers and switches to perform more services, such as access control, path isolation, and edge services. Internet Protocol security (IPsec) is an example of an edge service that secures IP communications by authenticating and encrypting each IP packet of a communication session. Routers and switches support globalization.

Clustering

Clustering means connecting multiple computers to make them work as a unified system (see Figure 1.9). Clustering increases a computer system's load balancing and redundancy.

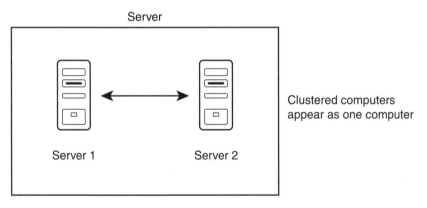

Figure 1.9
Clustered computers.
© 2014 Cengage Learning®.

Load balancing distributes processing across multiple servers, which is important when you do not know how many requests to expect for a group of servers or when the requests will arrive. Load balancing might allocate incoming requests evenly to all servers, or it might send requests to the next available server.

Redundancy is the ability of a cluster to respond gracefully to an unexpected hardware or software failure. Failover is the capability to switch to a redundant or standby server automatically when the active server fails. Failover automation occurs using a heartbeat network of two servers. Essentially, the second server monitors the main server, and it will immediately begin executing the functions of the main server if it detects a failure.

Role-Based Security

In addition to file-based security permissions, virtualization requires a new approach called *role-based security* that provides finer control over permissions in a virtualized environment. In this approach, groups of virtual machine instances determine which machines are available for particular user tasks. Administrators specify the operations that a user can perform for a group in which the user has membership. For example, when a user starts a virtual machine, a check is made to verify that the user has permission to do so.

For a specific example of role-based security, consider the self-service user role. Members of this role can manage their virtual machines under certain controls. The user is given a simplified view of his virtual machines and the tasks he can execute with them. These operations might include creating virtual machines that use particular templates and ISO image files. The role also can be used with a quota to limit the number of virtual machines that are available to a user.

Examples of Cloud Computing Services

Four types of services are available from a cloud service provider:

- **Infrastructure as a Service (IaaS):** In this approach, the service provider pays for servers, network equipment, storage, and backups. Customers pay only for the service, which allows them to build applications on the cloud without using their own company's computer resources. Amazon offers IaaS; the company characterizes its service as Amazon Elastic Compute Cloud (Amazon EC2), "a Web service that provides resizable comput[ing] capacity in the cloud." Rapid provisioning contributes to Amazon's ability to scale up by adding virtual machines to meet increased demand.

- **Platform as a Service (PaaS):** This service provider offers business solutions for users. For example, Salesforce.com distributes business software on a subscription basis and is best known for its customer relationship management (CRM) products. CRM aids sales personnel by tracking customers and sales while providing analytical reports.

- **Software as a Service (SaaS):** Customers pay to use the service provider's software, particularly application software. An example of SaaS is Google Apps, which provides a wide range of office applications such as mail, word processing, spreadsheets, and presentations from the Web.

- **Storage as a Service (STaaS):** Similar to IaaS, STaaS providers rent space in their storage infrastructure. Typically, this storage is used for off-site backups. Examples of this service are Carbonite and iDrive. Backups can be scheduled to occur when the local computer is not required for processing.

INSTALLING THE VIRTUALIZATION HOST SERVERS

In this section, you'll review the hardware and software requirements for your implementation of the private cloud. After verifying that you have the components available, you can cable the hardware components. With this completed, you are ready to install the OS on your three host computers.

Computer Hardware Requirements

Virtualization requires specific hardware to make the host computer's operating systems function properly. This section provides hardware requirements for three servers, networks, and the storage that will be needed to complete this exercise.

Figure 1.10 provides an overview of hardware requirements to build the private cloud referenced in this book. The private cloud implementation requires three servers. The cluster consists of two servers (COMPUTE1 and COMPUTE2) that provide fault tolerance for the virtual machines. A third server (MANAGE) manages the virtual machines in the private cloud. Around the periphery are network switches and routers that support the four required networks (Heartbeat, Storage, Management, and Service).

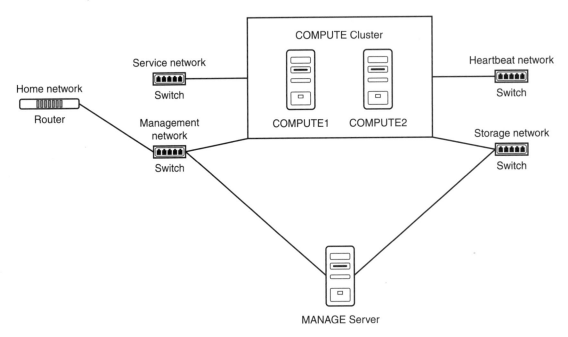

Figure 1.10
Hardware diagram for the private cloud.
© 2014 Cengage Learning®.

Dynamic Host Configuration Protocol (DHCP) and Network Address Translation (NAT) are required for the network. DHCP assigns dynamic IP configurations to devices on a network. NAT enables networks to use one set of IP addresses for internal traffic and a second set of addresses for external traffic. A home router provides this support for the three servers.

Processor Requirements

You'll find that X86 virtualization allows multiple operating systems to simultaneously share processor resources safely and efficiently. This virtualization is used to simulate a complete hardware environment, or virtual machine, where an unmodified guest operating system executes. Virtualization was added to most ×86 processors (Intel VT-x or AMD-V) in 2006.

To use hardware virtualization, the VT-x or AMD-V option must be enabled in the BIOS. You can access the BIOS settings menu by pressing the appropriate key (perhaps F2 or Delete) as the start-up flash screen is displayed. The BIOS settings for Intel VT or AMD-V are usually in the Chipset or Security menu.

Memory Requirements

The amount of memory required for effective processing is determined by the number of virtual machines that will run concurrently. Running Windows Server 2012 R2 requires at least 512MB of RAM; 1GB of RAM is suggested. To start the Hyper-V hypervisor, you need almost 300MB of memory. A good standard for determining the memory overhead of each virtual machine is to start with 32MB for the first 1GB of virtual RAM, and then add 8MB for each additional GB of virtual RAM. Use this standard when calculating how many virtual machines to host on a physical server.

Networking Requirements

The number of network adapter cards you need is determined by the minimum number of networks required for the creation of private clouds. To complete the exercises in this book, the following networks are required. (Color-coded cables are recommended to make device connection easier.)

- **Management:** Monitors and manages the host computers and virtual machines in the cluster. Blue cables are recommended.

- **Storage:** Provides shared storage for the virtual machines in the cluster. Green cables are recommended.

- **Heartbeat:** Communicates between the host computers in the cluster. Red cables are recommended.

- **Service:** Communicates between virtual machines running on each host computer. Yellow cables are recommended.

Most computers have one or perhaps two network adapters, but you will need a total of four adapters. Four gigabit Ethernet switches are required for the networks.

Storage Requirements

As you learned earlier, a SAN is a dedicated network that provides access to consolidated data storage. The iSCSI protocol supports the storage requirements for the lab activities in this book. You will learn more about iSCSI in Chapter 5, "Working with VMM Storage."

The disk controller in your host computer uses block-level access to read and write to the disks that are attached internally within the computer. In a SAN, where disks are external to the servers, read/write access is also at the block level. When connected to a SAN, disks appear to the operating system as resident (installed locally) to the computer. These devices can be partitioned and formatted with Windows Server 2012 R2 tools.

To conserve costs, this book uses Microsoft iSCSI Software Target Server to provide an iSCSI-based SAN. The iSCSI Software Target Server is available in Microsoft Windows Server 2012 R2. If you have an iSCSI SAN available, you do not need to install the iSCSI Software Target Server.

Installing the Virtualization Services

Using Table 1.1, complete the inventory and place checks in the Mark column to indicate that the hardware components are available.

Table 1.1   Hardware Inventory Worksheet

Mark	Quantity	Item Description
	2	Cluster Servers (COMPUTE1 and COMPUTE2) with minimum of 8GB of RAM memory and four RJ-45 network connections
	1	MANAGE server with minimum of 12GB of RAM memory and two RJ45 network connections. One additional hard drive of at least 1TB (1,000 gigabytes)
	4	5-port network gigabit switches with power supplies
	4	Blue network cables
	3	Green network cables
	2	Red network cables
	3	Yellow network cables
	1	LCD panel
	1	KVM switch with three cable sets (if required, a power supply)
	1	Keyboard
	1	Mouse
	2	6-outlet power strips

Wait to Insert Cables

Do *not* place network cables in the servers or switches until you are instructed to do so in future steps. You can't count on Windows Server to identify the network adapters in the same sequence on each host computer.

Computer Software Requirements

Windows Server 2012 R2 Datacenter Edition will be installed on each of the three servers. On the MANAGE server, you will install Hyper-V, Active Directory Domain Services (AD DS), and Domain Name Service (DNS). On the COMPUTE1 and COMPUTE2 servers, you will install Hyper-V. Windows Server 2012 R2 will be installed in a virtual machine to provide access to virtual machines. Hyper-V and Windows Server Failover Clustering will be installed on the two cluster servers. Windows Server Failover is designed to allow servers to work together as a computer cluster, which provides failover and increased availability of applications.

In Chapter 2, "The Microsoft Private Cloud," the System Center Virtual Machine Manager (VMM) 2012 R2 will be installed on the MANAGE server to manage the virtual machines running on the COMPUTE servers.

Using Table 1.2, complete the inventory and place checks in the Mark column to indicate that the components are available.

Table 1.2   Software Inventory Worksheet

Mark	Quantity	Item Description
	1	Microsoft Windows Server 2012 R2 Datacenter DVD
	3	Microsoft Windows Server 2012 R2 Datacenter licenses
	1	Microsoft Windows Server 2012 R2 Standard iso file
	12	Microsoft Windows Server 2012 R2 Standard licenses
	1	Microsoft SQL Server 2012 SP1 DVD
	1	Microsoft System Center Virtual Machine Manager 2012 R2 DVD
	1	Microsoft System Center Virtual Machine Manager 2012 R2 license
	1	Microsoft System Center Application Controller 2012 R2 DVD

© 2014 Cengage Learning®.

Consider Using the Microsoft 180-Day Evaluation Software

Microsoft provides 180-day evaluation copies for Windows Server 2012 R2, Microsoft SQL Server 2012 SP1, Microsoft System Center Virtual Machine Manager 2012 R2, and Microsoft System Center Application Controller 2012 R2. To locate this free software, perform a Web search for Microsoft 180-day free trial.

Cabling the Servers

Now that you have the required hardware and software available, you are ready to cable the KVM switch and the first network.

The suggested KVM port assignments are presented in Table 1.3.

Table 1.3 Suggested KVM Port Assignments

Server	KVM Port
MANAGE	1
COMPUTE1	2
COMPUTE2	3

© 2014 Cengage Learning®.

Wait to Insert Cables

Do not place network cables in the servers or switches until you are instructed to do so in each exercise.

To cable the KVM switch and the management network, complete these steps:

1. Connect a blue cable from port 5 of a 5-port network switch to the home router.

2. If required, place the USB connectors for the keyboard and mouse in the KVM switch. Also, connect the VGA cable.

3. If required, cable the power supply to the KVM switch and plug the power supply into the power strip.

4. Locate the server and then cable the KVM switch to the appropriate port.

5. Connect a blue cable between the top RJ45 connector on the management server and the next available port of the 5-port network switch.

6. Repeat steps 4 and 5 for the remaining servers (COMPUTE1 and COMPUTE2).

Label the Host Server Names

To make it easy to identify the host computers on the KVM switch, tape a note above the LCDs on the KVM switch.

Installing the Operating System on the Host Computers

As you progress through this book, you will put in place the software to build a private cloud. In this chapter, you will start building the MANAGE server. In addition, you will start the build out of the COMPUTE1 and COMPUTE2 servers.

Here's how to install Windows Server 2012 R2. When you get these 31 steps down, you will be ready to install Windows Server 2012 R2 for virtual machines in future chapters. You will need the Windows Server 2012 R2 DVD and three Datacenter licenses.

The suggested IP configurations appear in Table 1.4. Depending on your existing network, you may need to enter alternative IP addresses.

Table 1.4   Suggested IP Configurations for Servers

Server Name	IPv4 Address	IPv4 Gateway	IPv4 DNS	IPv6 Address
MANAGE	192.168.0.100	192.168.0.1	192.168.0.1	fd00::100
COMPUTE1	192.168.0.101	192.168.0.1	192.168.0.1	fd00::101
COMPUTE2	192.168.0.102	192.168.0.1	192.168.0.1	fd00::102

© 2014 Cengage Learning®.

1. Turn on the server and switch the KVM switch to the appropriate KVM port.
2. Insert the Windows Server 2012 R2 DVD and press the Reset button. (On some computers, you will need to recycle the power switch.)
3. When prompted to press any key to boot from the CD or DVD, press the spacebar.
4. If the Windows Boot Manager appears, press Enter. Wait for Windows to load files.
5. When the regional settings window appears, verify the selections for language, time, currency, and keyboard. Make corrections as needed and then click Next.
6. Click the Install now link.
7. If requested to enter a product key, enter a valid product key and press Enter.

Using the Microsoft 180-Day Evaluation Software

> If you are using the Microsoft 180-day evaluation software for Windows Server 2012 R2, you will not need a product key for the installation. Other editions require a product key.

8. To indicate which version to install, select Windows Server 2012 R2 Datacenter (server with a GUI) and then click Next.

9. When the license terms appear, click I accept the license terms and then click Next.

10. Click the Custom Install Windows only (advanced) link.

Remove Previous Partitions

> If any previous partition exists, click Drive 0 Partition 1: System Reserved. Click Delete and then click OK. Repeat for Drive 0 Partition 2.

11. Click Disk 0 Unallocated Space and then click Next.

12. Wait for Windows to copy and expand the files, install features and updates, and restart the computer to complete this step of the installation.

13. Wait while Windows prepares to start for the first time and then prepares the computer for use.

14. Remove the Windows Server 2012 R2 DVD.

15. When prompted for a password for the administrator account, enter Pa$$w0rd in the New password text box, press Tab, enter Pa$$w0rd in the Confirm password text box, and press Enter.

16. Press Ctrl+Alt+Delete, enter Pa$$w0rd, and press Enter.

17. When the Do you want to find PCs appears in the right pane, click Yes.

18. To go to the pane for this server, click Local Server in the Server Manager window.

19. To verify and set the screen resolution, minimize the Server Manager, right-click on the desktop, and click Screen Resolution. Click the Resolution chevron (down arrow to the right of the Resolution) and select the highest resolution. Click OK. Click Keep changes and then click OK. Maximize the Server Manager.

20. To configure IE Enhanced Security Configuration for administrators, click the On link (to the right of IE Enhanced Security Configuration) and click Administrators/ Off. Click OK.

21. To set the time zone, click the Time zone link. If necessary, click the Change time zone button, select the appropriate time zone, click the Change date and time button, change the time, and then click OK twice. The Date and time will change during the next refresh.

22. To name the physical Ethernet adapter, double-click the active Ethernet link. Right-click the active Ethernet connection. Click Rename, enter Management Physical Network, and press Enter.

Windows Identifies Network Adapters

Windows may not identify the Ethernet adapters in the same sequence on each host computer. You will want to work with a single network adapter at a time. Renaming the adapter will avoid future confusion as to which Local Area Connection matches each Ethernet adapter.

23. Right-click the active Management Physical Network and click Properties. Click the Internet Protocol Version 6 (TCP/IPv6) and click Properties. Click Use the Following IPv6 address, enter the suggested IPv6 address, and press Tab. Click OK.

24. Click Internet Protocol Version 4 (TCP/IPv4) and then click Properties. Click Use the following IP address, enter the suggested IP address, and then press Tab twice; the subnet mask will appear in the Subnet mask text box.

25. Next, enter the default gateway, press Tab twice, and enter the preferred DNS. Click OK and click Close. Close the Network Connections window.

26. To enter the computer name, click the Computer name link (located to the upper left), click the Change button, and enter the computer name (MANAGE, COMPUTE1, or COMPUTE2). Click OK twice, click Close, and then click Restart Now.

27. Wait for the computer to restart.

28. Press Ctrl+Alt+Delete and enter a password of Pa$$w0rd. Click Local Server on Server Manager.

29. To set the administrator password expiration properties, click TASKS in the upper-right corner and click Computer Management. Expand Local Users and Groups, click Users, right-click Administrator, and click Properties. Then click the Password never expires check box and click OK. Close the Computer Management window.

30. To add the Multipath I/O feature, which is required for future network communication, click Manage (upper-right corner of Server Manager), click Add

Roles and Features, click Next four times, and scroll and select Multipath I/O. Click Next and then click Install.

31. Wait for the Installation to complete and then click Close.

32. Repeat steps 1 through 31 for the remaining host servers (COMPUTE1 and COMPUTE2).

DESCRIBING THE HYPER-V VIRTUALIZATION ENVIRONMENT

In this section, you will learn about the Hyper-V Hypervisor, which provides virtualization for your private cloud.

Overview of Hyper-V Hypervisor

The Windows Server 2012 R2 hypervisor enables you to create a virtualized server computing environment. You can use this environment to implement a private cloud of guest virtual machines and then use Hyper-V to manage the virtual machines and their resources. Each guest runs in an isolated execution environment, which allows you to run multiple operating systems simultaneously on one physical computer.

The Hyper-V role in Windows Server 2012 R2 consists of several components, including the following:

- Hypervisor
- Parent and child partitions
- Virtual machines and guest operating systems
- Synthetic and emulated devices
- Integration services

The Hyper-V hypervisor is the core component of Hyper-V, and is responsible for creating and managing isolated execution environments called partitions. The hypervisor sits directly on the hardware and controls access from the partitions to the physical processors, as shown in Figure 1.11.

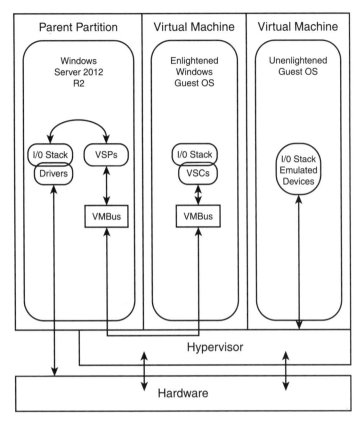

Figure 1.11
Hyper-V high-level architecture.
© 2014 Cengage Learning®.

When the Hyper-V role is enabled in Windows Server 2012 R2, the hypervisor uses the virtualization extensions built into the processors to place itself "under" Windows Server 2012 R2, giving it greater control of the physical hardware. When the Hyper-V hypervisor loads for the first time, it creates a partition called the *parent partition*. This parent partition, the first virtual machine, hosts the Windows Server 2012 R2 operating system that was running on the hardware before the Hyper-V role was enabled.

The parent partition is important for two main reasons:

- It controls all hardware devices, such as network adapters, hard disks, keyboards, mice, and graphics adapters, and is responsible for allocating physical memory to the partitions.

- It directs the hypervisor to create and delete child partitions. This activity is actually performed by the virtualization stack that runs in the parent partition.

Unlike the parent partition, child partitions do not have access to physical hardware. When a virtual machine is created, it is assigned a newly created child partition and a set of virtual devices that do not have direct access to the physical hardware. Instead, I/O requests from the virtual machine are routed through the parent partition to the physical adapters on the system.

The indirect I/O model used by Hyper-V allows virtual machines to be independent of the specific types of hardware devices used on the physical server. Because the drivers for these specific hardware devices of the physical computer run in the Windows Server 2012 R2 parent partition, only Microsoft drivers are installed in the hypervisor. This driver isolation improves the security footprint of the Microsoft hypervisor. The architecture allows Hyper-V to leverage the broad support available in Windows Server 2012 R2.

Operating systems installed within child partitions are commonly referred to as *guest operating systems*. The virtual devices that a virtual machine exposes to a guest operating system can be assigned to one of two broad categories. Emulated virtual devices are a software implementation of a typical PCI device. To the guest operating system, an emulated device appears as a physical PCI device. The second category of devices, synthetic virtual devices, only functions with Hyper-V and is also implemented in software. The devices are based on architecture that is unique to Hyper-V, and they use a high-performance channel called the VMBus as the VSP-VSC communication mechanism between the different partitions:

- **Virtualization Service Provider (VSP):** This component runs in the parent partition and directly communicates with the hardware drivers. VSP makes sure that the other virtual machines running on the same host can access the hardware successfully. VSP also ensures that hardware access and sharing by multiple virtual machines is secure. For example, VSP is responsible for sharing a common storage device across multiple virtual machines.

- **Virtualization Service Client (VSC):** VSC runs in the child partitions and presents the virtual device to each child partition. Each VSC has a corresponding VSP in the parent partition. In other words, VSP and VSC exist as pairs. For example, a storage device would have a VSP/VSC pair.

- **VMBus**: This point-to-point memory bus is used for communication between VSP and VSC.

Using synthetic devices creates less processor overhead than using emulated devices.

In general, implementations in virtual environments that reduce overhead and improve guest operating system performance are called *enlightenments* by Microsoft. The synthetic device model is an example of device enlightenment. Enlightenments within a guest operating system's kernel allow the OS to know it is running in a virtual environment. This knowledge changes the operating system's behavior and reduces the amount of overhead traditionally associated with running an OS. The operating systems used in this book have enlightenments for Hyper-V.

The drivers for synthetic devices are provided by Microsoft as part of its Integration Services for Hyper-V. Integration Services are available for all supported guest operating systems and are installed after the guest operating systems are installed.

Integration Services are meant to provide better integration between child and parent partitions. Along with providing drivers for synthetic devices, Integration Services provide additional enhancements such as mouse integration, time synchronization, and the ability to shut down the guest operating system from the management console.

Hyper-V Manager is the management console from which you operate Hyper-V. You use Hyper-V Manager to create, start, stop, delete, and configure all your virtual machines, and to set the default locations for storing your virtual hard disks and virtual machine configuration files.

Describing Virtual Hard Disks

A virtual hard disk can have the same contents as a physical hard disk drive, such as disk partitions and a file system. It is typically used as the hard disk of a virtual machine.

Two methods, called *disk format*, of storing virtual hard disks are supported. This controls the maximum file size for a virtual hard disk.

- **VHD:** Supports virtual hard disks up to 2,040GB in size.
- **VHDX:** Supports virtual hard disks up to 64TB in size. You may want to use this format for your virtual hard disks to take advantage of the performance improvements.

Types of Virtual Disks

Three types of virtual hard disks are supported. You can define the type you want when creating the virtual disk:

- **Dynamically expanding:** The virtual hard disk file grows as data is stored to the disk. When you create a dynamically expanding virtual hard disk, you specify a maximum file size that limits how large the virtual disk can become. For example, if you create a 1GB dynamically expanding virtual hard disk, the initial size of the virtual hard disk file will be about 32MB. As a virtual machine uses the virtual hard disk, the size of the virtual hard disk file grows to accommodate the new data. The size of a dynamically expanding disk only grows; it does not shrink, even when you delete data. You may be able to reduce the size of a dynamically expanding disk by compacting it. The default of 127GB can be used for an OS installed on a dynamically expanding disk.

- **Fixed size:** The virtual hard disk file uses the full amount of space specified during creation. You need to enter only a maximum size for the disk

- **Differencing:** The virtual hard disk file exists as a child disk in a parent/child relationship with an existing virtual hard disk. You can identify the parent file by looking for it with the Inspect Disk tool. The child file used as the differencing virtual hard disk stores all state changes to a virtual hard disk in a separate file. This allows you to isolate changes to a virtual machine and keep a virtual hard disk in an unchanged state. You do not specify a size for a differencing disk, which can be considered a special type of dynamically expanding disk. Differencing disks can grow as large as the parent disks to which they are associated. For production environments, a fixed-size virtual hard disk is recommended because it performs better than dynamically expanding and differencing disks.

When the operating system running in the virtual machine will benefit from direct access to the physical disk, a pass-through disk is often required. A pass-through disk is a physical disk mapped directly to a virtual machine. To the parent partition on the host computer, the disk is in an offline state. I/O requests from the virtual machine are passed through the parent partition to the disk. The parent partition no longer manages the disk, and additional CPU cycles are provided for virtual machine processing. When mapped to a pass-through disk, the guest operating system has direct access to the raw blocks of the physical storage device.

Describing Virtual Networks

A virtual network switch works like a physical network switch, except that the switch is implemented in software. Switch ports are added or removed automatically as virtual machines are connected to or disconnected from a virtual network switch.

Virtual Network Switches

When Windows Server 2012 R2 is installed on a system with three network adapters, Figure 1.12 shows what the Network Connections window looks like. To open this window, right-click the network icon in the taskbar's system tray, click Open Network and Sharing Center, and click Change adapter setting. In the figure, only the Ethernet adapter is active on the host computer. The next two network adapters do not have an Ethernet cable plugged into the adapter. These last two adapters will be added to network switches in future chapters.

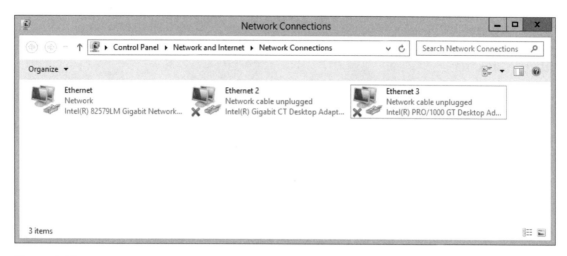

Figure 1.12
Network Connections window.
Source: Network and Sharing Center/Windows Server 2012 R2.

Figure 1.13 shows how your host computer is operating before a virtual switch is installed. The Ethernet network adapter (physical NIC) is attached directly to the physical network.

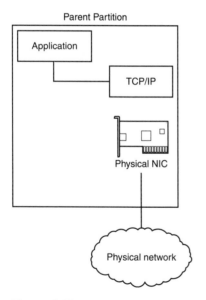

Figure 1.13
Network adapter attached directly.
© 2014 Cengage Learning®.

When the Virtual Switch Manager is used to create a virtual network, a virtual network switch is added to the host computer. Figure 1.14 shows what the Network Connections window looks like after the virtual network switch is installed. Ethernet is now the virtual network switch with only the Microsoft Virtual Network Switch Protocol enabled. The new vEthernet (virtual network switch to Ethernet) has the IP configuration of the previous Ethernet adapter.

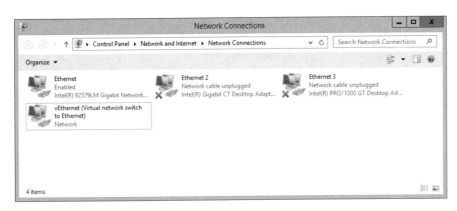

Figure 1.14
Network Connections window after the virtual network switch is added.

Source: Network and Sharing Center/Windows Server 2012 R2.

Figure 1.15 shows how your system is operating after the Virtual Switch Manager is used to create a virtual switch. As you can see, the parent partition (host operating system) is now using a virtual NIC to connect to the physical NIC through the virtual switch. The only protocol bound to this physical NIC Ethernet is the Microsoft Virtual Network Switch Protocol. The virtual machine is using the VMBus to access the virtual network switch. The logical adapter now has all of the standard protocols and services bound to it instead of the physical adapter. The IP configuration was transferred from the physical NIC to the logical NIC.

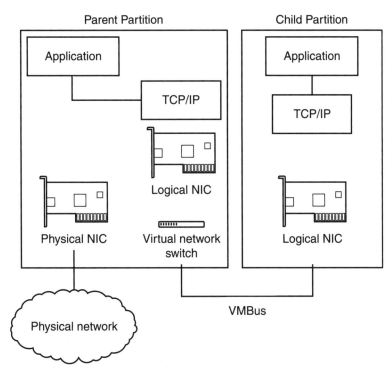

Figure 1.15
Network communications through virtual switch.
© 2014 Cengage Learning®.

Types of Virtual Networks

Virtual Network Manager is available from Hyper-V Manager, and it offers three types of virtual networks that you can use for guest virtual machines and the host computer:

- **External virtual networks:** This type of network provides virtual machines with access to a physical network to communicate with externally located servers and clients. External virtual networks also allow virtual machines on the same host computer to communicate with each other.

- **Internal virtual networks:** This type of network allows communication between virtual machines on the same host computer and between virtual machines and the host computer. You would use an internal virtual network to build a test environment.

■ **Private virtual networks:** This type of network allows communication only among virtual machines on the same host computer; the network is isolated from the host computer and from external servers and clients. A private virtual network is useful when you need to create an isolated networking environment, such as a test domain.

Table 1.5 summarizes the connectivity for three types of virtual networks. Use this table to choose the virtual network type for your situation. For example, if you wanted your virtual machine to have access to the host computer but not the Internet, you would choose the internal virtual network.

Table 1.5   Connectivity for Types of Virtual Networks

	Physical adapter	Host computer	Virtual machine(s)
External virtual network	Yes	Yes	Yes
Internal virtual network	No	Yes	Yes
Private virtual network	No	No	Yes

© 2014 Cengage Learning®.

INSTALLING THE HYPER-V ROLE

In these 17 steps, you will install the Hyper-V hypervisor role on each host computer, which will enable you to run virtual machines.

1. Switch the KVM switch to the appropriate port for MANAGE.

2. If necessary, log on to your server with a password of Pa$$w0rd.

3. Click Manage (upper-right corner of Server Manager) and then click Add Roles and Features. Click Next three times.

4. To add the Hyper-V role, click the Hyper-V check box and then click Add Features.

5. To install the virtual switch, click Next until Create virtual switches is displayed; then click Management Physical Network.

6. To select all of the defaults, click Next three times.

7. Click Restart the destination server automatically if required. Click Yes.

8. Review the Confirm installation selections and then click Install.

9. Wait for the Restart Pending message and then click Close.

10. Wait for the computer to complete the updates needed to install the Hyper-V hypervisor. The system will restart.

11. Press Ctrl+Alt+Delete and enter a password of Pa$$w0rd.

12. Click Local Server in Server Manager.

13. Wait for the installation to complete and click Close.

14. Right-click the Network icon on the Taskbar (right-side, terminal with RJ-45), click Open Network and Sharing Center, click Change adapter settings, right-click vEthernet (*physical adapter name*), click Rename, and type Management Logical Network. Press Enter. Close the Network Connection window.

15. To place a Hyper-Manager button on the taskbar, press the Windows key, type Hyper-V, right-click Hyper-V Manager, and click Pin to Taskbar. Press the Windows Key.

16. To open the Hyper-V Manager, click the Hyper-V Manager button (two green servers) on the Taskbar. Click on MANAGE.

17. To name the Management Logical Network, click Virtual Switch Manager, click the Virtual Switch identified in step 14, and enter Management Logical Network for the Name. Click OK.

18. Complete steps 1 through 17 for the remaining host servers (COMPUTE1 and COMPUTE2).

Operating Hyper-V Manager

Hyper-V Manager is located under Tools in Server Manager. See the upper-right corner for Tools. When you open Hyper-V Manager, the window shown in Figure 1.16 appears.

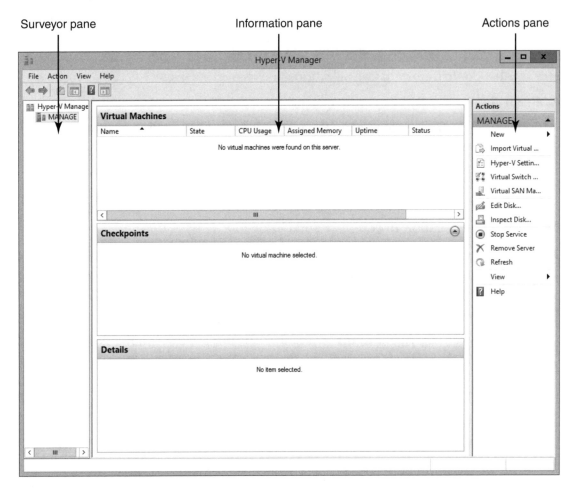

Figure 1.16
Hyper-V Manager with panes identified.
Source: Hyper-V Manager/Windows Server 2012 R2.

Take a moment to become familiar with this window; you use it to configure and operate your virtual machines.

1. To open the Hyper-V Manager, click Hyper-V Manager on the task bar.

2. Locate the Surveyor pane (left pane), which you use to select the host computer.

3. Locate the Information pane and identify the three subpanes (Virtual Machines, Checkpoints, and Details).

4. Locate the Actions pane (right pane), which shows available actions for the host computer (top half) and a selected virtual machine (bottom half).

Alternate Method to Select an Action

You can see the same actions by right-clicking the item in the Information pane or Surveyor pane.

5. To see how the Actions pane links to a wizard, click New and then click Virtual Machine.

6. Review the Before You Begin text and then click Cancel.

Reviewing the Actions Pane

The following overview summarizes the actions (refer back to Figure 1.16) you can perform from the Actions pane when Hyper-V is running on the host computer:

- **New:** You can create a virtual machine, hard disk, or floppy disk. These procedures are covered later in this chapter.

- **Import Virtual Machine:** Add an existing virtual machine to be managed by Hyper-V Manager. See Chapter 3, "Configuring the Fabric Resources," for details.

- **Hyper-V Settings:** Update or change settings that affect all virtual machines, as explained later in this section.

- **Virtual Switch Manager:** Create and remove virtual networks. These procedures are covered later in this chapter in the section on creating virtual network switches.

- **Virtual SAN Manager:** Create and remove virtual Fibre Channel storage area networks. This topic is beyond the scope of this text.

- **Edit Disk:** Modify virtual hard disks. This procedure is covered later in this chapter in the section on creating virtual hard disks.

- **Inspect Disk:** Obtain information about an existing Hyper-V virtual hard disk, such as its current size, maximum size, image file location, and disk type. For details, see the section on creating virtual hard disks.

- **Stop Service:** Stop the Virtual Machine Management service. You might want to stop the service when troubleshooting the Hyper-V management interface.

- **Remove Server:** Drop the existing Hyper-V host computer prior to adding another host computer.

- **Refresh:** Refresh the Hyper-V Manager window.

- **View:** Customize the Hyper-V view by showing or hiding items.

- **Help:** Get assistance for using Hyper-V.

Creating and Configuring Virtual Machines

In this section, you will learn to create virtual machines with the New Virtual Machine Wizard and to configure existing virtual machines. Figure 1.17 shows a Before You Begin page.

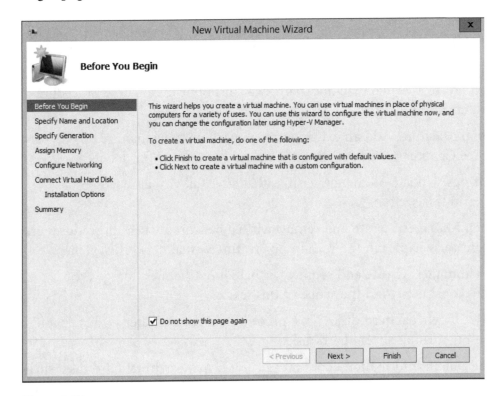

Figure 1.17
New Virtual Machine Wizard Before You Begin page.
Source: Hyper-V Manager/Windows Server 2012 R2.

1. To start the New Virtual Machine Wizard, click New in the Actions pane and click Virtual Machine.

2. Read the instructions on the page, click Do not show this page again, and then click Next.

Specifying the Name and Location

As shown in Figure 1.18, you enter the name for the virtual machine. A common convention is to name the virtual machine the same as the computer name. A folder will be created to store the files associated with the virtual machine. Also, this is the default name for the virtual hard disk that will contain the OS files.

To store the virtual machine in a folder other than the default location, click the "Store the virtual machine in a different location" check box, click the Browse button, and navigate to the folder you want.

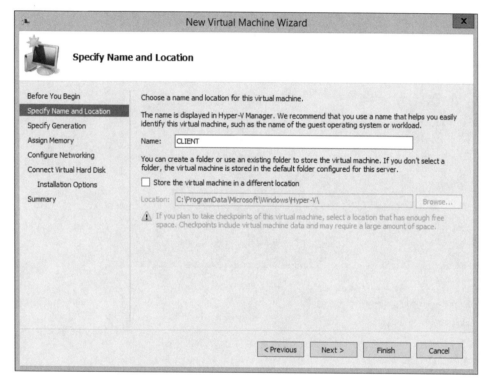

Figure 1.18
New Virtual Machine Wizard Specify Name and Location page.
Source: Hyper-V Manager/Windows Server 2012 R2.

1. Enter CLIENT over New Virtual Machine.
2. Click Next.

Specifying Generation

On the next page, you select the Generation for the virtual machine. Generation 1 is OK (see Figure 1.19). Generation 2 is beyond the scope of this book.

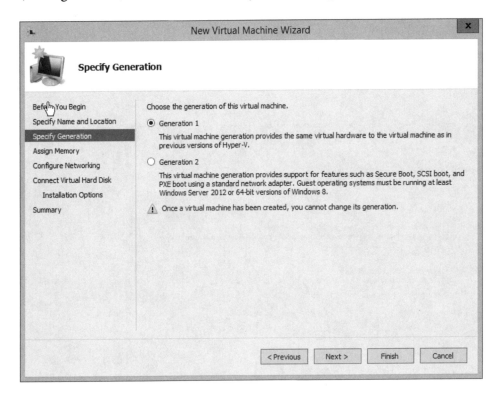

Figure 1.19
New Virtual Machine Wizard Specify Generation page.
Source: Hyper-V Manager/Windows Server 2012 R2.

1. Retain Generation 1.
2. Click Next.

Assigning Memory to a Virtual Machine

A virtual machine needs enough memory to run the anticipated workload; however, each virtual machine consumes memory only when it is running or paused. You can install Windows Server 2012 R2 with a minimum of 512MB, but the performance of the virtual machine will improve with additional memory. The memory setting is a compromise between a larger memory allocation and the total number of virtual machines running on the Hyper-V server.

You want to check the Use Dynamic Memory for this virtual machine check box, as shown in Figure 1.20. This permits the virtual machine to communicate memory requirements to the Hypervisor. More about this in the section, "Memory Settings."

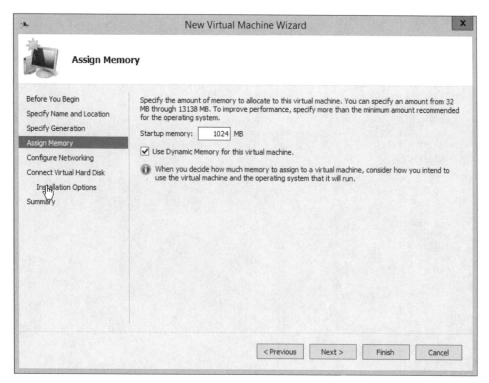

Figure 1.20
New Virtual Machine Wizard Assign Memory page.
Source: Hyper-V Manager/Windows Server 2012 R2.

1. Enter 1024 for the Startup memory.

2. Click Use Dynamic Memory for this virtual machine.

3. Click Next.

Adding a Network Connection

Providing a virtual machine with networking capabilities requires the same two basic components that a physical computer requires: a network adapter and an available network. When you create a virtual machine, it is automatically configured with one network adapter. If one or more virtual network switches are available on the host computer running Hyper-V, you can connect the network adapter to one of those networks when you create the virtual machine. Additional network adapters can be added later. A completed Configure Networking page is shown in Figure 1.21.

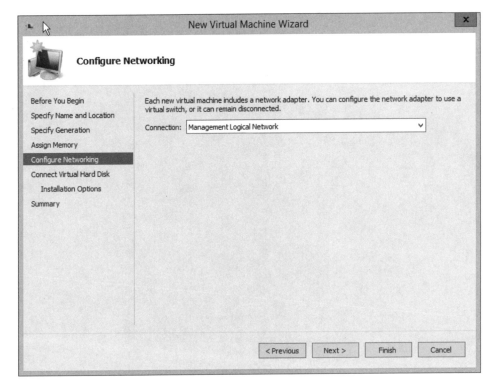

Figure 1.21
New Virtual Machine Wizard Configure Networking page.
Source: Hyper-V Manager/Windows Server 2012 R2.

1. Click the Connection chevron (down arrow on right).

2. Select Management Logical Network.

3. Click Next.

Adding a Virtual Hard Disk

The next window, as shown in Figure 1.22, allows you to add the first hard disk to the virtual machine. The default virtual hard disk will use the same name as the virtual machine, and it will have a .vhdx extension.

You also have the option of connecting to an existing virtual hard disk, which is useful if you need to attach a copy of a previous .vhdx file for a virtual machine. The final option allows you to connect the virtual hard disk after the virtual machine is created.

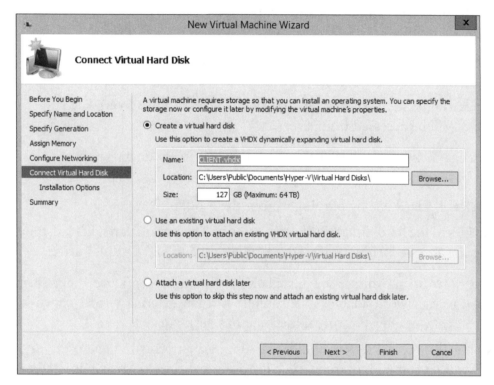

Figure 1.22
New Virtual Machine Wizard Configure Virtual Hard Disk page.

Source: Hyper-V Manager/Windows Server 2012 R2.

1. Review the default selection for a virtual hard disk.

2. Click Next.

Specifying the Location of OS Installation Files

Figure 1.23 shows the Installation options for installing the operating system files. You can install and run guest operating systems in virtual machines. Before you can install the guest operating system, however, you must specify the location of the installation media using one of the following four options:

- **Install an operating system later:** The installation files will be available later.

- **Install an operating system from a boot CD/DVD-ROM:** Use this option if you have burned the installation files from the .iso file to a CD/DVD-ROM or if you have copied the .iso file to a hard drive on the host computer.

- **Install an operating system from a boot floppy disk:** Install the guest operating system from a floppy disk image (.vfd file).

- **Install an operating system from a network-based installation server:** The installation files will be accessed from a server.

The most likely scenario is to use installation files that you have downloaded to a file server. When you have the .iso file, you have two choices:

- Create a physical DVD-ROM by burning it from the .iso file.

- Copy the .iso files to the hard disk of the host computer. The installation takes less time when the files are accessed from the hard drive rather than the DVD-ROM drive.

If you want to perform a network-based installation, you must configure the virtual machine to use a legacy network adapter and connect it to an external virtual network. You can perform these tasks after the virtual machine has been created.

The last window, not shown, in the wizard displays summary information about the new virtual machine. If you see something wrong, click Previous to return to a previous window of the wizard and fix the problem. Otherwise, click Finish to create the virtual machine.

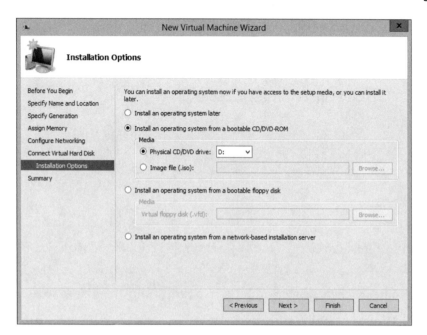

Figure 1.23
New Virtual Machine Wizard Installation Options page.
Source: Hyper-V Manager/Windows Server 2012 R2.

1. Click Install an operating system from a bootable CD/DVD-ROM.

2. Retain the Physical CD/DVD drive.

3. Click Next.

4. Review the Summary. Click Previous to make corrections and then click Finish.

5. Wait for the virtual machine to be created.

Installing an Operating System

Installing an operating system in a virtual machine is like installing it on a physical computer. To access a physical machine, you position yourself before the monitor, keyboard, and mouse. Then you power on the computer. The equivalent steps for a virtual machine are click Start to boot the virtual machine from the operating system installation files, connect to the virtual machine, and work with the virtual machine using the monitor, keyboard, and mouse.

By completing these 27 steps, you can install Windows Server 2012 R2 in the CLIENT virtual machine.

1. Insert the Windows Server 2012 R2 DVD in the MANAGE server.

2. To start the CLIENT, click CLIENT in the Information pane and then click Start in the Actions pane.

3. To connect to the CLIENT, click Connect in the Actions pane.

4. Wait for the files to be loaded.

5. When the regional settings window appears, verify the selections for language, time, currency, and keyboard. Make corrections as needed and then click Next.

6. Click the Install now link.

7. If requested to enter a product key, enter a valid product key and press Enter.

8. To indicate which version to install, select Windows Server 2012 R2 Standard (Server with a GUI) and then click Next.

9. When the license terms appear, click I accept the license terms and then click Next.

10. Click the Custom Install Windows only (advanced) link.

11. Click Disk 0 Unallocated Space and then click Next.

12. Wait for Windows to copy and expand files, install features and updates, and restart the computer to complete this step of the installation.

13. Wait while Windows prepares to start for the first time and then prepares the computer for use.

14. To remove the Server 2012 R2 DVD from the virtual machine, click the Media menu in the Virtual Machine Connection window, point to DVD Drive, and then click Release D.

15. When prompted for a password for the administrator account, enter Pa$$w0rd in the New password text box, press Tab, enter Pa$$w0rd in the Confirm password text box, and press Enter.

16. Click Action on the Menu, click Ctrl+Alt+Delete, enter Pa$$w0rd, and press Enter.

Three Finger Salute

Do not press Ctrl+Alt+Delete when working with a virtual machine. This sequence will be sent to the host computer and not to the virtual machine. Use Ctrl+Alt+Delete on the Action menu.

17. When the Do you want to find PCs appears in the right pane, click Yes.

18. To go to the pane for this server, click Local Server.

19. To configure IE Enhanced Security Configuration for administrators, click the On link. Click Administrators/Off. Click Users/Off. Click OK.

20. To set the time zone, click the Time zone link. If necessary, click the Change time zone button, select the appropriate time zone, click the Change date and time button, change the time, and then click OK twice. The Date and time will changed during the next refresh.

21. To enter the IP configuration, click the Ethernet link, right-click Ethernet and click Properties, click the Internet Protocol Version 6 (TCP/IPv6) and click Properties, click Use the Following IPv6 address, enter the FD00::109 IPv6 address, and press Tab. Click OK.

22. Click Internet Protocol Version 4 (TCP/IPv4) and then click Properties. Click Use the following IP address, enter the 192.168.0.109 for the IP address, and then press Tab twice; the subnet mask will appear in the Subnet mask text box.

23. Next, enter 192.168.0.1 for the default gateway, press Tab twice, and enter 192.168.0.1 for the preferred DNS. Click OK and then click Close. Close the Network Connections window.

24. To enter the computer name, click the Computer Name link, click the Change button, and enter CLIENT for the computer name. Click OK twice, click Close, and then click Restart Now.

25. Wait for the computer to restart.

26. Click Action on the Menu and click Ctrl+Alt+Delete. Enter a password of Pa$$w0rd. Click Local Server.

27. To set the administrator password expiration properties, click Tools in the upper-right corner and click Computer Management. Expand Local Users and Groups, click Users, right-click Administrator and click Properties, click the Password never expires check box, and then click OK. Close the Computer Management window.

Configuring Virtual Machines

The virtual machine settings allow you to adjust the configuration of a virtual machine after you have created it. From Hyper-V Manager, click a virtual machine in the Virtual Machines pane, and then click Settings in the Actions pane for the virtual machine. Figure 1.24 shows the settings for a selected virtual machine. The machine has one hard drive, which was created to store the operating system and is attached to the first Integrated Drive Electronics (IDE) controller. The DVD drive is attached to the second IDE controller. The network adapter is connected to the virtual network that was created in a previous section in this text.

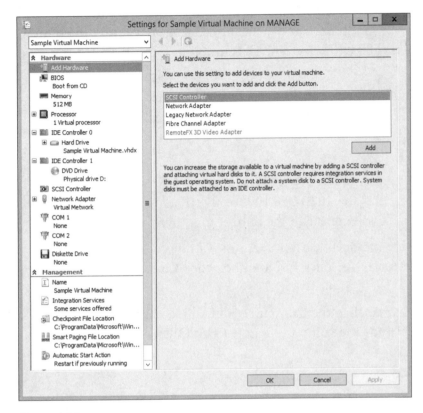

Figure 1.24
Settings for a Sample Virtual Machine window.
Source: Hyper-V Manager/Windows Server 2012 R2.

Adding Hardware Devices

From the initial configuration window shown in Figure 1.24, you can add the following hardware devices to a virtual machine:

- **SCSI Controller:** Attach additional virtual hard disks for data storage. (An operating system cannot be started from a SCSI device.) The SCSI controller uses the VMBus for faster I/O transfers.

- **Network Adapter:** Add another network adapter to an existing virtual network switch (synthetic device).

- **Legacy Network Adapter:** Add a network adapter to perform a network-based installation of the guest operating system. Some older operating systems, such as Windows Vista, require these adapters.

- **Fibre Channel Adapter:** Add a Fibre Channel adapter to the virtual machine that supports Fibre Channel communications.

- **RemoteFX 3D Video Adapter:** Add a rich graphics experience in a guest operating system. A 3D video adapter must be installed in the server.

Just like your host computer system, a virtual machine has a Basic Input Output System (BIOS). Although the range of options for a virtual machine is considerably narrower than those for a physical computer's BIOS, you can change the virtual machine BIOS settings.

Figure 1.25 shows the BIOS settings, which appear when you click BIOS in the Hardware list. You can change the boot order by clicking a device in the Startup order list and then using the up and down arrows. For a network-based installation, move the Legacy Network adapter to the top of the boot order.

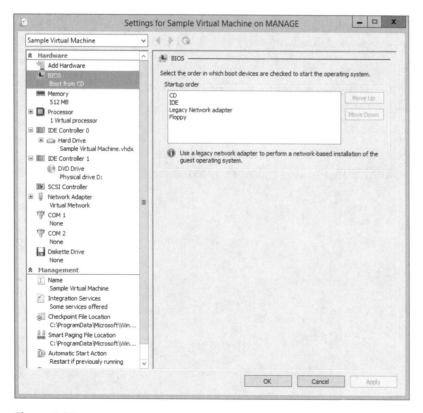

Figure 1.25
BIOS settings window.
Source: Hyper-V Manager/Windows Server 2012 R2.

Memory Settings

Virtual machines use the memory of the host computer on which Hyper-V is running. You can specify the amount of memory allocated to a virtual machine by clicking Memory in the Hardware list. Figure 1.26 shows the options for memory management. To specify static memory, enter the amount of memory you need in the RAM text box.

Hyper-V manages dynamic memory using the following settings:

- **Startup RAM:** Specify the amount of memory needed to start the virtual machine. Consider this value carefully. The Startup RAM must be adequate so that the guest operating system will start, but to allow additional virtual machines to run, it should be set as low as possible.

- **Minimum RAM:** Specify the amount of memory needed by the virtual machine to run. Consider this value carefully. This value is equal to or less than the Startup RAM.

- **Maximum RAM:** Specify the maximum amount of memory that the virtual machine can use. This value can range from the Startup RAM value up to 64GB; however, the maximum memory cannot exceed the amount of memory supported by the guest operating system. For example, Windows Server 2012 R2 Standard Edition has a limit of 32GB.

- **Memory buffer:** Specify the amount of memory that Hyper-V tries to assign to the virtual machine compared with the memory needed by the virtual machine. Enter the Memory buffer value as a percentage.

- **Memory weight:** Provide Hyper-V with a way to rank and distribute memory among virtual machines when insufficient physical memory is available for them on the host computer.

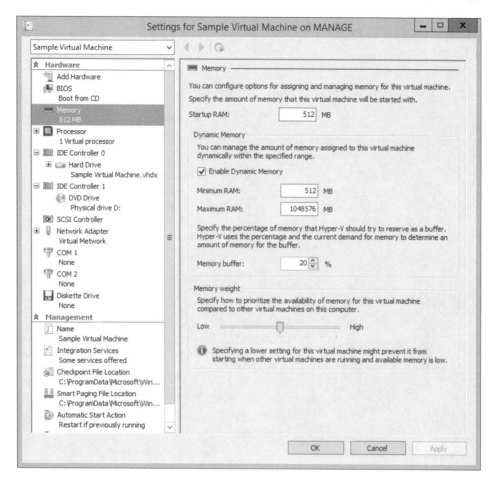

Figure 1.26
Memory settings window.
Source: Hyper-V Manager/Windows Server 2012 R2.

Logical Processor Settings

Hyper-V lets you control the number of individual "cores," or logical processors, that are assigned to a virtual machine. A quad processor has four cores, or four logical processors. If Intel Hyper-Threading is available, a quad-core processor can support up to eight logical processors. (Hyper-Threading makes each processing core appear to have two processors.) If you attempt to exceed the limit of logical processors on the host computer, the virtual machine will not start. The enlightened operating systems used in this book can have one or more logical processors. Figure 1.27 shows the window in which you can set the number of logical processors: to access this window, click Processor in the Hardware list.

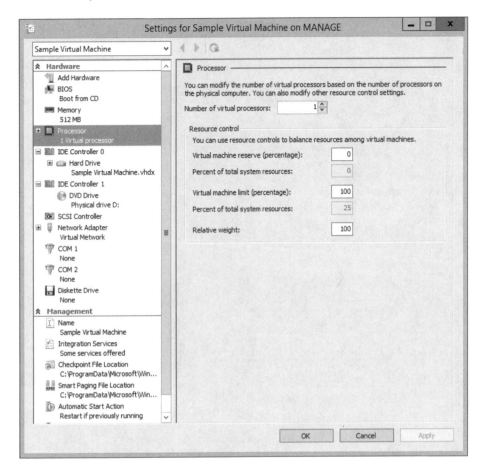

Figure 1.27
Processor settings window.

Source: Hyper-V Manager/Windows Server 2012 R2.

You have several options for controlling how Hyper-V allocates logical processors to virtual machines:

- **Virtual machine reserve (percentage):** Specifies the percentage of processing resources to reserve for the virtual machine. This setting guarantees that the percentage you specify will be available to the virtual machine. This setting can also affect how many virtual machines you can run at one time.

- **Percentage of total system resources:** Specifies the percentage of total logical processors available to reserve for the virtual machine.

- **Virtual machine limit (percentage):** Specifies the maximum percentage of processing resources that the virtual machine can use. This setting is applied regardless of whether other virtual machines are running.

- **Percentage of total system resources:** Specifies the percentage of total logical processors available to reserve for the virtual machine.

- **Relative weight:** Provides Hyper-V with a way to rank and distribute logical processors to the selected virtual machine when more than one is running and the virtual machines compete for resources.

Hard Disk Controller Settings

Virtual machines have two IDE controllers and two IDE devices per controller, just like physical computers. However, up to 64 hard drives can be connected to a SCSI controller. The most typical configuration is to place the virtual hard disk for the guest operating system on IDE Controller 0 and a DVD drive on IDE Controller 1, as shown in Figure 1.28.

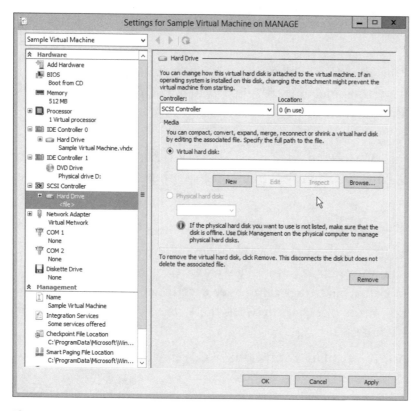

Figure 1.28
Hard Drive settings window.

Source: Hyper-V Manager/Windows Server 2012 R2.

To connect a physical disk to a virtual machine as a pass-through disk, click the Physical hard disk option button and then click the Physical hard disk arrow if necessary. The physical disk must be offline on the host computer, which you can verify using the Disk Management tool on the host computer. You will create a pass-through disk in Chapter 5.

To remove a virtual or physical hard disk, click the hard drive in the Hardware list and then click Remove. Remember that removing a hard disk does not delete the files from the host computer. You must delete the .vhd files using Windows Explorer.

The SCSI Controller functions are similar to the IDE Controller functions described earlier in this section. For SCSI support, Hyper-V uses a SCSI controller that is not emulated.

Instead, the synthetic SCSI controller uses the VMBus, which is much faster and requires less CPU overhead than an emulated IDE controller. An IDE controller must be used for the guest operating system. For data drives, SCSI is a better alternative.

Network Adapter Settings

In order to connect a virtual machine to a virtual network, you need to have a virtual network adapter connected to the virtual machine. A single virtual machine can use multiple virtual network adapters, although each of these adapters can be connected to only one virtual network switch.

To change settings for a virtual network adapter, click Network Adapter in the Hardware list, as shown in Figure 1.29. You can modify the following settings in the window that appears:

- **Virtual switch:** Each virtual switch can be connected as a single network connection.

- **VLAN ID:** The IEEE 802.1Q standard for VLAN tagging was created to allow you to use a network connection to transmit multiple streams of isolated network traffic. For example, two virtual machines cannot see each other's packets after configuration. However, if a router is used between the VLANs, the packets will be visible to both virtual machines.

- **Bandwidth Management:** By enabling Bandwidth Management, the minimum and maximum bandwidth in Mbps is specified.

- **Remove:** An existing virtual switch port is dropped from the virtual machine.

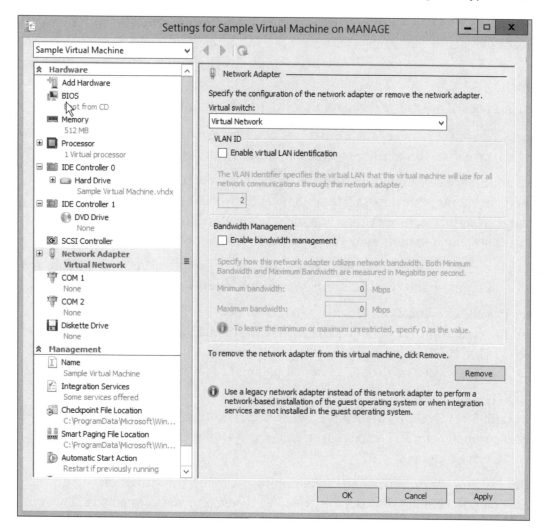

Figure 1.29
Network Adapter settings window.
Source: Hyper-V Manager/Windows Server 2012 R2.

Communication Ports

Microsoft does not support connections from virtual machines to physical COM ports. Microsoft does support piping between virtual machines, but the topic is beyond the scope of this book.

Diskette Drives

Each virtual machine has a single virtual floppy diskette drive; there is no access to a physical diskette drive. Therefore, you must use virtual floppy disks (VFDs), which can be created with the Virtual Disk Wizard. To start the wizard, click New and then click Floppy Disk in Hyper-V Manager.

Management

You have a number of options for managing your virtual machines:

- **Name:** Change the name of the virtual machine. This option is useful if you need to change a virtual machine name to avoid confusion with similar machine names.

- **Integration Services:** Limit one or more of the five Integration Services for the selected virtual machine: Operating system shutdown, Time synchronization, Data exchange, Heartbeat, and Backup (volume snapshot). All of the enlightened operating systems used in this book are capable of using each of the services.

- **Checkpoint File Location:** Change the location of snapshots from their default location of C:\ProgramData\Microsoft\Windows\Hyper-V.

- **Smart Paging File Location:** Change the location of the Smart Paging file for a virtual machine from the default location of C:\ProgramData\Microsoft\Windows\ Hyper-V. During virtual machine start-up, additional memory is required by the virtual machine, which is dropped later. A paging file provides this memory during start-up.

- **Automatic Start Action:** Change the option for restarting the virtual machine when the host computer starts. The default selection is Automatically start if it was running when the service stopped.

- **Automatic Stop Action:** Change the option for stopping the virtual machine when the host computer stops. The default selection is Save the virtual machine state.

Operating Virtual Machines

Operating a virtual machine is like operating a physical computer. You can start them, shut them down, and turn their power off. However, because they are virtual machines, you can perform additional tasks depending on whether the machine is off, running, or paused. To interact with a virtual machine, connect to it using the Virtual Machine Connection tool.

Table 1.6 describes the actions you can perform on a virtual machine that is not running. This table will come in handy as you work with virtual machines in future chapters.

Table 1.6 Actions You Can Perform When the Virtual Is Off

Action	Description
Connect	Connects to a virtual machine to install the guest operating system or interact with it.
Settings	Reviews and updates virtual machine settings.
Start	Turns on and boots a virtual machine.
Checkpoint	Saves a virtual machine's state, data, and configuration at a given point in time.
Export	Prepares the virtual machine's files for importing to another host computer later.
Rename	Changes the name of the virtual machine.
Delete	Deletes the virtual machine configuration. (Note that .vhd files will remain.)
Enable Replication	Configures replication to a replication server.
Help	Obtains help for using Hyper-V.

Source: Hyper-V Manager/Windows Server 2012 R2.

Table 1.7 describes the actions you can perform on a virtual machine that is running or paused. You will use this table as you work with virtual machines in future chapters.

Table 1.7 Actions You Can Perform When the Virtual Is Running or Paused

Action	Description
Connect	Connects to a virtual machine to install the guest operating system or interact with it.
Settings	Reviews the virtual machine settings.
Turn Off	Allows a "noncontrolled power-off" of a virtual machine, which is equivalent to pulling the power plug on a physical computer.
Shut Down	Allows a controlled power-off of a virtual machine, which requires Integration Services support.
Save	Stops virtual machine processing and saves the memory and processor state to a file.

(Continued)

Table 1.7 Actions You Can Perform When the Virtual Is Running or Paused (*Continued*)

Action	Description
Pause	Suspends virtual machine processing.
Resume	Restarts virtual machine processing after pausing it.
Reset	Allow a noncontrolled restart of a virtual machine, which is equivalent to pushing the reset button on a physical computer.
Checkpoint	Saves a virtual machine's state, data, and configuration at a given point in time.
Rename	Changes the name of the virtual machine.
Help	Obtains help for using Hyper-V.

Source: Hyper-V Manager/Windows Server 2012 R2.

Connecting to a Virtual Machine

Use the Virtual Machine Connection tool to connect to a virtual machine and then install the guest operating system or interact with it. You can use the Virtual Machine Connection tool to perform the following tasks:

- Connect to the video output of a virtual machine.
- Control the state of a virtual machine.
- Modify the settings of a virtual machine.

To connect to a virtual machine, right-click the virtual machine name in the Virtual Machines pane of Hyper-V Manager and then click Connect. The Virtual Machine Connection window appears with the desktop of the running guest operating system. If the virtual machine is not currently running, you will see the black screen and message shown in Figure 1.30. To start the virtual machine, click the Action menu and then click Start.

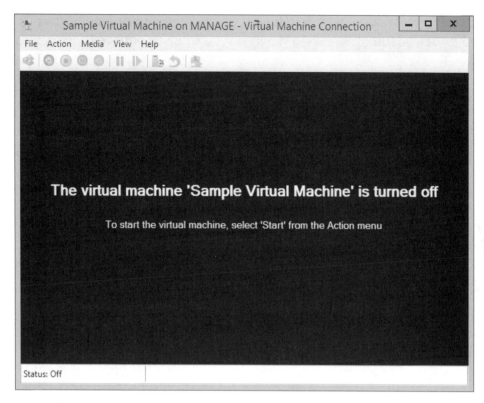

Figure 1.30
Virtual Machine Connection window.
Source: Hyper-V Manager/Windows Server 2012 R2.

You may find the following tips to be helpful when using the Virtual Machine Connection tool:

- Until a guest operating system is installed, press the mouse release key combination and then move the mouse pointer outside the virtual machine window. The default release key combination is Ctrl+Alt+Left arrow.

- You can move the mouse pointer easily between the operating systems running on the host computer and the virtual machine. If the mouse pointer appears as a small dot when you connect to a running virtual machine, click anywhere in the virtual machine window.

- You cannot press Ctrl+Alt+Delete on the keyboard to send the key combination to a virtual machine, because it will interrupt the host computer. Use the menu command instead; from the Action menu, click Ctrl+Alt+Delete. You can also press Ctrl+Alt+End.

- You can switch from a window view to a full-screen view by selecting Full Screen Mode from the View menu of Hyper-V Manager. To switch back to window mode, press Ctrl+Alt+Break.

The Virtual Machine Connection window contains a menu bar with the following options:

- **File:** Accesses the settings for the connected virtual machine. If you select Exit to close the Virtual Machine Connection session, the virtual machine will continue to run in the background.

- **Action:** Sends the Ctrl+Alt+Del sequence to the guest operating system. Other actions in the menu allow you to start, shut down, save, pause, and reset the virtual machine, take a snapshot of it, and revert to a previous state of the virtual machine. If the virtual machine is not currently running, most of these options will be disabled (grayed out).

- **Media:** Connects an .iso image file to a CD/DVD drive assigned to the virtual machine. You can also capture CD/DVD drives on the host computer for use by the virtual machine, eject currently mounted media, and specify a .vfd image to be connected to the virtual machine as a floppy disk.

- **Clipboard:** Pastes text from the clipboard of the parent partition into the guest operating system. You can also take a screen shot of the current image of the virtual machine, which is placed into the clipboard of the parent partition.

- **View:** If you switch the view to Full Screen Mode, a small toolbar appears at the top of the screen. If you click the pushpin, the toolbar disappears. Move the mouse pointer to the top of the screen to make the toolbar reappear. To verify the remote connection, click the lock. To return to the normal window view, press Ctrl+Alt +Break. To hide the Virtual Machine Connection toolbar, you can also click the Toolbar option on the View menu.

SUMMARY

- Cloud computing is the use of multiple server computers on a digital network that work together as if they were one computer. Cloud computing differs from the traditional client/server model by providing applications from a server that are executed and managed by a client's Web browser.

- Virtualization uses software to simulate a physical computing environment and uses virtual hardware on which you can install a number of OSs and interact with them. With virtualization technology, you can run a range of OSs on top of an OS. Virtualization requires specific hardware, X86 virtualization (Intel VT-x or AMD-V), for the host computers to function properly.

- The amount of memory required for effective processing is determined by the number of virtual machines that will run concurrently. For example, Windows Server 2012 R2 requires at least 512MB of RAM; however, 1GB is suggested.

- The number of network adapter cards you need is determined by the minimum number of networks required for the creation of private clouds.

- The Internet Small Computer System Interface (iSCSI) is an IP-based storage networking standard for linking host computers to data storage facilities.

- Hyper-V Manager provides a user interface for the Hyper-V virtualization environment.

- You can use Hyper-V Manager to create and configure virtual machines with virtualized hardware components.

- You can use wizards to create virtual hard disks and virtual networks. (A virtual hard disk can have the same contents as a physical hard disk drive, such as disk partitions and a file system, which in turn can contain files and folder.) (A virtual network works like a physical network switch, except that the switch is implemented in software.)

- Using the Virtual Machine Connection tool, you can turn on a virtual machine and boot it, log off and power down a virtual machine, stop processing and save the memory and processor status, review machine settings, and install a guest operating system.

- Several operating systems must be installed to support the lab activities in this book. Windows Server 2012 R2 Datacenter Edition will be installed on each of the three servers.

CASE PROJECTS

Case 1-1: Locating Software for the Activities

You are eager to start building your private cloud. You have located the hardware; however, you have a limited budget for software. Your task is to search the Web for affordable sources for this software. To get you started, consider the search key "DreamSpark."

Case 1-2: Exploring Information About Hyper-V

You would like to read additional information about a number of topics in this book. What you're looking for is a Microsoft technical site dedicated to the Hyper-V hypervisor. Consider this search term: "server 2012 hyper-v."

Case 1-3: Exploring Information About Generation 2

You are intrigued about the Generation 2 hardware capabilities that are available in the Create Virtual Machine wizard. Do a Web search for Windows Server 2012 Generation 2 Overview.

CHAPTER 2

THE MICROSOFT PRIVATE CLOUD

After reading this chapter and completing the exercises, you will be able to do the following:

- Describe Microsoft's private cloud strategy.
- Describe the VMM 2012 R2 components.
- Identify the requirements for VMM 2012 R2.
- Deploy VMM prerequisites.
- Install VMM server.

In this chapter, you will learn to describe Microsoft's private cloud strategy, which builds on the virtualization you learned in Chapter 1, "Introduction to the Private Cloud." You'll describe the components for System Center Virtual Machine Manager (SCVMM) 2012 R2, a Microsoft product that manages a series of host computers and virtual machines from a central console. From this point forward, the term *VMM* corresponds to System Center Virtual Machine Manager 2012 R2. Next, you'll identify the requirements required by VMM and install the VMM perquisites. The last step will be to install the VMM server.

VMM provides the capability to manage virtualization components for an Infrastructure as a Service (IaaS) model of a private cloud. In successive chapters, you will add needed components to complete a working private cloud. VMM must be purchased from Microsoft, but the product helps you take a big step toward fulfilling the requirements for a working private cloud. You will gain the skills needed to scale up the private cloud to meet the needs of IT organizations.

Microsoft Private Cloud Strategy

Microsoft articulated the Microsoft cloud strategy at TechShare 2013 in New Orleans. The annual TechShare conferences provide Microsoft with the opportunity to communicate the direction that the company will take in the development of future products. Also, product announcements usually accompany these communications.

This strategy for the Microsoft private cloud is best described as a pool of compute, network, and storage resources available on demand with a component to manage the pool of resources.

These four components, as shown in Figure 2.1, coordinate activities to produce the private cloud environment:

- **Manage:** Contains the software to manage the cloud environment. This includes the VMM support software, such as Microsoft SQL Server (which stores the databases) and Active Directory Domain Services (which stores the directory data for the management of users and computers).

- **Compute:** Contains multiple clustered servers, where servers appear to users as unified computing resources, with each running multiple virtual machines.

- **Network:** Contains the software to integrate the physical network resources into the private cloud environment where network resources are virtualized.

- **Storage:** Contains the hardware and software to provide the private cloud with virtualized storage and to permit optimization of disk resources.

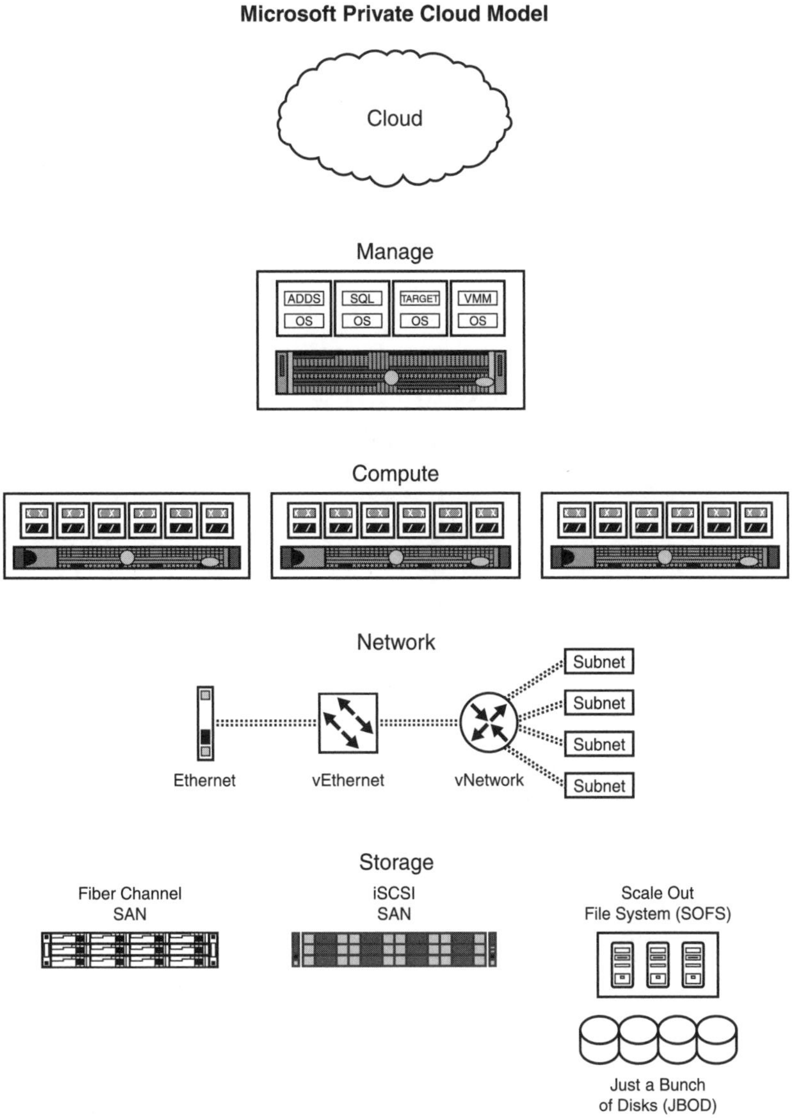

Microsoft Private Cloud Model

Figure 2.1
Microsoft private cloud.
© 2014 Cengage Learning®.

Manage

VMM ties together the following components and resources to manage the private cloud:

- **Virtualization management:** The key responsibility for VMM is the management of the virtual environment.

- **Fabric management:** A fabric controller oversees cloud resources across host servers. In addition, the fabric controller provides networking configurations and storage to virtual machines automatically as they are deployed.

- **Resource management:** One of the best features of VMM is the library. The library provides a source of reusable components: hardware profiles, software profiles, virtual machine templates, and ISO files. You will use the library to simplify the creation of virtual machines.

- **PowerShell:** A scripting solution for VMM. With PowerShell, you can script repetitive tasks to support VMM operations. In addition, VMM uses PowerShell scripts to automate management tasks. You will learn to use PowerShell in Chapters 9, "Introducing PowerShell," and 10, "Working with PowerShell Scripts."

- **Cloud management:** You use VMM to create and manage the private cloud. You control the resources of the cloud by specifying the permissions to deploy virtual machines.

- **App Controller:** With the App controller, you provide a self-service interface for the users of the private cloud. You will learn more about this component in Chapter 8, "Working with Application Self-Service Users."

The MANAGE server, in our project environment, supports the management component for multiple virtual machines (refer to Figure 2.1). Microsoft's philosophy remains to virtualize everything. These virtual machines are providing the following services:

- **Active Directory Domain Services:** Organizes and manages directory components such as users' and computers' accounts while providing security for network resources.

- **SQL Server:** A Microsoft database server, which provides storage for VMM resources such as virtual machine configurations.

- **iSCSI Software Target:** Provisions a Windows Server 2012 R2 virtual machine to act as a storage area network (SAN) that provides access to consolidated, block level data storage so that the devices appear as locally attached devices to the operating systems running on other host computers and virtual machines.

- **VMM:** Virtual Machine Manager component, which manages the private cloud environment.

Compute

The Compute component consists of multiple Hyper-V Host servers where each are running multiple virtual machines. Each virtual machine enables an OS to provide support to run user applications (refer to Figure 2.1). The Compute component is scalable, meaning that additional compute host servers are added to the private cloud as demand dictates.

The Compute component in our project environment consists of two host computers called COMPUTE1 and COMPUTE2, which form the COMPUTE cluster. These host computers run the virtual machines for the users of the private cloud.

Network

The Network component provides networking that supports your virtual machines. VMM enhances and extends the ways in which you work with IP addressing, subnets, switches, and other elements of networking.

In the previous chapter, you used the Virtual Switch Manager of Hyper-V Manager to create a logical network. You added a virtual switch to map the vEthernet logical network to the Ethernet physical adapter (refer to Figure 2.1). Virtual machines can't connect directly to physical adapters. You create virtual switches to permit virtual machines to use networks.

VMM provides a second layer of abstraction above that provided by the Virtual Switch Manager (refer to Figure 2.1). This is useful when you need to create independent subnets for groups of virtual machines. For example, you could isolate the virtual machines for one user from another user by placing the virtual machines on isolated networks. The vEthernet logical network is divided into multiple virtual networks (shown as subnets) by the virtual network router. This will be covered in detail in Chapter 4, "Working with Networks Using VMM."

The Network component in our project environment provides a number of virtualized network components:

- **Logical networks:** Map the physical network using Hyper-V Switches. The Management, Storage, and Heartbeat networks are provided directly by Hyper-V switches.

- **Virtual networks:** Provide network connectivity for the virtual machines. VMM provides a software-based layer 3 switch with DHCP allocators to provide IP addresses for the indicated subnets. The Service network is an example of a virtual network.

Storage

Microsoft offers a number of storage solutions (refer to Figure 2.1). These storage devices store the massive amounts of data required by the private cloud. Remote storage units off-load work from the host servers to external storage, which provides capacity and scaling to meet future growth. VMM supports block-level storage devices that use LUNs to indicate connections between host servers and storage devices.

- **Fibre Channel SAN:** Storage devices connected through Fibre Channel switches to Fibre Channel adapters in the host servers.
- **iSCSI SAN:** Storage devices connected by IP networks supporting SCSI device commands.
- **Scale Out File Servers (SOFS):** Clustered file servers offering file shares with some form of block-level shared storage, which is often called *just a bunch of disks* (JBOD).

The Storage component in our project environment uses the Microsoft iSCSI Software Target running within a virtual machine on the MANAGE host computer to provide virtualized storage. The Microsoft iSCSI Software Target provides storage (disks) over a TCP/IP network. It turns a computer running Windows Server 2012 R2 into a storage device. You need this storage to enable high availability and live migration for virtual machines. You will learn more about storage in Chapter 5, "Working with VMM Storage."

Describe the VMM 2012 R2 Components

VMM provides a comprehensive solution for building the Microsoft private cloud. VMM scales to manage hundreds of host computers running thousands of virtual machines. Figure 2.2 shows a typical implementation of the server roles for VMM. At the center of the figure, the VMM server functions as the controller of the virtual management environment. Access to the VMM servers is through the VMM administrator console.

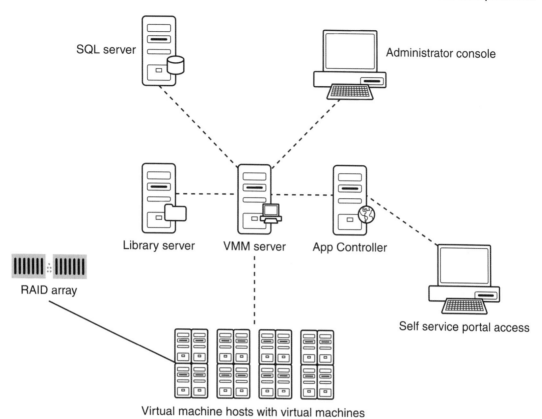

SQL server

Administrator console

Library server   VMM server   App Controller

RAID array

Self service portal access

Virtual machine hosts with virtual machines

Figure 2.2
Typical VMM implementation.
© 2014 Cengage Learning®.

The VMM server provides a number of services, including management of the host computers. To perform these management tasks, such as creating virtual machines, jobs are created by VMM in Windows PowerShell and then run. Recall that PowerShell is a Microsoft scripting language that interfaces with the operating system to perform most management tasks.

Microsoft SQL Server provides the database to store various configurations. The library server manages the reusable components, which are typically stored on a storage area network (SAN) for access by the host computers and virtual machines.

App Controller supports a VMM self-service portal that provides Web access to the VMM environment. From the Internet Explorer Web browser, users can create and manage their virtual machines in a controlled environment. The VMM App Controller with the self-service portal provides access to the virtual machines supporting the private cloud. Of course, the virtual machine hosts provide virtualization to run the guest operating systems. You will learn more about these components later in this section.

The VMM consolidated implementation used in this book is shown in Figure 2.3. Other than the hosts for the virtual machines, the various server roles have been consolidated on the management MANAGE server. The Microsoft iSCSI Target, a Microsoft implementation for iSCSI-based SAN storage, replaces the RAID device. The two host computers (COMPUTE1 and COMPUTE2) continue to provide the virtualization services to run the virtual machines. You will build this configuration as you work through this chapter and succeeding chapters, and you will finish the configuration with the component installations in future chapters.

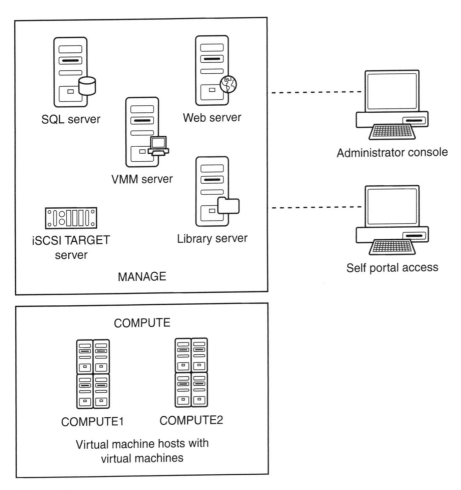

Figure 2.3
Consolidated VMM implementation.
© 2014 Cengage Learning®.

VMM Server and VMM Database

The VMM database is a Microsoft SQL database. The SQL server must be installed prior to the installation of the VMM server. When you install the SQL, you will use SQL Server 2012 SP1. Because the VMM engine interacts directly with the Microsoft SQL database, you will not need to interact with the database. The VMM setup procedure will define the database schema, which specifies the database fields and attributes.

The VMM server component is crucial to the VMM environment, and it should be the second component installed. Within the VMM server is the VMM engine, which connects to the VMM database stored on the SQL server. The VMM database stores all of the configuration and management information that VMM requires. The VMM engine performs three major tasks:

- It handles requests for information and updates to the VMM database. For example, when the VMM console needs information, the VMM engine contacts the VMM database for the data.

- It communicates and executes commands with the VMM agents on the host computers. Such commands include requesting that a VMM agent start a virtual machine on a host computer.

- It coordinates the execution of VMM jobs. Every operation in the VMM environment is handled by a VMM job. In addition, the VMM engine monitors jobs and reports their progress, and then informs you whether the jobs succeed or fail.

VMM Administrator Console

You use the VMM administrator console to manage the VMM environment. The console resembles Hyper-V Manager and has three panes. The pane on the left side of the window contains three sections that let you control the information shown in the console. Depending on the management view you select at the bottom of this pane, the entire console window changes. The VMM administrator console has five management views, and you will learn to work with these views in Chapter 3, "Configuring the Fabric Resources":

- **Hosts view:** Manages the host computers that run the virtual machines.

- **Virtual Machines view:** Manages and changes the settings for individual virtual machines.

- **Library view:** Lists the resources for building virtual machines.

- **Jobs view:** Provides the status of the current running jobs and the history of past jobs.

■ **Administration view:** Includes the administrative components of VMM. For example, it shows graphs for four summary categories: Hosts, Virtual Machines, Recent Jobs, and Library Resources.

Windows PowerShell Interface

Before the VMM engine can perform management tasks, such as the addition of host computers, jobs must be created in Windows PowerShell and run to perform these tasks. Microsoft describes PowerShell as a task-based command-line shell and scripting language designed especially for system administration. Because PowerShell is built on the .NET Framework, a library of software that provides access to operating system functionality, VMM has access to the required Windows Server 2012 R2 resources to manage the VMM environment. To perform these management tasks, PowerShell provides a wide range of cmdlets, small scripting commands that can be invoked in PowerShell scripts.

The VMM wizards allow you to display these generated scripts by clicking the View Script button on any wizard summary page. Although you can view a script to see how VMM performs a task, you do not need to write PowerShell scripts. In Chapter 10, "Working with PowerShell Scripts," you will learn to extend PowerShell scripts to automate tasks. For example, you will extend a script that creates one virtual machine to create multiple virtual machines.

VMM Agents

VMM communicates with the VMM agents installed on the host computers, and it provides an automatic method for deploying remote agents. When host computers are added to the VMM environment from the VMM administrator console, a job is run to deploy the agents to the selected host computers. The only requirement is that the host computer be a member of the same Active Directory domain with the appropriate user credentials.

VMM Library

The VMM library is the central location for the building blocks necessary to construct virtual machines. *Rapid provisioning* takes advantage of the VMM library to deploy virtual machines in the private cloud. A hardware profile, software profile, and stored image are combined to construct a new virtual machine in a matter of minutes; the same operation might take several hours using conventional operating system installations. The library can be used to store all file-based resources, including virtual hard disks, ISO images, operating system and hardware profiles, and PowerShell scripts.

VMM App Controller

The VMM App Controller, a self-service portal, provides Web access to the VMM environment. From the Internet Explorer Web browser, users can create and manage their virtual machines in the private cloud in a controlled environment. You can create self-service roles from VMM to control this access. You will learn more about the self-service portal in Chapter 8.

VMM Architecture

In this section, you will learn about the communications protocols and port assignments used by VMM system components. This information is useful when you need to troubleshoot problems in the VMM environment. Figure 2.4 shows the communications protocols used between the various VMM system components.

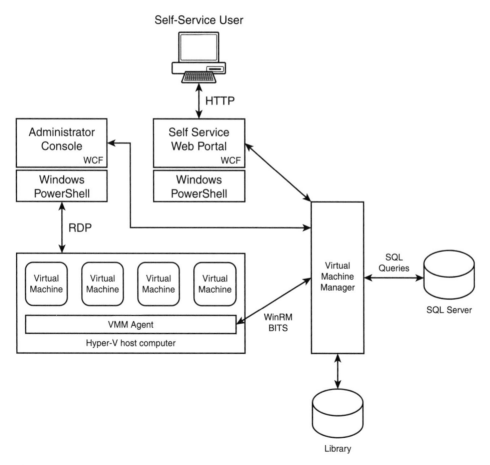

Figure 2.4
VMM communications between components.
© 2014 Cengage Learning®.

VMM Protocols

VMM combines a number of Microsoft communications protocols and Internet protocols to communicate between components. You may find this information helpful when you troubleshoot problems in the VMM environment. The central hub of these communications is the VMM server. The following list summarizes VMM communications and the protocols used:

■ VMM communicates with VMM agents on the host computers using Windows Remote Management (WinRM), the Microsoft implementation of the WS-Management protocol, which is a public standard for remotely exchanging management data between computers. VMM always initiates this communication by polling for information or sending commands.

■ VMM uses the Background Intelligent Transfer Service (BITS) for transferring data files between server roles. BITS maximizes the transfer of files between machines using idle network bandwidth.

■ For communications between the VMM server, administrator console, and PowerShell cmdlets, VMM uses the Windows Communication Foundation (WCF). Microsoft describes the WCF as a part of the .NET Framework for rapidly building Internet applications, such as online sales and order tracking, customer relations management, and health management.

■ VMM uses the Remote Desktop Protocol (RDP) to connect to a virtual machine and provide a console session to the user. The RDP was developed by Microsoft to provide a GUI from a connected remote computer.

■ For private cloud users, VMM uses the HyperText Transfer Protocol (HTTP), an Internet protocol for the transmission and formatting of Web pages. For secured Web pages, VMM uses HyperText Transfer Protocol Secure (HTTPS), which is the secure version of HTTP.

Table 2.1 shows the communication ports required by VMM. As you run the setup procedure to install VMM, the required ports are opened in the Windows firewall. The default communication ports will work.

Table 2.1   Communication Ports for VMM Environment

VMM Components	Network Port	Protocol
VMM server	80	HTTP, WinRM
	443	BITS
	8100	WCF
SQL Server	1433	Remote SQL
	1434	SQL Browser
Windows host	80	HTTP, WinRM
	443	BITS
	3389	RDP
Hyper-V host	2179	RDP port listener
Internet Information Server (IIS)	80	HTTP
	443	HTTPS

© 2014 Cengage Learning®.

IDENTIFYING REQUIREMENTS FOR VIRTUAL MACHINE MANAGER

VMM is Microsoft's suite of management tools for the virtualized environment of Hyper-V host computers. This section outlines the hardware and software that are required to implement the VMM environment.

Requirements for VMM Server

You can install VMM on a single computer; this minimal configuration can serve up to 10 host computers. For heavier workloads, Microsoft recommends that the server roles be distributed on dedicated computers.

The VMM administrator console is normally installed on the VMM server or any accessible computer running the Windows Server 2012 R2 Standard or Enterprise edition. However, you could install the console on a desktop computer that is running Windows 8.1.

Requirements for VMM Database Server

VMM uses a Microsoft SQL Server database to store data for the managed virtual machines, host computers, jobs, and other related data. This data is the basis for the information that you view in the VMM administrator console. You have a number of choices when selecting the location of this SQL server. For example, you can select an existing local or remote supported version, or you can install SQL Server 2012 SP1.

Requirements for VMM Library Server

If a VMM object is not stored in the SQL database, it is stored on the VMM library server. You can expect to find a wide range of files stored on this server:

- **Virtual machine templates:** Standardized hardware and software settings, including an installed OS that can be used to provision virtual machines in the private cloud.
- **Virtual hard disk:** Virtualized hard disk with a file system.
- **Virtual floppy disk:** Virtualized floppy disk with a file system.
- **PowerShell scripts:** Programs written to use the PowerShell cmdlets to perform tasks with the Windows Server 2008 operating system.
- **Hardware profiles:** Hardware settings that will be used by a virtual machine.
- **Guest operating system profiles:** Operating system settings to ensure constant configurations for virtual machines.
- **Stored virtual machines:** Virtual machines that have been removed from the hard disks of host computers and stored in the library.

When you install VMM, the setup procedure automatically adds the management computer as the default library server with a default library share of "MSSCVMMLibrary." Because you cannot delete or rename it, be careful when specifying the location and name for the default library share. After you complete the setup procedure, you can add more library shares.

Requirements for App Controller

The VMM App Controller requires a Web server with Windows Server IIS. This is available as a role service from Windows Server 2012 R2. In Chapter 8, you will install and work with the App Controller to access virtual machines running in the private cloud.

Requirements for PowerShell CLI

The PowerShell command-line interface (CLI) is implemented as a support component for scripting on computers running Windows Server 2012 R2. The administrator console and self-service portal are built using PowerShell components. The VMM PowerShell CLI component is installed as the administrator console is installed.

Requirements for VMM Virtual Machine Hosts

The Hyper-V virtualization environment used in this book, Windows Server 2012 R2, is fully supported by VMM. Support also exists for other virtualization environments, such as Citrix XenServer and VMware ESXi Server, but these environments are beyond the scope of this book.

Network Requirements for VMM

As virtual machines run, the virtual hard disk files can grow from 4GB to as large as 15GB, depending on the operating system, applications, and services. For this reason, Microsoft recommends network connections of 1 gigabit (Gb). In addition, a SAN device is needed to store the virtual hard disk files in the private cloud. You will implement iSCSI SAN storage in Chapter 5.

The computer you select to run VMM must be a member of a domain in Active Directory Domain Services. Microsoft recommends using a domain controller that is at the Windows Server 2012 R2 domain functional level.

DEPLOY ACTIVE DIRECTORY DOMAIN SERVICES (AD DS)

AD DS provides a distributed database that stores and manages information about network resources. You can use AD DS to organize elements of a network, such as users, computers, and other devices, into a hierarchical structure. This structure includes the Active Directory forest, domains in the forest, and organizational units (OUs) in each domain. A server that runs AD DS is called a *domain controller.*

Security is integrated with AD DS through logon authentication and access control to resources in the directory. Using a single network logon, you can manage the AD DS directory data and organization throughout your network. Authorized users can also use a single network logon to access resources anywhere in the network.

Policy-based administration expands the role of AD DS to centralize the management of computers. Similar to how permissions are used to control access to computing resources, Group Policy defines the settings and allowed actions for users and computers.

The AD DS server role requires DNS to be running so that network resources and services can be located. For example, the AD DS structure uses DNS domain names for forests and domains.

With the DNS server role, you provide a name resolution process that enables users to locate network computers by querying for a user-friendly name instead of an IP address. A computer that runs the DNS server role can host the records of a DNS database and use the records to resolve DNS name queries sent by DNS client computers. These queries can include requests such as the names of websites, network computers, or computers on the Internet. The local DNS server will forward name queries for computers on the Internet.

Install ADDS Server

In this exercise, you will create a virtual machine on the MANAGE server and Add the Active Directory Domain Services role after installing Windows Server 2012 R2 Standard.

You need the Windows Server 2012 R2 Standard .iso file and one standard license. Also, the Virtual Switch for the Management Logical Network must be completed (see "Installing the Virtualization Host Servers" in Chapter 1).

1. Copy the Windows Server 2012 R2 .iso file to the **C:\ISOFiles** folder.

2. Using Chapter 1 as a guideline, launch the New Virtual Machine Wizard and create a virtual machine conforming to the requirements in Table 2.2.

Table 2.2 Suggested Settings for ADDS Virtual Machine

Item	Suggested Setting
Name	ADDS
Generation	Generation 1
Start-up memory	1024
Use Dynamic Memory for this virtual machine	Selected
Connection	Management Logical Network
Virtual hard disk	ADDS.vhdx
Install an operating system from a bootable CD/DVD	Selected
Image files (.iso)	C:\ISOFiles\ Windows Server 2012 R2 .iso

© 2014 Cengage Learning®.

3. Using Chapter 1 as a guideline, start the ADDS virtual machine and install the OS in the ADDS virtual machine with the suggested settings in Table 2.3.

Table 2.3   Suggested Settings for ADDS Virtual Machine Installation

Item	Suggested Setting
Password	Pa$$w0rd
IPv6 Address	FD00::103
Subnet prefix length	64
IPV4 Address	192.168.0.103
Subnet Mask	255.255.255.0
Default Gateway	192.168.0.1
IPv4 DNS Server	192.168.0.1
Computer name	ADDS
Domain name	Test.Local

© 2014 Cengage Learning®.

4. After the reboot of the virtual machine, click the Media menu, point to DVD Drive, and click Eject.

5. To log on, click the Action menu, click Ctrl+Alt+Delete, and then enter Pa$$w0rd.

6. Continue with steps in Chapter 1 using the suggested settings in Table 2.3.

Problems with Internet Connectivity

If you have problems with Internet connectivity, replace the 192.168.0.1 for the IPv4 DNS Server with your Internet Service Provider's DNS Server IP address.

7. Wait for the install to complete and complete the configuration of the ADDS virtual machine.

8. To add the Active Directory Domain Services, click Manage on the Server Manager window, click Add Roles and Features, click Server Selection, and then click Next.

9. Check Active Directory Domain Services. Click Add Features, click Next three times, and click Install.

10. Wait for the installation to complete and then click Close.

11. To promote the server to a Domain Controller, click AD DS in the left pane, click More in the yellow bar, and then click Promote this server to a domain controller.

12. Select Add a New Forest, enter Test.Local for the Root domain name, and then click Next.

13. Enter Pa$$w0rd for Password and Confirm password and then press Enter.

14. To ignore the DNS delegation message, click Next.

15. Continue with the Wizard and review the NetBIOS domain name. Click Next three times.

16. Review the results of the prerequisites check, scroll and locate the All prerequisite checks passed successfully, and then click Install. The system will restart.

17. To log on, click the Action menu, click Ctrl+Alt+Delete, and then enter Pa$$w0rd.

18. To establish a user account for VMMAdmin, click Tools (upper-right corner of Server Manager) and then click Active Directory Users and Computers.

19. Navigate to the User folder. Click Action, point to New, and then select User.

20. Enter the account details for VMMAdmin with a password of Pa$$w0rd. Check Password never expires.

21. Make the VMMAdmin a member of the Domain Admins security group.

22. Repeat steps 18 through 21 for VMMStore and VMMRun.

23. To create the container for Distributed Key Management with ADSI Edit, press the Windows key, type adsi on the desktop, and then double-click ADSI Edit.

24. Right-click on ADSI Edit, click Connect to, click on Select a well-known Naming Context, and then click OK.

25. To add a new container, expand Default naming context (ADDS.Test.Local), right-click DC=Test, DC=Local, point to New, click Object, click Container, and click Next. Enter VMMDKM for the Value and then click Next. Click Finish and close the ADSI Editor window.

26. To add security details to the VMMDKM container, return to Active Directory Users and Computers. Click View and then click Advanced Features.

27. Right-click on VMMDKM and then click Properties. Click the Security tab, click Add, type vmmadmin, and then click OK. Select Allow: Read, Write, and Create all child objects.

28. Click Advanced, select VMMAdmin, and then click Edit. Click Applies to and then select This object and all descendant objects. Click OK three times.

29. When finished, close the Active Directory Users and Computers window.

30. To open Group Policy Management, click Tools and then click Group Policy Management.

31. Expand Forest.Test.Local, expand Domains, expand Test.Local, click Default Domain Policy, and click OK.

32. To locate the network policy, right-click Default Domain Policy and click Edit.

33. Under Computer Configuration, expand Policies, expand Windows Settings, expand Security Settings, and then click Network List Manager Policies.

34. To set the policy to configure unidentified networks as Private, right-click Unidentified Networks, click Properties, click Private, and then click OK.

35. Close the two open windows.

36. Record the VMMAdmin, VMMStore, and VMMRun user accounts for use in future activities. Also record VMMDKM details for Distributed Key Management.

Microsoft SQL Server 2012 Requirements

Microsoft SQL (pronounced *sequel*) Server is a relational database management system. Database management systems (DBMSs) are specially designed server applications that interact with other applications, such as VMM and the database. Most relational databases use the SQL data definition and query language. The software requirements for SQL are listed in Table 2.4.

Table 2.4   Software and Hardware Requirements for SQL Server

Component	Requirement
.Net Framework	.NET 3.5 SP1
Windows PowerShell	PowerShell 2.0
	(Continued)

Table 2.4 Software and Hardware Requirements for SQL Server (*Continued*)

Component	Requirement
Virtualization	Windows Server 2012 R2
Internet Software	IE 7.0 or later
Hard Disk	6GB
Memory	1GB

© 2014 Cengage Learning®.

Install SQL Server

In this exercise, you will create a virtual machine on the MANAGE server and install SQL Server 2012 SP1 after installing Windows Server 2012 R2 standard. You need the Windows Server 2012 R2 Standard .iso and one standard license.

1. Using Chapter 1 as a guideline, launch the New Virtual Machine Wizard and create a virtual machine with the suggested settings in Table 2.5.

Table 2.5 Suggested Settings for SQL Virtual Machine

Item	Suggested Setting
Name	SQL
Generation	Generation 1
Start-up memory	1024
Use Dynamic Memory for this virtual machine	Selected
Connection	Management Logical Network
Virtual hard disk	SQL.vhdx
Install an operating system from a bootable CD/DVD	Selected
Image files (.iso)	C:\ISOFiles\ Windows Server 2012 R2 .iso

© 2014 Cengage Learning®.

2. Using Chapter 1 as a guideline, start the SQL virtual machine and install the OS in the SQL virtual machine using the suggested settings in Table 2.6.

Table 2.6 Suggested Settings for SQL Virtual Machine Installation

Item	Suggested Setting
Password	Pa$$w0rd
IPv6 Address	FD00::104
Subnet prefix length	64
IPV4 Address	192.168.0.104
Subnet Mask	255.255.255.0
Default Gateway	192.168.0.1
IPv4 DNS Server	192.168.0.103
Computer name	SQL

© 2014 Cengage Learning®.

3. After the reboot of the virtual machine, click the Media menu, point to DVD Drive, and click Eject.

4. To log on, click the Action menu, click Ctrl+Alt+Delete, and then enter Pa$$w0rd.

5. Continue with the installation steps in Chapter 1 using the suggested settings in Table 2.6.

6. Wait for the install to complete and complete the configuration of the SQL virtual machine.

7. To join the domain, from the Server Manager, click the Workgroup link. Click Change, click Domain, and enter Test. Log in as the Administrator with Pa$$w0rd.

8. Wait for the Welcome to the Test domain message and restart the machine.

9. To change to the domain administrator account, click the Action menu, click Ctrl+Alt+Delete, click the back arrow, and click Other user. Enter test\administrator and Pa$$w0rd.

10. Return to the Server Manager and click Local Server.

11. To install .NET Framework 3.5, click Manage in the Server Manager window, click Add Roles and Features, click Server Selection, click Next, click Features, check .NET Framework 3.5 Features, click Next, and then click Install.

12. Wait for the installation to complete and then click Close. Minimize Server Manager.

13. Insert the SQL DVD and click Media, point to DVD Drive, and click Capture D.

14. Open the Windows Explorer (yellow folder on the task bar), right-click DVD Drive (D:), and then select Install or run program from your media.

15. To start the SQL installation, click Installation and then select New SQL Server stand-alone installation (first link).

16. When the Setup Support Rules check completes successfully (first time), click OK.

17. Proceed through the install setup files wizard to install the setup files.

18. When the Setup Support Rules check completes successfully (second time), click Next twice.

19. Select Database Engine Services, scroll and select Management Tools – Complete. Click Next.

20. When the Installation Rules check completes successfully, click Next.

21. Review and record the Instance Configuration for the Instance ID of MSSQLSERVER.

22. Click Next until the Database Engine Configuration page appears.

23. To specify user accounts to access the Database Engine, click Add Current User. Click Add, add the VMMAdmin account, click OK, and then click Next twice.

24. When the Installation Configuration Rules check completes successfully, click Next and then click Install.

25. When the installation completes close the SQL Server Setup window.

26. To eject the SQL DVD, click the Media menu, point to DVD Drive, and then click Release D.

27. To open the firewall for the port used by VMM to communicate with SQL, click Tools in Server Manager, click Windows Firewall with Advanced Security, and then click Inbound Rules.

28. In the Action panel, click New Rule, click Port, and then click Next.

29. Enter 1433 for the Specified local ports and click Next three times. Enter Open1433 for the Name and then click Finish. Close the Windows Firewall with Advanced Security window.

SQL Server Management Studio Installed

If you are researching a problem with the database on your SQL server, you may be asked to enter SQL commands to correct the problem. The SQL Server can be accessed from the Start screen by typing SQL Server Management Studio.

INSTALLING VMM DEPENDENCIES

Before the VMM role can be added, a number of dependencies must be met:

- The VMM server must be a member of the Test domain.

- Download and install the Windows Assessment and Deployment Kit (ADK). The Windows Assessment and Deployment Kit (ADK) customizes and deploys the virtual machines that you deploy in the private cloud. In addition, the ADK supports the deployment of bare metal installations of Hyper-V hosts. The ADK will use the existing SQL server to store its database.

- Download and install the SQL 2012 SP1 Server Connectivity Feature Pack. With this package, your VMM connects to the SQL server with the SQL server native client and uses the SQL server command line utilities.

- Configure the distributed key management (DKM), which is used to store VMM encryption keys in Active Directory Domain Services. The DKM is required to store keys for future use by the failover cluster.

Install VMM Server Prerequisites

In this exercise, you'll create a virtual machine on the MANAGE server and Add the VMM Server Perquisites after installing Windows Server 2012 R2 Standard. You need the Windows Server 2012 R2 Standard .iso file and one standard license. Also, the Virtual Switch for the Management Network must be completed (see Chapter 1, "Introduction to the Private Cloud").

1. Using Chapter 1 as a guideline, launch the New Virtual Machine Wizard and create a virtual machine conforming to the requirements in Table 2.7.

Table 2.7 Suggested Settings for VMM Virtual Machine

Item	Suggested Setting
Name	VMM
Generation	Generation 1
Start-up memory	4096
Use Dynamic Memory for this virtual machine	Selected
Connection	Management Logical Network
Virtual hard disk	VMM.vhdx
Install an operating system from a bootable CD/DVD	Selected
Image files (.iso)	C:\ISOFiles\ Windows Server 2012 R2 .iso

2. Using Chapter 1 as a guideline, start the VMM virtual machine and install the OS in the VMM virtual machine with the suggested settings in Table 2.8.

Table 2.8 Suggested Settings for VMM Virtual Machine Installation

Item	Suggested Setting
Password	Pa$$w0rd
IPv6 Address	FD00::105
Subnet prefix length	64
IPV4 Address	192.168.0.105
Subnet Mask	255.255.255.0
Default Gateway	192.168.0.1
IPv4 DNS Server	192.168.0.103
Computer name	VMM
Domain name	Test.Local

3. After the reboot of the virtual machine, click the Action menu, point to DVD Drive, and click Eject.

4. To log on, click the Action menu, click Ctrl+Alt+Delete, and then enter Pa$$w0rd.

5. Continue with the installation steps in Chapter 1 using the suggested settings in Table 2.8.

6. Wait for the install to complete and complete the configuration of the VMM virtual machine.

7. To join the domain, from the Server Manager, click the Workgroup link. Click Change, click Domain, and enter Test.Local. Log in as the Administrator with Pa$$w0rd. Wait for the Welcome to the Test domain message and restart the machine.

8. To change to the domain administrator account, click the Action menu, click Ctrl+Alt+Delete, click the back arrow, and click Other user. Enter test\administrator and Pa$$w0rd.

9. To add accounts to the local Administrators group, click Tools, click Computer Management, expand Local Users and Groups, click Groups, double-click Administrators, click Add, click Advanced, enter VMM for Starts with, click Find Now, click VMMAdmin and VMMRun. and click OK three times. Close the Computer Management window.

10. Open the Internet Explorer, click Settings (blue gear), click Internet Options, click Security, click Custom level, scroll and locate File download, and then click Enable. Click OK, click Yes, and then click OK.

11. From the Internet Explorer, search for Download Windows Assessment and Deployment Kit (ADK) for Windows 8.1 and then click Save.

Use Windows Assessment and Deployment Kit (ADK) for Windows 8.1

You must download the Windows Assessment and Deployment Kit (ADK) for Windows 8.1 because other versions will be rejected during the installation of the VMM server.

12. To install the ADK, click Run, click Next twice, click Accept, clear all checkboxes with the exception of Deployment Tools and Windows Preinstallation Environment (Windows PE), and click Install.

ADK Install Takes Time

The installation of the ADK is a time-consuming process. You will want to take a break after it starts!

13. Wait for the ADK to be installed and click Close.

14. From the Internet Explorer, search for the SQL Server 2012 SP1 Feature Pack. Click Download. Scroll and check ENU/x64/SqlCmdLnUtils.msi. Scroll and check ENU/x64/sqlncli.msi. Scroll and click Next, and click Save twice. Click View Downloads.

15. To install the SQL client, click Run for ENU/x64/sqlncli.msi., click Next, click I accept the terms of the license agreement, click Next twice, click Install, and then click Finish.

Install the SQL Client first

You must install the SQL Client first, which is used by the SQL command line utilities.

16. To install the SQL command line utilities, click Run for ENU/x64/SqlCmdLnUtils.msi, click Next, click I accept the terms of the license agreement, scroll and click Next, click Install, and then click Finish. Click Close.

17. To add the Multipath I/O feature, click Manage, click Add Roles and Features, click Next four times, scroll and select Multipath I/O, scroll and select Telnet Client, click Next, and then click Install.

18. Wait for the installations to complete and click Close.

19. To restart the VMM virtual machine, click TASKS, select Shut Down Local Server, click the What do you want to do chevron, select Restart, click the Option chevron, and then select Operating System Reconfiguration (Planned). Click OK.

Do Not Select Operating System Recovery (Planned)

If you select Operating System Recovery (Planned), you will place the operating system in an unrecoverable loop. Be sure you select Operating System Reconfiguration (Planned) to shut down or restart your virtual machine.

20. To log on, click Action, click Ctrl+Alt+Delete, and then enter Pa$$w0rd.

INSTALLING THE VMM SERVER

The VMM server is the core of VMM. In this section, you will install the VMM management component.

Before starting this install, you need to be sure that the previous activities were completed successfully. Also, the ADDS and SQL virtual machines must be running. You will need the System Center 2012 R2 Virtual Machine Manager .iso file and a System Center 2012 R2 Virtual Machine Manager product key.

Start the installation from the System Center 2012 R2 Virtual Machine Manager .iso file. The initial screen is shown in Figure 2.5. You can install a VMM Agent to a machine in the COMPUTE group by clicking the Local Agent link. To install the VMM management server and VMM Console, click the Install link.

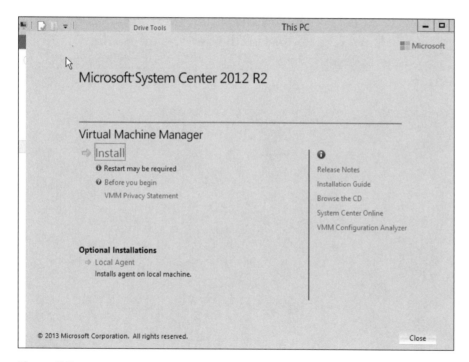

Figure 2.5
Microsoft System Center 2012 R2 Splash screen.
Source: VMM Install/Windows Server 2012 R2.

1. Insert the System Center 2012 R2 Virtual Machine Manager DVD.

2. Return to the VMM Server Virtual Machine. Click Media and click Capture D.

3. Open the Windows Explorer, double-click DVD Drive (D:) SC2012R2VMM, and then click Install.

Steps for VMM 2012 R2 Evaluation

If you are using the SCVMM 2012 R2 evaluation software, replace Step 3 with these steps:

1. Click Media on the menu bar, point to DVD Drive, and click Capture D.

2. To extract the VMM files, click the Windows Explorer icon, double-click DVD Drive (D:), double-click SC2012_R2_SCVMM, and click Next.

3. Change D:\SC2012_R2_SCVMM to C:\ SC2012_R2_SCVMM and click Next. Click Extract.

4. Wait for the extraction to complete. Click Finish.

5. Navigate to the C:\SC2012 R2 SCVMM folder and double-click setup. Click Install.

6. Click Media, click DVD Drive, and then click Release D.

Select VMM Management Server

Figure 2.6 shows the features to install. When you check the VMM management server, the VMM console is installed. You could install the console to another available server, which allows the console to be used to access the VMM server from an adjacent server or perhaps a desktop.

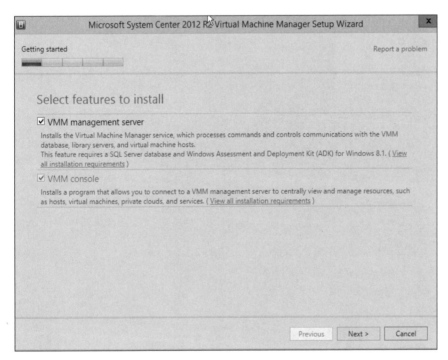

Figure 2.6
VMM Setup Wizard VMM components to install page.
Source: VMM Install/Windows Server 2012 R2.

1. Click VMM management server.

2. Click Next.

Product Registration

In the next step, the Product registration info is added (see Figure 2.7). You can identify the responsible party. The organization is optional and may be skipped. You may enter the Product key or wait and activate it at a later date. You have a grace period of 30 days. If you are using the 180-day evaluation version, you don't need to enter a product key.

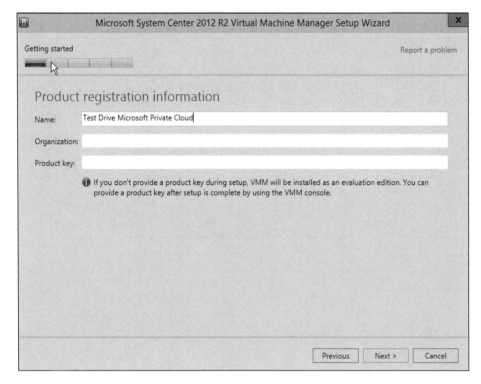

Figure 2.7
VMM Setup Wizard VMM Product registration page.
Source: VMM Install/Windows Server 2012 R2.

1. Enter Test Drive Microsoft Private Cloud for Name.

2. If necessary, enter the Product key.

3. Click Next.

Accept License Agreement

Now, you can see the license agreement shown in Figure 2.8. Using your judgment, select I have read, understood, and agree with the terms of the license.

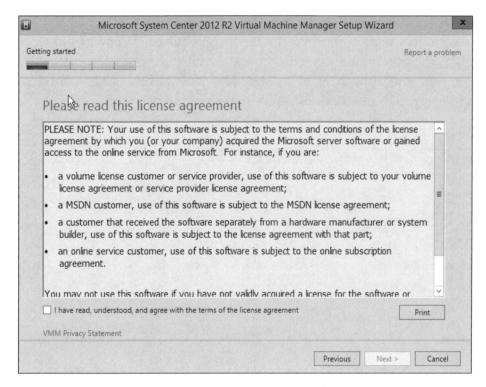

Figure 2.8
VMM Setup Wizard license agreement page.
Source: VMM Install/Windows Server 2012 R2.

1. Click I have read, understood, and agree with the terms of the license agreement.

2. Click Next.

Decide on Customer Experience Improvement Program

To participate in the Customer Experience Improvement Program (CEIP), choose Yes or No to opt out (see Figure 2.9). Microsoft describes the interaction with your computer this way: When you choose to participate in the CEIP, your computer automatically sends information to Microsoft about how you use VMM. Information from your computer is combined with other CEIP data to help Microsoft solve problems and to improve the products and features customers use most often.

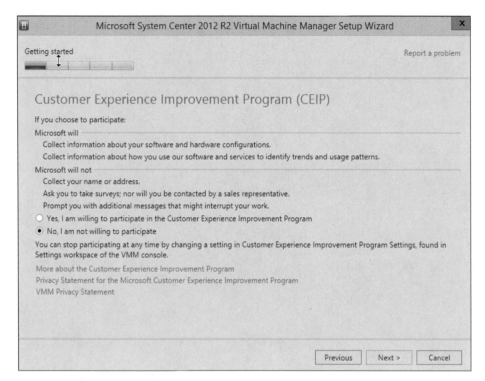

Figure 2.9
VMM Setup Wizard Customer Experience Improvement Program (CEIP) page.
Source: VMM Install/Windows Server 2012 R2.

1. Click No, I am not willing to participate.

2. Click Next.

Select Microsoft Update

On the next page, see Figure 2.10, you have the opportunity to add VMM to the Microsoft Update list. By doing this, you are assured that your VMM server has the latest security fixes and software updates.

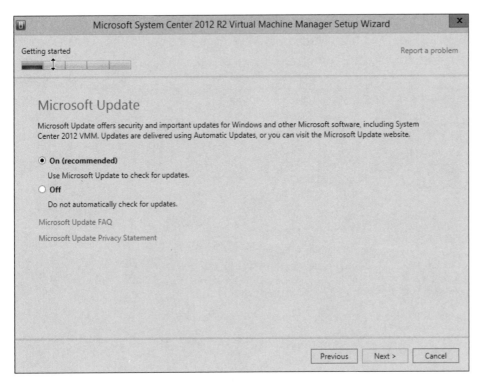

Figure 2.10
VMM Setup Wizard Microsoft Update page.
Source: VMM Install/Windows Server 2012 R2.

1. Click On (recommended).

2. Click Next.

Review Installation Location

Figure 2.11 shows the location of the installation folder. If you have additional physical disks available, you should consider moving the location to an underused drive.

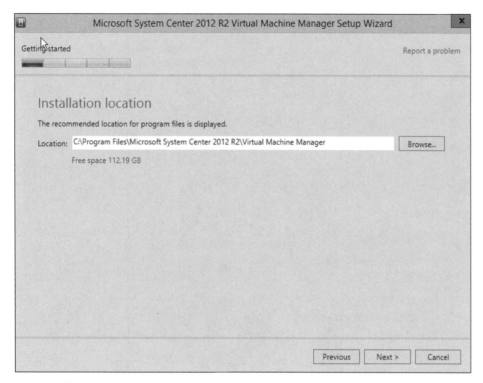

Figure 2.11
VMM Setup Wizard Installation location page.
Source: VMM Install/Windows Server 2012 R2.

1. Review the Installation location and click Next.

2. Wait for the prerequisites check to complete.

Configure SQL Database

The information that you enter on this page, as shown in Figure 2.12, connects VMM to the SQL server. Start by entering the fully qualified domain name (FQDN) for the SQL server. With this information, the VMM install establishes contact with the SQL server. After establishing contact, the VMM database is created on the SQL server. This task will take several moments. Next, you enter the communication port number. After a short period of time, you may enter the Instance name that will be used. You recorded the Instance name when you installed SQL Server.

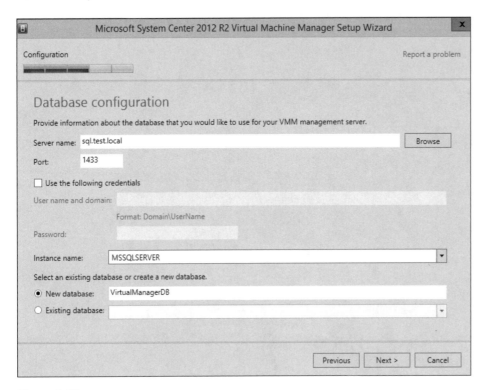

Figure 2.12
VMM Setup Wizard Database configuration page.
Source: VMM Install/Windows Server 2012 R2.

1. Enter SQL.Test.Local for the Server name.

2. Wait for communications to be established to the SQL server.

3. Enter 1433 for the Port and enter MSSQLSERVER for the Instance name.

4. Click Next.

Experience Unresponsiveness Entering Configuration

You may experience unresponsiveness when you are entering this information. Be patient, you will be able to enter the information.

Configure Service Account and Distributed Key Management

Figure 2.13 shows the Configure service account and distributed key management page. You entered this in Active Directory. The VMM service account is required when multiple host computers share common files on a storage device. The VMMDKM container in AD DS is used to share encryption keys for the VMM database. These entries are needed for the activities in Chapter 7.

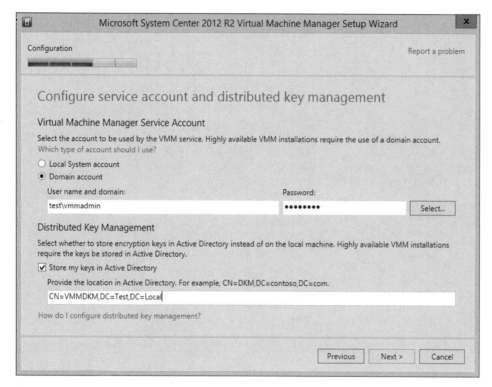

Figure 2.13
VMM Setup Wizard Configure service account and distributed key management page.
Source: VMM Install/Windows Server 2012 R2.

1. Enter test\vmmadmin for the User name and domain; then enter Pa$$w0rd for the Password.

2. Select Store my keys in Active Directory. Enter CN=VMMDKM,DC=Test,DC=local for the location to store the private keys.

3. Click Next.

Review Ports

On the next page, shown in Figure 2.14, you can see the ports that are assigned for communication with the VMM management server. Pay attention to port 443. This port is also used for HTTPS transfers. You may need this information for troubleshooting in the future.

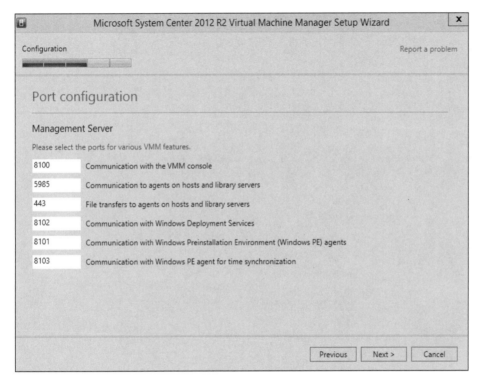

Figure 2.14
VMM Setup Wizard Port configuration page.
Source: VMM Install/Windows Server 2012 R2.

1. Review the Port configuration.
2. Click Next.

Configure Library Share

Figure 2.15 shows the Library configuration page. You select Create a new library share. If you restart the installation, the library share may be created. If this occurs, select the Use an existing library share. In either case, the name MSSCVMMLibrary works.

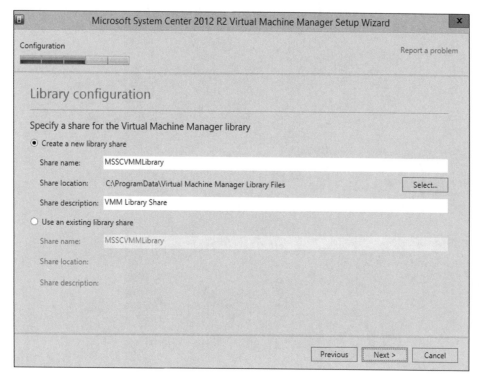

Figure 2.15
VMM Setup Wizard Library configuration page.
Source: VMM Install/Windows Server 2012 R2.

1. Click Create a new library share.

2. Click Next.

Review Installation Summary

Review the installation summary (see Figure 2.16). This summary is provided before the actual VMM management server is installed, and it might be useful in diagnosing a potential problem. You have choices: Previous (to back up and correct a problem), Install, or Cancel the install.

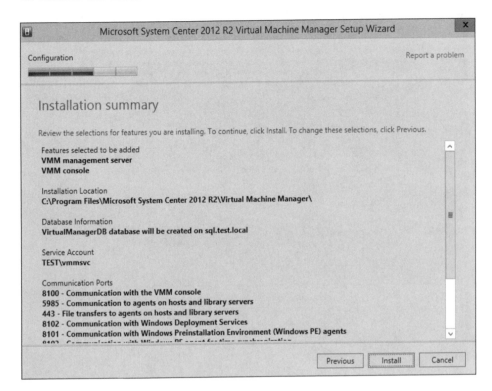

Figure 2.16
VMM Setup Wizard Installation summary page.
Source: VMM Install/Windows Server 2012 R2.

1. Review the Installation summary.

2. Click Install.

Installing Features

After setting the various configuration options, you arrive at Installing features, as shown in Figure 2.17. If the install fails, consult the "Troubleshooting the VMM Installation" section in this chapter.

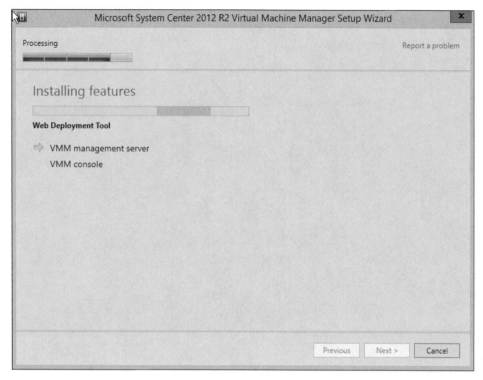

Figure 2.17
VMM Setup Wizard Installing features page.
Source: VMM Install/Windows Server 2012 R2.

1. Wait for the VMM management server and VMM console to install.

2. Click Close

Setup Completed Successfully

After about 20 minutes, you should see Figure 2.18. You succeeded! The VMM management server and the VMM console are installed. See Figure 2.19 for the Connect to Server page. You are ready to go to Chapter 3.

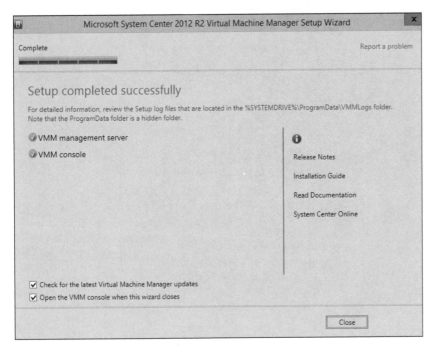

Figure 2.18
VMM Setup Wizard Setup page completed successfully.

Source: VMM Install/Windows Server 2012 R2.

Figure 2.19
Connect to server page.

Source: VMM console/Windows Server 2012 R2.

TROUBLESHOOTING THE VMM INSTALLATION

In the event that the VMM installation didn't complete successfully, you need to review the VMM log files, which are in the hidden C:\Program Data\ folder. To see the hidden folders, from the Control Panel, click View by and select Small icons; click Folder Options; click the View tab; click Show hidden files, folders, and drives; and then click OK.

Click the yellow folder on the taskbar and navigate to C:\Program Data\VMMLogs. Start with the Setup Wizard file. Every step that the Setup Wizard takes is summarized in the log. Scroll to the end of this log to locate the component that caused the failure. You may be told to continue with one of the other logs.

For example, the PrereqCheck contains the information on the conditions that must be met to install successfully. Figure 2.20 shows the check for the Windows Assessment and Deployment feature.

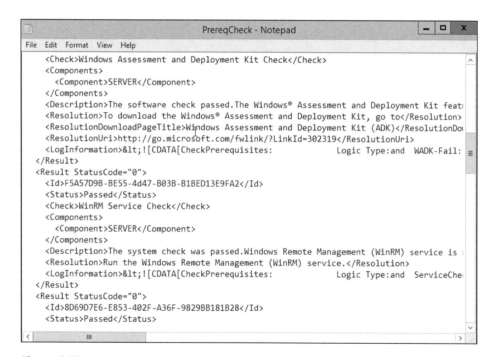

Figure 2.20
PrereqCheck log showing the status of the Windows Assessment and Deployment Kit page.
Source: VMM install/Windows Server 2012 R2.

You need to make the necessary corrections. Recall in Figure 2.4, the line *restart may be required*. The correction may be as simple as restarting the VMM virtual machine and redoing the install configuration.

SUMMARY

- This strategy for the Microsoft private cloud is best described as a pool of Compute, Network, and Storage resources available on demand with a component to manage the pool of resources.

- Virtual Machine Manager (VMM) 2012 R2 is a Microsoft product that manages a series of host computers and virtual machines from a central console. The VMM server functions as the controller of the virtual management environment. Access to the VMM servers is through the VMM administrator console.

- VMM uses PowerShell, a Microsoft scripting language, to perform management tasks. Microsoft SQL Server provides the database to store various configurations. The library server manages the virtual hard disks, which are typically stored on a SAN for access by the host computers and virtual machines.

- VMM combines a number of Microsoft communications protocols, such as Windows Remote Management, Background Intelligent Transfer Service, and Remote Desktop Protocol, with Internet protocols to communicate between components. The central hub of these communications is the VMM server.

- As a part of the VMM installation process, VMM determines that the required prerequisites are completed. The VMM server must be a member of the Test domain. Other requirements are the Windows Assessment and Deployment Kit (ADK), the SQL 2012 SP1 Server Connectivity Feature Pack, and a container in Active Directory to store VMM encryption keys.

CASE PROJECTS

Case 2-1: Identifying the Cost of Virtual Machine Manager

Microsoft does not provide System Center Virtual Machine Manager 2012 R2 for free. You need to determine the cost of System Center Virtual Machine Manager 2012 R2. Search on the Web for pricing for five host computers. There are a number of firms that market this software. To get started, consider these firms: CDW, Newegg Business, Provantage, and TigerDirect.

Case 2-2: Resolving an Installation Error

You get a screen saying that your installation cannot continue and this message: Windows Assessment and Deployment Kit (ADK) for Windows 8.1 is not present on this computer. You know that you downloaded an ADK and ran this as you prepared to install the VMM management server. How will you resolve this problem? Refer to the section on Troubleshooting the VMM Installation.

Case 2-3: Communications Between the VMM Server and the SQL Server

You suspect that there is a problem with the communications between the VMM server and the SQL server. You open the Command Prompt on the VMM server and type

```
telnet sql.test.local
```

What port number will you want add to the telnet command? Refer to Figure 2.12.

CHAPTER 3

CONFIGURING THE FABRIC RESOURCES

After reading this chapter and completing the exercises, you will be able to do the following:

- Describe the VMM Administrator console.
- Configure the COMPUTE servers.
- Set up the VMM Library.

In this chapter, you will start learning about Fabric Resources. You learned about the features of the VMM Administrator console that you installed in Chapter 2, "The Microsoft Private Cloud." One of the key resources in your private cloud is COMPUTE where the virtual machines that do work for your users execute. You will set up the COMPUTE1 and COMPUTE2 servers as the COMPUTE resource. The VMM Library holds resources that you can use to build virtual machines, so you will start to populate your Library.

You'll learn about Networking in Chapter 4, "Working with Networks Using VMM," and in successive chapters: Storage, Hyper-V Cluster, and Private Cloud.

DESCRIBING THE VMM ADMINISTRATOR CONSOLE

In this section, you will start with a "25,000 foot flyover" of the VMM Administrator console. As you fly over the console, rest assured that many of the features are covered in subsequent chapters.

In Chapter 2, you installed the VMM Administrator console. Figure 3.1 shows the VMM Connect to Server window. From the VMM server, you connect to the VMM Administrator console from here. You have a choice of logon credentials—either the Microsoft Windows current session identity or an alternate identity. Since you logged on with the test\administrator user account, the current logon is OK. The alternate identity could be used to connect to the VMM server from another computer.

Figure 3.1
You can connect to the server here.

Source: VMM Administrator Console/Windows Server 2012 R2.

1. To bypass this window in the future, click Automatically connect with these settings.

2. Click Connect.

Default View of Administrator Console

By default, the VMM Administrator console displays the VMs and Services view, as shown in Figure 3.2, but additional management views are available. In the Surveyor pane, you will find these management views in the lower-left corner below the double bar separator.

- **VMs and Services:** Switches to views of Tenants, Clouds, VM Networks, Storage, and Hosts.

- **Fabric:** Displays the pool of resources: Managed servers, Networking, and Storage.

- **Jobs:** Displays a list of the Running jobs and History list of previous jobs.

- **Settings:** Defines the settings for the VMM environment.

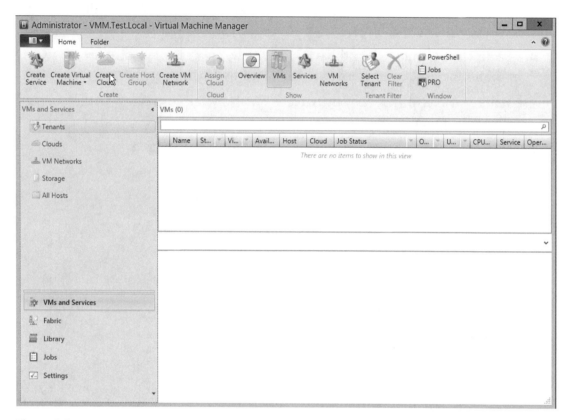

Figure 3.2
The default view of the Administrator console.
Source: VMM Administrator Console/Windows Server 2012 R2.

Notice that the icons are grouped on the ribbon. For this view, the groups are Create, Cloud, Show, Tenant Filter, and Window. These groupings make it easier to locate the desired icon.

In the ribbon for the VMs and Services management view, you will find these icons:

- **Create Service:** Uses a server template to create and deploy a server. In addition, the Service Designer can be used to create a new service template.

- **Create Virtual Machine:** Launches the Virtual Machine Wizard to create a new virtual machine.

- **Create Cloud:** Launches the Create a Cloud Wizard to specify the cloud components for future virtual machines.

- **Create Host Group:** From the All Hosts view, creates a new host group, which indicates the host computers to be managed by VMM.

- **Create VM Network:** Starts the Create VM Network to create a virtual machine network from an existing logical network.

- **Assign Cloud:** Launches the Assign Cloud Resources Wizard.

- **Overview:** Displays summary graphs for the various VMs and Services.

- **VMs:** Lists the VMs running by Tenant, Cloud, or Host.

- **Services:** Lists the Services running by Tenant, Cloud, or Host.

- **VM Networks:** Lists the VM network assignments.

- **Select Tenant:** Selects a Tenant (a delegated administrator) to use as a filter.

- **Clear Filter:** Clears the current Tenant filter.

- **PowerShell Window:** Opens a PowerShell window.

- **Jobs Window:** Lists the recent jobs run.

- **PRO Window:** When System Center Operations Manager (SCOM) is deployed, PRO tips are displayed. Microsoft defines System Center Operations Manager (SCOM) as a cross-platform data center management system for operating systems and hypervisors. From a single interface, it shows state, health, and performance information of computer systems.

As you go from management view to management view, the icons in the ribbon change.

Fabric Management View

Switching to the Fabric management view, as shown in Figure 3.3, you can see the Fabric resource pool: Servers, Networking, and Storage. The default is Servers with the VMM server being managed.

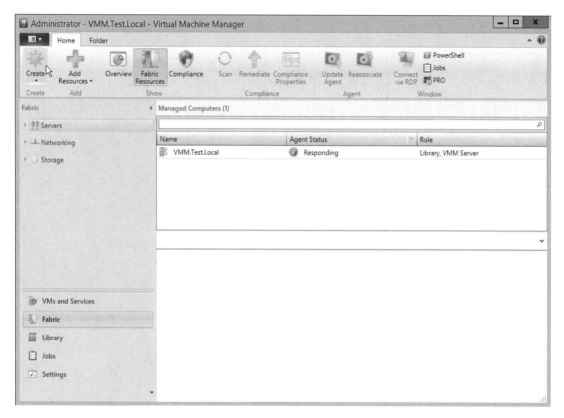

Figure 3.3
Fabric management view.
Source: VMM Administrator Console/Windows Server 2012 R2.

1. To switch to the Fabric view, click Fabric in the Surveyor pane below the double bar separator.

2. Observe the Servers, Networking, and Storage resources at the top of the Surveyor pane.

3. Notice that the ribbon content changed.

Create Resources Within the Fabric Management View

From the Create icon, shown in Figure 3.4, you can create a wide range of resources. For example, you can create resources that you previously created in the Hyper-V Manager from this location. You will find this feature useful in order to create a virtual machine.

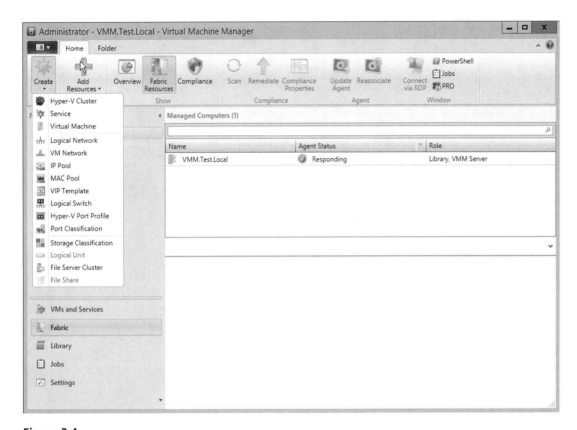

Figure 3.4
Create on Fabric management view.

Source: VMM Administrator Console/Windows Server 2012 R2.

1. Click the Create icon.

2. Observe the various objects that you can create.

3. Click the Add Resources icon.

4. Note the Resources that you bring into your private cloud.

Networking on Fabric Management View

Figure 3.5 shows Networking on the Fabric management view. From this view, you manage VMM networking. Notice that you can create a wide range of networking components. You'll learn about the creation and management of these in Chapter 4, "Working with Networks Using VMM."

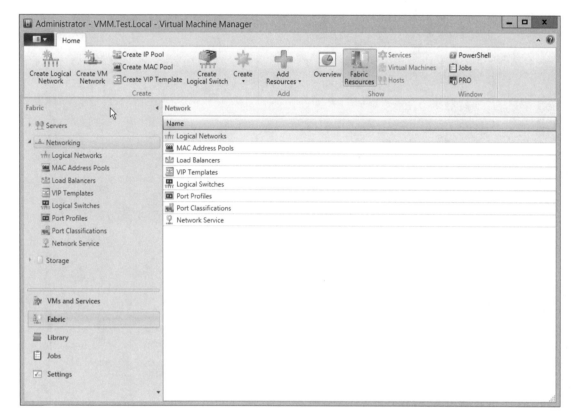

Figure 3.5
Networking on the Fabric management view.
Source: VMM Administrator Console/Windows Server 2012 R2.

1. To switch to Networking node, click Networking.

2. Expand the Networking node.

3. Observe the networking components.

Storage on Fabric Management View

As shown in Figure 3.6, you can see the information regarding Storage. In Chapter 5, "Working with VMM Storage," you'll learn to work with Storage.

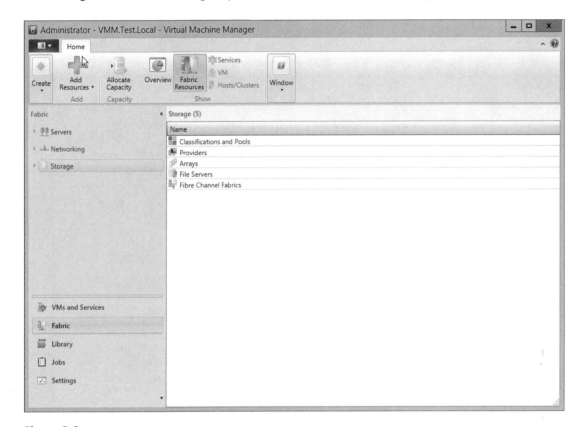

Figure 3.6
Storage on Fabric management view.
Source: VMM Administrator Console/Windows Server 2012 R2.

1. To switch to Storage node, click Storage.

2. Expand the Storage node.

3. Observe the Storage components

Library Management View

Moving on to the Library view, you can see the options for this view, as shown in Figure 3.7. Later in this chapter, you'll learn to work with the Library where the resources for virtual machine deployment are stored.

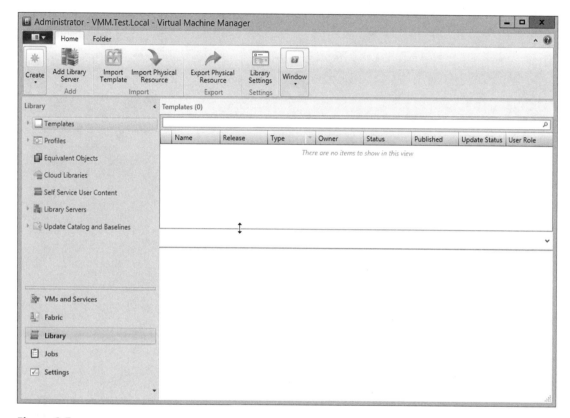

Figure 3.7
Library management view.

Source: VMM Administrator Console/Windows Server 2012 R2.

1. To switch to the Library view, click the Library node.

2. Observe the wide range of objects available in the Library view.

Jobs Management View

Figure 3.8 shows the Jobs management view, where you can view the running jobs. You will find this useful to track the status of running PowerShell jobs. Recall that VMM uses PowerShell scripts to create resources. Use the History view to view jobs that have completed execution.

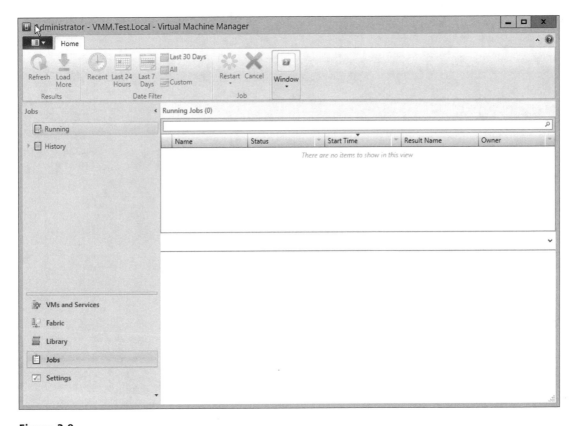

Figure 3.8
Jobs management view.
Source: VMM Administrator Console/Windows Server 2012 R2.

Settings Management View

The last management view, as shown in Figure 3.9, is a place where you configure the settings for the VMM environment. As an example, Database Connection shows which SQL server is being used. Consider the User Roles that are located by expanding Security, which you'll learn about in Chapter 7. You will find this type of information useful when troubleshooting problems with VMM.

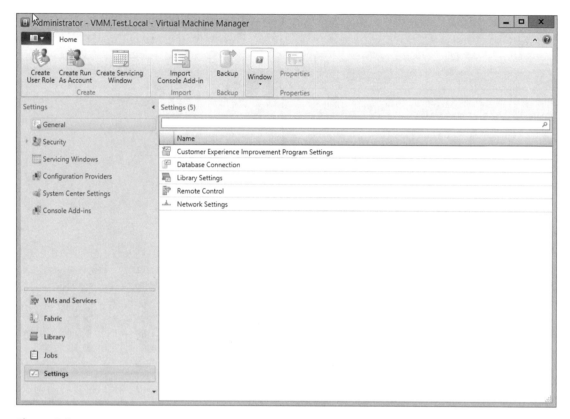

Figure 3.9
Settings management view.

Source: VMM Administrator Console/Windows Server 2012 R2.

CONFIGURING THE SERVERS

This section is all about setting up the host servers for the VMM Fabric.

Figure 3.10 shows the current state of your private cloud implementation. In the previous chapters, you created these resources:

- MANAGE server with ADDS (Active Directory Domain Services), SQL server, VMM (Virtual Machine Manager), and CLIENT virtual machines.
- COMPUTE host servers (COMPUTE1 and COMPUTE2)
- NETWORK with the Management Logical Network (Hyper-V logical network)

You'll create additional resources in future chapters. For example, in Chapter 4, you will create additional networking resources. In Chapter 5, you will create the iSCSI storage resource.

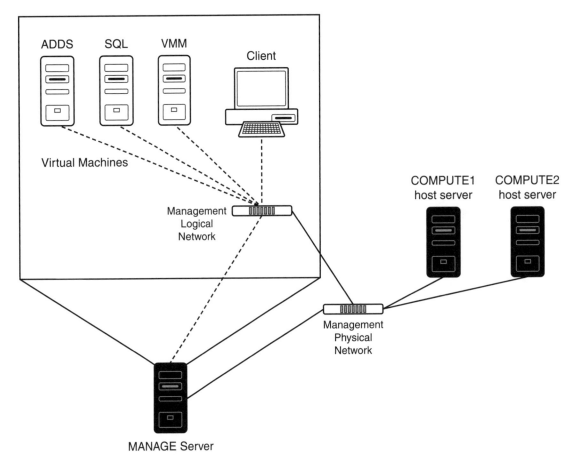

Figure 3.10
Private cloud implementation.
© 2014 Cengage Learning®.

Configuring the COMPUTE Servers

Now that the Active Directory Domain Services is available, the COMPUTE1 and COMPUTE2 host computers can be brought to the domain level. To do this, you will need to complete the following steps:

1. Log on to the COMPUTE1 host server as compute1\administrator.

2. To access Network Connections, right-click the Network icon in the taskbar, click Open Network and Sharing Center, and then click Change adapter settings.

3. To update the name of the vEthernet connection, right-click vEthernet and select Rename. Type Management Logical Network.

4. To change the DNS entry to the new DNS, right-click Management Logical Network and then click Properties. Click Internet Protocol Version 4 (TCP/IPv4), click Properties, and change the Preferred DNS server to 192.168.0.103. Click OK and click Close. Close the Network Connections window.

5. To change the name of the virtual switch, click Tools and select Hyper-V Manager. Click COMPUTE1. Click Virtual Switch Manager in the Actions pane. Click the network adapter under Virtual Switches, type Management Logical Network for the Name, and then click OK. Minimize the Hyper-V Manager window.

6. To join the domain, from the Server Manager, click the Workgroup link. Click Change, click Domain, and enter Test.local. Click OK. Log in as test\ administrator with Pa$$w0rd. Click OK.

7. Wait for the Welcome to the Test domain message. Click OK twice. Click Close and then click Restart Now.

8. To change to the domain administrator account, click the Action menu, click Ctrl+Alt+Delete, click the back arrow, and click Other user. Enter test\administrator and Pa$$w0rd.

9. To access network discovery and file sharing, right-click the Network icon in the Taskbar, click Open Network and Sharing Center, and then click Change advanced sharing settings.

10. To turn on network discovery and file sharing, click the Private Chevron, click Turn on Network Discovery, and click Turn on file and printer sharing.

11. Repeat steps 9 and 10 for the Domain. Click Save changes. Close the Network and Sharing Center window.

12. To add the VMM user accounts to the local Administrators group, click Tools, click Computer Management, expand Local Users and Groups, double-click Groups, and then right-click Administrators. Click Add to Group, click Add, click Advanced, enter vmm for Starts with, and then click Find Now. Select VMMAdmin, VMMRun, and VMMStore, and then click OK three times. Close the Computer Management window.

13. Repeat steps 1 through 12 for COMPUTE2.

Create COMPUTE Host Group

You can use host groups to group host computers. You do this to isolate sets of servers to simplify the management of host computers. Figure 3.11 shows the completed host group.

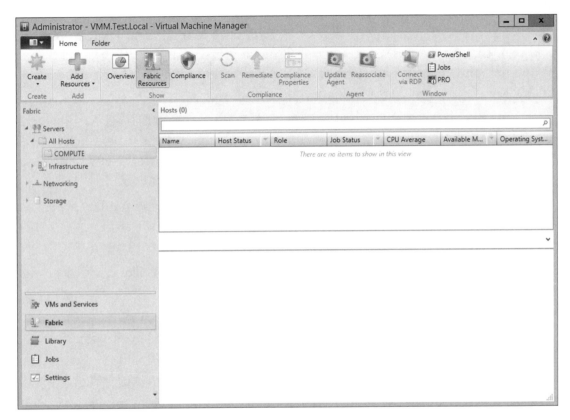

Figure 3.11
COMPUTE host group created.
© 2014 Cengage Learning®.

1. Return to MANAGE and connect to the VMM Administrator console in the VMM virtual machine.

2. Click the Fabric management view.

3. To create the COMPUTE host group, expand Servers and right-click All Hosts. Click Create Host Group and type COMPUTE over New host group. Press Enter.

Add COMPUTE1 and COMPUTE2 to Host Group

After the Add Resource wizard is started, the Resource Location is displayed, as shown in Figure 3.12. Since your host computers are in a trusted domain, the default is OK. There are other options that indicate the versatility of VMM. The last option is interesting—Physical computers to be provisioned as virtual machine hosts. You could use this to expand the compute resources by adding host computers. The baseboard management controller (BMC) permits a host computer to be powered-on and managed remotely. It also permits images to be installed remotely to remote servers.

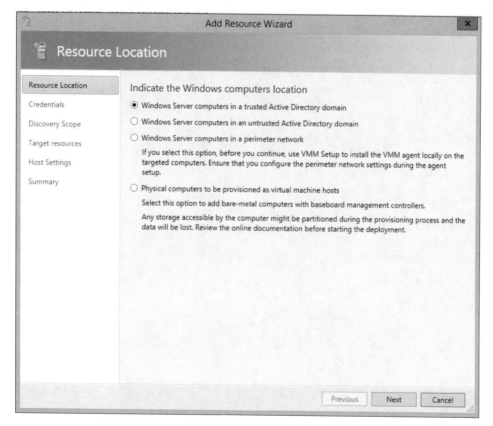

Figure 3.12
Resource location.

Source: VMM Administrator Console/ Windows Server 2012 R2.

1. To start the Add Resource Wizard click the Add Resources icon and select Hyper-V Hosts and Clusters.

2. Review the options to select the host computers.

3. Retain Windows Server computers in a trusted Active Directory domain.

4. Click Next.

Specify Credentials to Discover Host Computers

For the Credentials, you create a Run As account. In Chapter 2, you created a VMMRun host account in the Active Directory, and in this chapter, you added the account to the local Administrators group on COMPUTE1 and COMPUTE2.

Now, you use the existing VMMrun account to create a Run As account. The credentials that you provide in a Run As Account are used to run scripts on servers in the COMPUTE host group. While adding a new host server to VMM, specify this Run As account to be used to add the host computer. Figure 3.13 shows the Run As account added to Credentials.

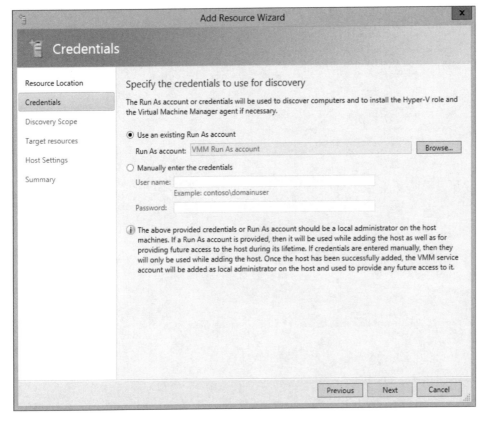

Figure 3.13
Add Resource Wizard Credentials to use for discovery.

Source: VMM Administrator Console/ Windows Server 2012 R2.

1. To create a Run As account, click Browse, click Create Run As Account, enter VMM Run As account as the name, enter test\VMMrun as the User name, and enter Pa$$w0rd for the Password and confirm password. Click OK twice.

2. Click Next.

Enter Computers to Add

Figure 3.14 shows the two host computer names entered. If you have numerous computers, you could use an Active Directory query. To do this, select Specify an Active Directory query to search for Windows Server computers. Then click Generate an AD Query. From the Advanced tab, click Field and select Name, enter the first few characters for the Value.

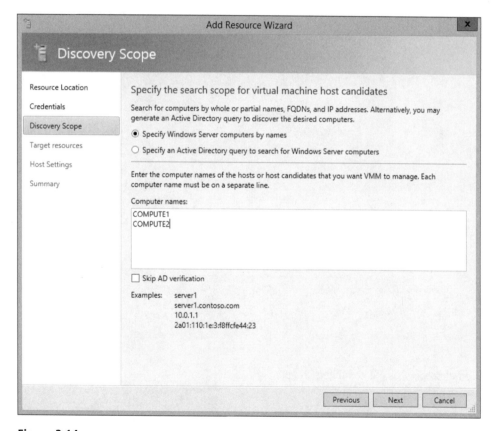

Figure 3.14
Add Resource Wizard Computers to add are entered.
Source: VMM Administrator Console/ Windows Server 2012 R2.

1. To specify the Windows host servers, enter COMPUTE1 and COMPUTE2 (one per line) for the Computer names.

2. Click Next.

Add Discovered Host Computers

When the Target resources are displayed, select the host computers to add, as shown in Figure 3.15. Of course, you could click Select all if the computer Names were correct.

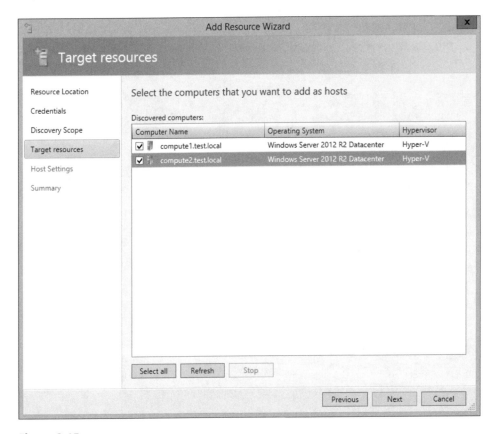

Figure 3.15
Add Resource Wizard Target Scope showing computers to add.

Source: VMM Administrator Console/ Windows Server 2012 R2.

1. When the Discovered computers appear, select the compute1.test.local and compute2.test.local entries.

2. Click Next.

Specify Host Group

To select the COMPUTE host group, click All Hosts and select COMPUTE. Figure 3.16 shows the Host Settings. This adds both computers to the COMPUTE host group.

By default, VMM stores virtual machines in c:\Users\Public\Public Documents\Hyper-V\ Virtual hard disks. To improve disk efficiency you may want to store virtual machines in another path on a separate physical hard drive. For example, you could use E:\Virtual Machines.

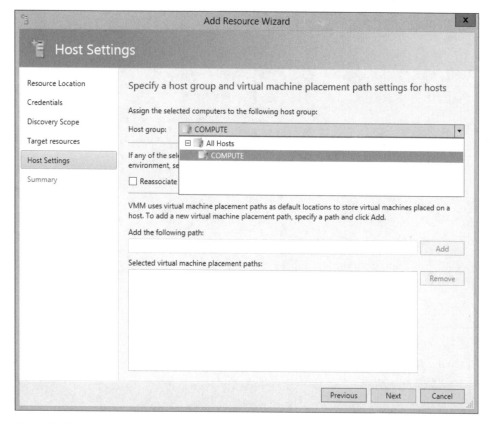

Figure 3.16
Add Resource Wizard Host Settings with COMPUTE.
Source: VMM Administrator Console/ Windows Server 2012 R2.

1. Click the Host group chevron and then select COMPUTE.
2. Click Next.

Review Summary

Figure 3.17 shows the Summary where you determine if your entries appear correctly. Of course, the Previous button provides an opportunity to make a correction.

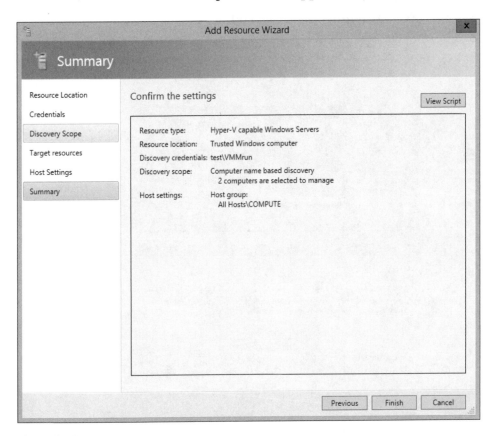

Figure 3.17
Add Resource Wizard Summary page.

Source: VMM Administrator Console/ Windows Server 2012 R2.

View PowerShell Script

VMM will run a PowerShell script to add the host computers to the COMPUTE host group, as shown in Figure 3.18.

Figure 3.18
PowerShell script to add host computers.
Source: VMM Administrator Console/ Windows Server 2012 R2.

1. To view the script in Notepad, click View Script.

2. Review the PowerShell script for Get and Add cmdlets.

3. Close the NotePad window.

4. Click Finish.

View Execution of PowerShell Script

Figure 3.19 shows the progress for the PowerShell script to add the host computers to the COMPUTE host group.

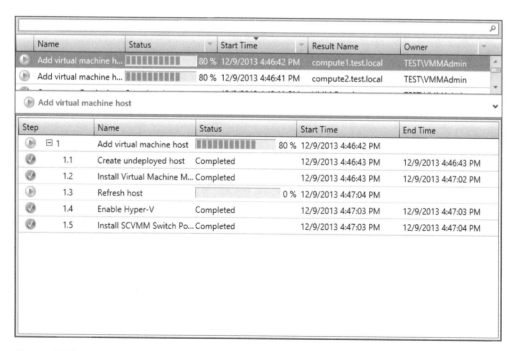

Figure 3.19
Jobs showing PowerShell script running.
Source: VMM Administrator Console/ Windows Server 2012 R2.

1. To view the running job, click the Jobs management view and select Running.

2. To see the details for a job, click the green chevron for the job.

3. Wait for the job to complete.

4. Close the Jobs window.

Completion Messages

You may encounter warning messages, which can be safely ignored. If you receive an error message, rerun the Add Resources wizard. You will not need to create the Run As account again.

Host Computers Added

Returning to the Fabric management view, you see two host computers added, as shown in Figure 3.20. Additional tasks are available from the remaining icons.

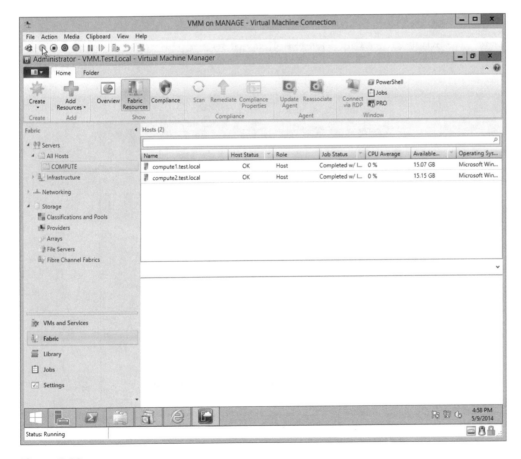

Figure 3.20

Fabric management view showing added computers.

Source: VMM Administrator Console/ Windows Server 2012 R2.

Overview Host and Virtual Machines

From the Overview, you can see the information regarding the number of host computers and virtual machines, as shown in Figure 3.21. You will want to check on the status of the agents running on the host computers. You can see the counts for Access Denied, Not Responding, Responding, and Stopped. If you see that the number of host and hosts responding does not agree, the other counters give a general reason for the failure.

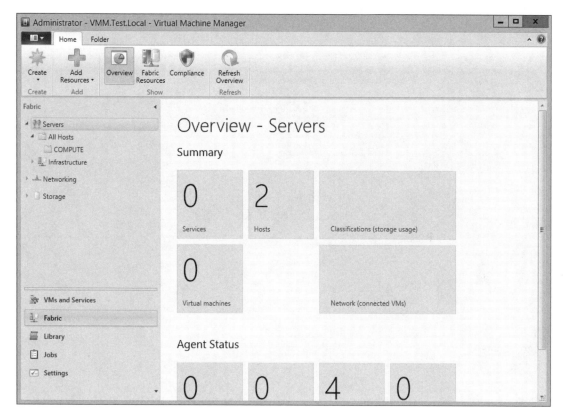

Figure 3.21
Count of managed computers.
Source: VMM Administrator Console/ Windows Server 2012 R2.

1. To see the overview, click the Overview icon.

2. Wait for the refresh to occur. (Blue orbs no longer spin.)

Performance Counters

Scrolling down, you can see the performance counters, as shown in Figure 3.22. It is critical that your host computers maintain acceptable performance levels. Daily and monthly performance counters are graphed for these critical measures: CPU performance (%), Memory (GB), Storage (MBps), and Network (MBps).

To refresh the view, click the Refresh Overview icon.

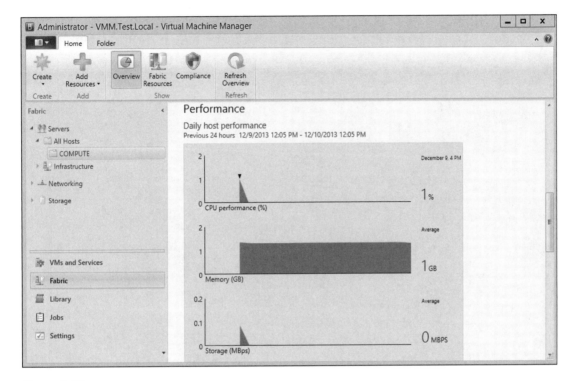

Figure 3.22
Performance counters.

Source: VMM Administrator Console/ Windows Server 2012 R2.

1. To see Daily host performance, scroll down until Daily host performance shows.

2. To see Monthly host performance, scroll down to the end.

You'll learn about Compliance in a future section.

SETTING UP THE VMM LIBRARY

The VMM Library provides central, secure storage for the resources that you use to create virtual machines. Using the Library promotes the reuse of virtual machine files and configurations.

Contents of MSSCVMMLibrary share

When you installed VMM, a Library was created on the VMM server and shared as the MSSCVMMLibrary. You can use the Library tools to work with these files. Notice that there are backup files for each of the provided VHD or VHDX files.

Recall that VHDX is the preferred file type offering better performance, reliability, and enhanced storage capacity. You will use these files to create virtual machines, which are stored in the Library. Figure 3.23 shows other resources in the Library workspace.

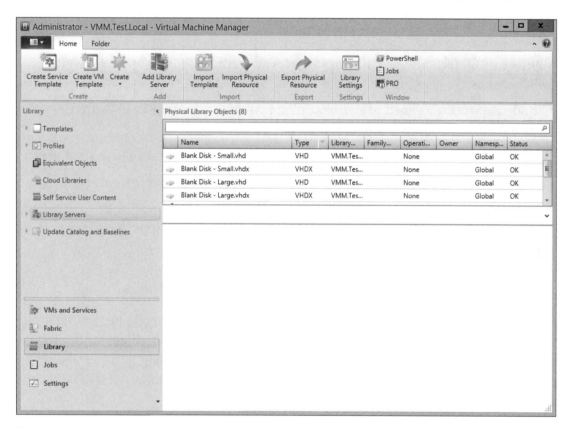

Figure 3.23

Library management view showing virtual hard disks.

Source: VMM Administrator Console/ Windows Server 2012 R2.

1. Click the Library node.

2. To see the VHD and VHDX entries, click Library Servers.

3. Observe the other Library resources in the Surveyor pane for the Library.

You use these Library resources as you work with VMM:

- **Templates:** Consists of configuration components. These components, with the exception of VHDs, are stored in the VMM database on the SQL server.

- **Profiles:** Hardware and Guest OS profiles contain specifications for the creation of virtual machines.

- **Equivalent Objects:** Equates Library objects at multiple sites as being equivalent, which avoids the copying of the same file between sites.

- **Cloud Libraries:** Assigned to a private cloud where self-service users with appropriate permissions store virtual machines.

- **Self Service User Content:** Consists of Library objects created by self-service users.

- **Library Servers:** List of individual Library servers, which shows the content on each server.

- **Update Catalog and Baselines:** Contains Library objects to support WSUS compliance.

Adding Files to the Library

You must add file-based resources such as VHDs and ISOs manually. When you add files to the Library, they will not appear until the next Library refresh. By default, the refresh interval is one hour. To make files appear sooner, you must manually refresh the Library. During a Library server refresh, VMM indexes the files in the Library and updates the Library workspace.

To get started adding files to the Library, you will create a new folder for ISO files.

1. To add file-based resources, expand the Library Servers, expand vmm.test.local, right-click MSSCVMMLibrary, and select Explore.

2. From the Explorer window, right-click in the whitespace, click New, and point to Folder and Type ISOFiles.

Copying Files to the Library

To copy files between hosts and other virtual machines, you must copy the file over a network share. To do this for the Windows Server 2012 R2 file, complete these steps:

1. Return to MANAGE for the iso file.

2. Open the Windows Explorer.

3. Navigate to the C:\ISOFiles folder, right-click the Windows Server 2012 R2 file, and select Copy.

4. To paste the file in the Library, press the Windows Key, type \\vmm\MS, click \\vmm\MSSCVMLibrary, right-click ISOFiles, and select Paste.

5. Wait for the file to copy and then close Windows Explorer windows.

6. Return to the VMM virtual machine.

7. To force a refresh or index of the Library, right-click MSSCVMMLibrary and click Refresh.

8. To verify that the Windows Server 2012 R2 file is available, wait for the ISOFiles to appear. Double-click ISOFiles.

You may encounter these file types after VMM indexes the Library:

- **Virtual hard disks:** .VHD and .VHDX files
- **ISO image files:** .ISO files containing installation files for operating systems
- **PowerShell scripts:** .ps1 files containing scripts of cmdlets
- **Driver files:** .inf files for hardware
- **Answer files:** .inf or .xml used to configure installs
- **Custom resources:** .cr folders are used to force indexing of files that would not normally be indexed by VMM.

Adding Profiles to the Library

To eliminate reentry of configuration data, you use profiles. A profile is a Library resource that contains a number of configuration components. Usually, templates are stored in the VMM database but appear in the Library. An exception exists—.vhd and .vhdx files used as templates are stored in the Library.

Profiles that you will work with in VMM include the following:

- Hardware profiles
- Guest operating-system profiles

- Capability profiles
- Virtual hard disks

With profiles consisting of hardware and software settings, you can create multiple new virtual machines with the same settings. This not only eliminates manual configuration errors, but it also results in consistency as you reuse the templates.

Creating a Hardware Profile

Hardware profiles contain the most common settings for a virtual machine. To create a hardware profile, right-click Hardware Profiles under the Profiles node of the Library view and then select Create Hardware Profile. You can create a hardware profile and configure the number of processors and dynamic memory. At this time, you will accept the defaults for the remaining hardware options, which will be covered in future chapters.

Name the Hardware Profile

Create a name for the hardware profile that identifies the settings within the profile. The completed General node is shown in Figure 3.24. After entering the profile name, add a descriptive paragraph that identifies the configured components.

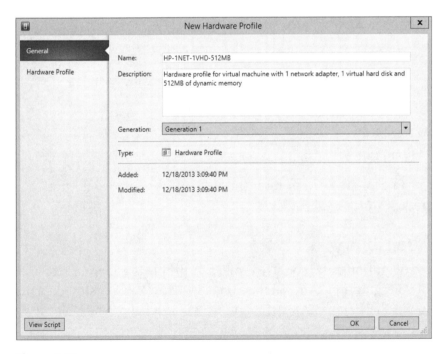

Figure 3.24
Completed General tab.

Source: VMM Administrator Console/ Windows Server 2012 R2.

1. Click the Library management view and then expand Profiles.

2. To create a hardware profile, expand Profiles, right-click Hardware Profiles, and then select Create Hardware Profile.

3. To describe the hardware profile, enter HP-1NET-1VHD-512MBD for the Name. Enter Hardware profile for virtual machine with 1 network adapter, 1 virtual hard disk, and 1GB of dynamic memory for the Description.

Specify the Number of Processors

Click on the Hardware Profile node to access the hardware settings, as shown in Figure 3.25.

Start with the Cloud Capabilities (not shown). Choose from the three hypervisor compatibilities:

- **ESX Server:** VMware cloud servers
- **XenServer:** Citrix cloud servers
- **Hyper-V:** Microsoft cloud servers

Of course, you will select Hyper-V for Microsoft cloud servers.

Next, specify the number of virtual processors. You are specifying the number of virtual processors, which is determined by the configuration of the physical processor. For example, an Intel Xeon quad processor with hyper threading has four cores with two threads per core or eight virtual processors.

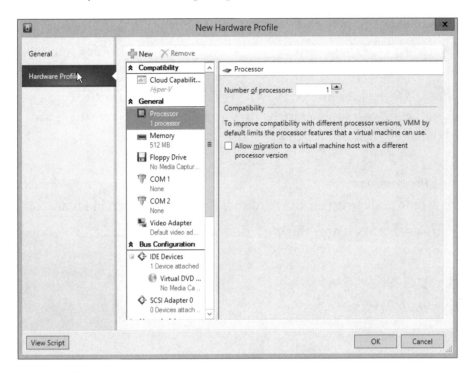

Figure 3.25
Number of processors shown.

Source: VMM Administrator Console/ Windows Server 2012 R2.

1. Click Hardware Profile.

2. To indicate Hyper-V Cloud Compatibility, check Hyper-V.

3. Retain 1 as the Number of processors.

Number of Available Processors

Since your processor availability may be limited, you most likely can only assign one virtual processor to each virtual machine. For example, two host computers running quad processors without hyper-threading limits the number of running virtual machines to eight.

Configure the Memory

The settings for dynamic memory are shown in Figure 3.26. In this scenario, the basic assumptions are that the virtual machine starts with 768MB of memory. Startup memory is the minimum amount of memory that a virtual machine must have to start. However,

Windows requires more memory during startup than the steady state. The Minimum memory is the amount of memory needed during the steady state. After the virtual machine reaches the steady state, the Hyper-V hypervisor reclaims the excess memory. You can configure a maximum memory amount for a virtual machine, and Hyper-V continues to ensure that this amount is always available to the running virtual machine.

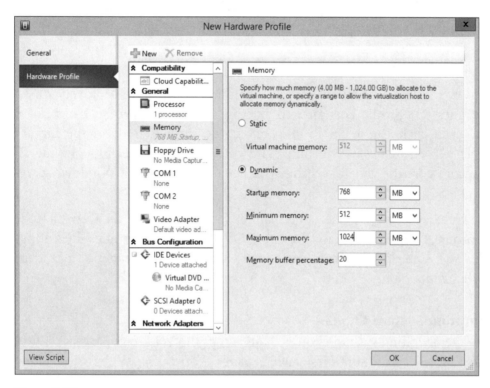

Figure 3.26
Memory settings.
Source: VMM Administrator Console/ Windows Server 2012 R2.

1. To specify the Memory, click Memory, click Dynamic, enter 768 for the Startup memory, enter 512 for the Minimum memory, and enter 1024 for the Maximum memory.

2. Observe the remaining options.

3. Click View Script, review the PowerShell script, and then close the Notepad window.

4. To run the script, click OK.

5. Wait for the script to run and build the hardware profile.

The Memory buffer percentage requires additional explanation. Dynamic memory adds memory to a virtual machine as required, but there is a chance that an application running within a virtual machine might demand memory more quickly than dynamic memory can allocate it. This is where the memory buffer makes the memory available. The percentage is based on the amount of memory that is actually needed by the application running on the virtual machine. It is expressed as a percentage because it changes depending on the virtual machine requirements.

Creating a Guest OS Profile

By creating guest OS profiles, you can ensure that operating systems are deployed consistently. Creating a guest OS profile is similar to creating a hardware profile. To create a Guest OS profile, right-click Guest OS Profiles under the Profiles node of the Library view and then select Create Guest OS Profile. The Guest OS node settings provide an opportunity to preconfigure the general settings you need for installing a Windows server operating system.

You complete the General settings in the same manner that you created the General node on the hardware profile. Create a name for the Guest OS profile that identifies the settings within the profile. After entering the profile name, add a descriptive paragraph that identifies the configured component.

Select from Operating System Choices

Figure 3.27 shows the operating system choices. Notice that the Windows Server 2012 R2 Standard was selected. Microsoft supports a wide range of operating systems, including flavors of Linux.

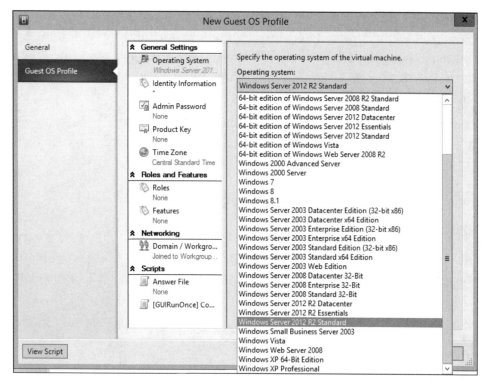

Figure 3.27
Operating system choices.
Source: VMM Administrator Console/ Windows Server 2012 R2.

1. To create a Guest OS profile, right-click Guest OS Profiles and then select Create Guest OS Profile.

2. Enter W2K12R2STD for the Name; enter Windows Server 2012 R2 Standard for the Description.

3. To see the Linux offerings, click the Compatibility chevron and then select Linux. Click Guest OS Profile node. Click the Operating systems chevron.

4. Observe the list.

5. To return and select Microsoft Windows, click General, click the Compatibility chevron, and select Microsoft Windows.

6. Click Guest OS Profiles, click the Operating systems chevron, and then scroll and select Windows Server 2012 R2 Standard.

Enter Local Administrator Password

The next task is to set the administrator password. Figure 3.28 includes three options for the credentials. You may choose to delay the signification of the password associated with the local administrator account. The second option is to supply a password. Or you may choose a Run As account from AD DS.

Figure 3.28 shows the administrator's password set and confirmed. Recall that you are using Pa$$w0rd in this book. In the workplace, you need to create passwords that are consistent with your organization's standards.

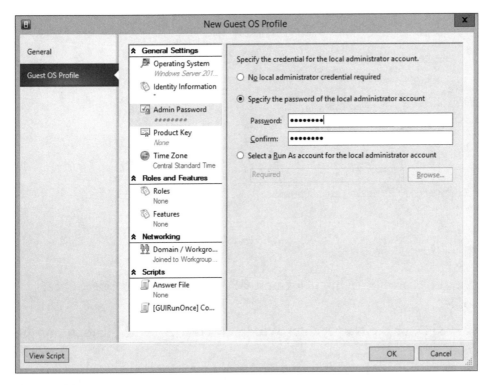

Figure 3.28
Credentials options.
Source: VMM Administrator Console/ Windows Server 2012 R2.

1. Click Admin Password. Click Specify the password of the local administrator account and enter Pa$$w0rd for the Password.

2. Enter Pa$$w0rd for the Confirm password.

Select Time Zone

When you install a Windows operating system, you need to select the time zone where the virtual machine will reside. This selection ensures that the time offset from Greenwich Mean Time (GMT) will be correct. Notice that the default is the same as the VMM server, as shown in Figure 3.29.

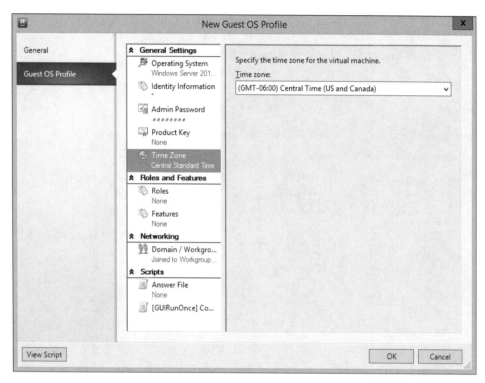

Figure 3.29
Specify Time Zone.

Source: VMM Administrator Console/ Windows Server 2012 R2.

1. If necessary, correct the Time Zone.

2. When entry is completed, click OK.

The remaining options will be covered in future chapters.

Creating a Virtual Machine Template

An easy way to create a template is to start with an existing virtual hard disk. To start the process with the New Template Wizard, click the Create VM Template icon on the ribbon.

Select Source Virtual Hard Disk

Figure 3.30 shows the Select Source window, which lets you select the location of an existing virtual hard disk. VMM provides blank disks for this purpose.

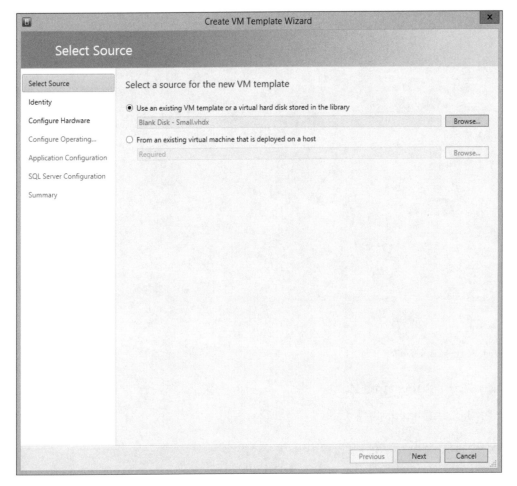

Figure 3.30
Create VM Template Wizard showing the source selected.
Source: VMM Administrator Console/ Windows Server 2012 R2.

1. To create a VM Template, expand Templates, right-click VM Templates, and select Create VM Template.

2. To select a source .vhdx file, click Browse, select Blank Disk - Small.vhdx and then click OK.

3. Click Next.

4. To provide an identity, enter W2K12R2STDBase for the VM Template Name, Enter Template to build a Windows Server 2012 R2 Standard server for the Description, and then click Next.

Modify Hardware Profile

Figure 3.31 shows the hardware profile modified with the Virtual DVD Drive linked to the existing Windows 2012 R2 Standard .iso file. In order to provide standardized installs, you can use the existing hardware profile.

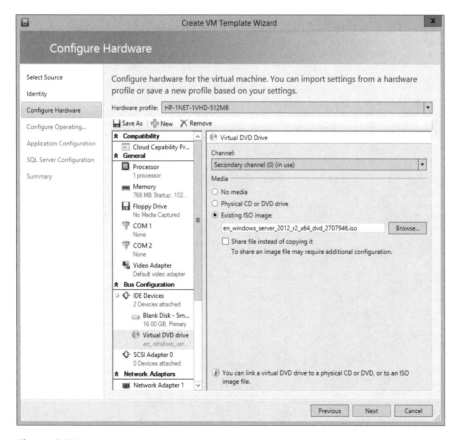

Figure 3.31
Modified hardware profile.
Source: VMM Administrator Console/ Windows Server 2012 R2.

1. To load the hardware profile, click the Hardware profile chevron and select HP-1NET-1VHD-512MB.

2. To link an existing .iso file to the template, click Virtual DVD Drive and then click Existing ISO image. Click Browse and select the ISO image for Windows Server 2012 R2 Standard. Click OK.

3. Click Next.

Link Guest OS Profile

On the next page, you will link up the existing Guest OS profile, as shown in Figure 3.32. In order to provide standardized installs, you can use the existing software profile.

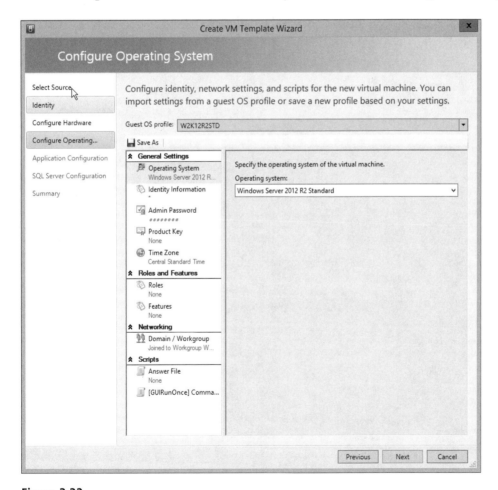

Figure 3.32
Linked software profile.

Source: VMM Administrator Console/ Windows Server 2012 R2.

1. To load the Guest OS profile, click the Guest OS profile chevron and select W2K12R2STD.

2. Click Next three times.

3. Review the Summary.

4. To view the PowerShell script, click View Script.

5. After viewing the script, close the Notepad window.

6. To run the script, click Create.

7. When the job completes, close the Jobs window.

Removing Resources from the Library

You can remove resources from the Library. When you no longer need a file in the Library, right-click the file and select Delete. Click Yes to confirm the deletion. Microsoft recommends that you remove the file through the VMM console. If you delete a file using the Windows Explorer, VMM will not be able to remove the related references and dependencies.

SUMMARY

- You learned about the various management views in the VMM Administrator console: VMs and Services, Fabric, Library, Jobs, and Settings.

- VMM uses host groups to group host computers for management. You created the COMPUTE host group and added the COMPUTE1 and COMPUTE2 host servers.

- The Library is the central location for resources that you use to build virtual machines. After setting up the Library, you created Hardware and Guest OS Profiles, which you integrated into a VM Machine Template.

CASE PROJECTS

Case 3-1: System Center Operations Manager (SCOM)

VMM is just one part of the Microsoft System Center. Microsoft System Center is a set of server products aimed specifically at helping corporate IT administrators manage a network of Windows Servers. Microsoft states the SCOM is a cross-platform data center management system for operating systems and hypervisors. To learn more about SCOM, do a Web search for: Microsoft SCOM.

Case 3-2: System Center Data Protection Manager (DPM)

DPM, another of the System Center products, is a disk-based backup system. A key feature of DPM is its ability to back up and restore virtual machines in the Hyper-V environment. To see how DPM works with Hyper-V, do a Web search for: protect Hyper-V virtual machines.

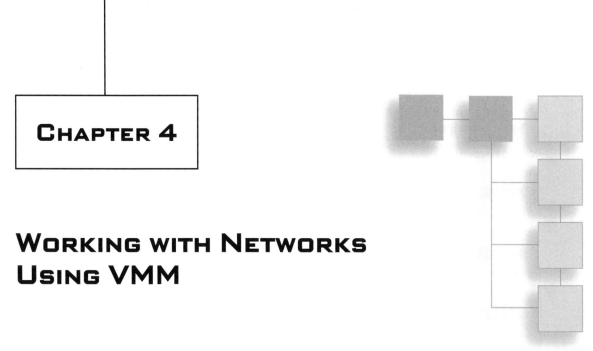

CHAPTER 4

WORKING WITH NETWORKS USING VMM

After reading this chapter and completing the exercises, you will be able to do the following:

- Cable physical networks.
- Create logical networks.
- Create virtual machine networks.
- Create port profiles and logical switches.

In this chapter, you will see how VMM maps logical networks to physical networks for host computers. Building on these concepts, you will learn how these logical networks will be extended as VM networks are made available for virtual machines. Then you can learn the steps to fine-tune your VM networks to provide optimal efficiency.

CABLING PHYSICAL NETWORKS

This section is all about naming your physical networks and configuring IP addresses. Proper management of networks is the key to success as you build your private cloud.

The host computers in the COMPUTE host group have four physical network adapters installed. Figure 4.1 shows the Network Connections window for COMPUTE1 with four network adapters with identifying names, such as Management Physical Network, Storage Physical Network, Heartbeat Physical Network, and Service Physical Network. You will name your own networks in exercises in this section.

You named the Management Physical Network, created a switch, and named the Management Logical Network in Chapter 1, "Introduction to the Private Cloud." However, only the Management Logical Network shows an identified network, because a DNS server IP address was configured for this network. The other networks do not have an assigned DNS server IP address. This will be OK since DNS lookups are not required on networks where only static IP addresses are used.

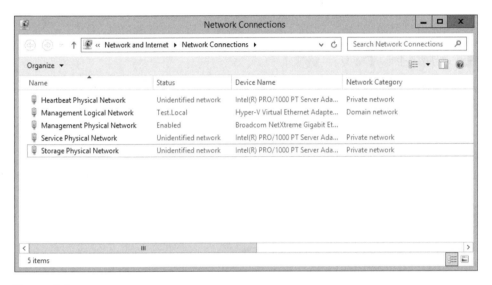

Figure 4.1
Network Connections window showing five networks.
Source: Network and Sharing Center/Windows Server 2012 R2.

In the following exercises, you will cable network adapters to physical switches for the remaining networks. In addition, you will enter IP Addresses for the Storage Physical Network, Heartbeat Physical Network, and the Service Physical Network. For these exercises, you'll need three additional 5-port Ethernet switches, three green cables, two red cables, and two yellow cables.

Wait to Place Ethernet Cables

Do not place network cables in the servers or switches until you are instructed to do so in this exercise. Because of the indiscriminate way that Microsoft Windows identifies network adapters, you should only work with one adapter at a time. To save yourself some confusion, be patient and follow instructions.

Cable Physical Storage Network

You use the Storage Physical Network for data communications between the iSCSI Target server and host computers in the COMPUTE resource. The suggested IP addresses for the Storage network appear in Table 4.1.

Table 4.1 Suggested IP Configurations for the Storage Physical Network

Server name	IPv4Address	Subnet mask
MANAGE	192.168.10.100	255.255.255.0
COMPUTE1	192.168.10.101	255.255.255.0
COMPUTE2	192.168.10.102	255.255.255.0

© 2014 Cengage Learning®.

1. Locate the MANAGE server and the Ethernet switch for the Storage Physical Network.

2. If required, cable the power supply to the Ethernet switch and plug the power supply into the power strip.

3. Connect a green cable between the next RJ45 connector on the MANAGE server and the next available port of the 5-port network switch for the Storage Physical Network.

4. Right-click the Network icon on the task bar, click Open Network and Sharing Center, and then click Change adapter settings.

5. To change the view, right-click in the whitespace, point to view, and click Details.

Adjust Column Sizes

To make it easier to see the device names, adjust the column widths by pulling the right side of the column headers.

6. Right-click the Unidentified network and click Rename. Enter Storage Physical Network.

7. Right-click the Storage Physical Network and click Properties. Click Internet Protocol Version 4 (TCP/IPv4) and click Properties. Enter the IP Address and subnet mask for the MANAGE server from Table 4.1.

8. Repeat steps 1 through 7 for the COMPUTE1 and COMPUTE2 host computers.

Cable Heartbeat Physical Network

The Heartbeat Physical Network exists for the clustered host servers in the COMPUTE resource to maintain status between the servers. Table 4.2 shows the suggested IP addresses for the Heartbeat Physical Network.

Table 4.2 Suggested IP Configurations for the Heartbeat Physical Network

Server Name	IPv4Address	Subnet mask
COMPUTE1	192.168.20.101	255.255.255.0
COMPUTE2	192.168.20.102	255.255.255.0

© 2014 Cengage Learning®.

1. Locate the COMPUTE1 server and the Ethernet switch for the Heartbeat Physical Network.

2. If required, cable the power supply to the Ethernet switch and plug the power supply into the power strip.

3. Connect a red cable between the next RJ45 connector on the COMPUTE1 server and the next available port of the 5-port network switch for the Heartbeat Physical Network.

4. Right-click the Unidentified network and click Rename. Enter Heartbeat Physical Network.

5. Right-click the Heartbeat Physical Network and click Properties. Click Internet Protocol Version 4 (TCP/IPv4) and click Properties. Enter the IP Address for the COMPUTE1 server from Table 4.2.

6. Repeat steps 1 through 5 for COMPUTE2.

Cable Service Physical Network

The Service Physical Network exists for communicating between virtual machines in the COMPUTE resource. The suggested IP addresses for the Service Physical Network appear in Table 4.3.

Table 4.3   Suggested IP Configurations for the Service Physical Network

Server Name	IPv4Address	Subnet mask
COMPUTE1	192.168.30.101	255.255.255.0
COMPUTE2	192.168.30.102	255.255.255.0

© 2014 Cengage Learning®.

1. Locate the COMPUTE1 server and the Ethernet switch for the Service Physical Network.

2. Connect a yellow cable between the next RJ45 connector on the COMPUTE1 server and the next available port of the 5-port network switch for the Service Physical Network.

3. If required, cable the power supply to the Ethernet switch and plug the power supply into the power strip.

4. Right-click the Unidentified network and click Rename. Enter the Service Physical Network.

5. Right-click the Service Physical Network and click Properties. Click Internet Protocol Version 4 (TCP/IPv4) and click Properties. Enter the IP Address for the COMPUTE1 server from Table 4.3.

6. Repeat steps 1 through 5 for COMPUTE2.

CREATING LOGICAL NETWORKS

One Fabric resource that VMM manages is Logical Networks, as shown in Figure 4.2. VMM maps logical networks to the equivalent physical networks. By using logical networks, you ensure that networks used by host computers are equivalent. VMM changes the Network Compliance entry from Fully compliant when a host IP configuration differs from the settings specified during the creation of the logical network.

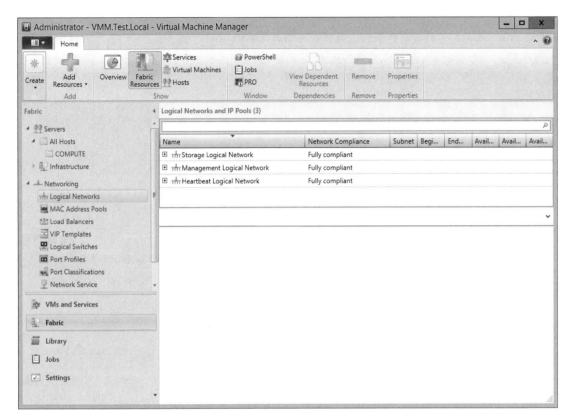

Figure 4.2
VMM Fabric showing Logical Networks.

Source: VMM Administrator Console/Windows Server 2012 R2.

In Figure 4.3, you see the Management Physical Network used by the COMPUTE host group. Recall that the COMPUTE host group consists of the COMPUTE1 and COMPUTE2 host servers.

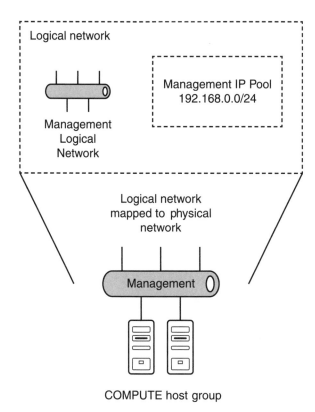

Logical network

Management IP Pool
192.168.0.0/24

Management
Logical
Network

Logical network
mapped to physical
network

Management

COMPUTE host group

Figure 4.3
VMM maps physical networks.
© 2014 Cengage Learning®.

Logical networks represent an abstraction of the underlying physical network. You can model the physical network without going into the intricate details of the physical network. Referring back to Figure 4.3, you can see the Management Logical Network created by VMM. Notice that an IP pool was defined for this logical network. Within this IP pool definition, you can configure the IP address range (192.168.0.1–192.168.0.254), a gateway (192.168.0.1), and a DNS server IP address (192.168.0.103).

How to Create Logical Networks

As you might suspect, the Create Logical Network Wizard is used to create logical networks. Figure 4.4 shows a completed name and description for the Storage Logical Network. Enter a recognizable Name. While the Description is optional, it is a good practice to enter a short description. The default is One connected network, which is OK for an existing physical network connected to host computers. VM Networks for virtual machines use the remaining options.

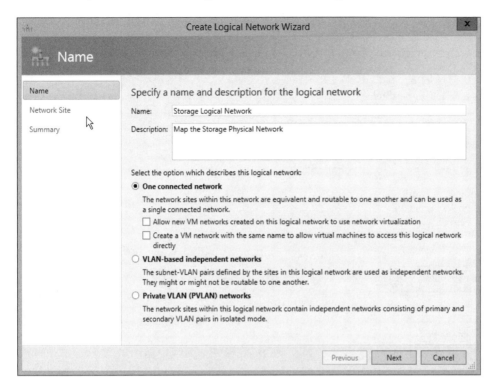

Figure 4.4
Create Logical Network Wizard Name page.
Source: VMM Administrator Console/Windows Server 2012 R2.

1. On the MANAGE server, move to the VMM Virtual Machine Manager console.

2. Click the Fabric View, expand Networking, and then click Logical Networks.

3. To start the Create Logical Network Wizard, click Create on the ribbon and then click Create Logical Network.

4. Enter Storage Logical Network for the Name and Map the Storage Physical Network for the description.

5. Click Next.

Associate Logical Network with Network Site

On the next page, you associate the Storage Logical Network with a Network site. A completed page is shown in Figure 4.5. Since there is only one site in the design, only All Hosts appears. If multiple sites existed, you could choose the site from the list of Host groups.

To complete this association, you enter the IP subnet. The /24 indicates that a 24-bit network is used. The /24 CIDR is the same as a subnet of 255.255.255.0. Since this physical network does not use VLANs, the VLAN entry is not required.

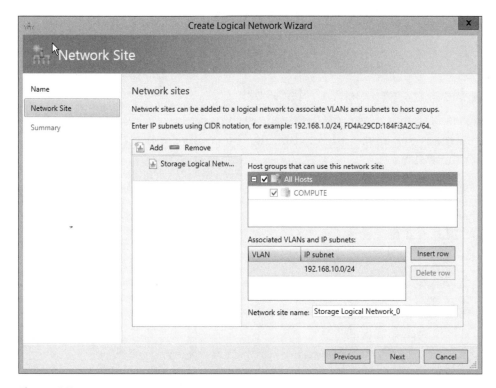

Figure 4.5
Create Logical Network Wizard Network Site page.
Source: VMM Administrator Console/Windows Server 2012 R2.

1. To add a Network Site, click Add, and then check All Hosts.

2. To associate an IP subnet with this logical network, click Insert row and enter 192.168.10.0/24 for the IP subnet.

3. Click Next.

Review Summary

Review the Summary on the next page. Of course, you can go to previous pages to correct errors. Since the Storage Logical Network is a non-routed network, you have completed the logical network.

1. Review the Summary.

2. To view the script, click View Script. Scroll the Notepad window. Close the Notepad window.

3. Click Finish.

4. Close the Jobs window.

Configure the Heartbeat Logical Network

The Heartbeat Logical Network connects the two host computers in COMPUTE to determine if the two machines are alive and functioning. To configure the Heartbeat Logical Network, complete these steps:

1. To start the Create Logical Network Wizard, click Create on the ribbon and then click Create Logical Network.

2. Enter Heartbeat Logical Network for the Name.

3. Click Next.

4. To add a Network Site, click Properties, click Add, and then check Compute.

5. To associate an IP subnet with this logical network, click Insert row and enter 192.168.20.0/24 for the IP subnet.

6. Click Next.

7. Review the Summary.

8. Click Finish.

9. Close the Jobs window.

Configure the Service Logical Network

The Service Logical Network supports virtual machines. The configuration resembles the other logical network with one addition—this network will support virtual machines. This requires the Allow new VM networks created on this logical network to use network virtualization option to be selected.

To configure the Service Logical Network, complete these steps:

1. To start the Create Logical Network Wizard, click Fabric, right-click Logical Networks, and then click Create Logical Network.

2. Enter Service Logical Network for the Name.

3. To enable Network virtualization, check the Allow new VM networks created on this logical network to use network virtualization option. Click Next.

4. To add a Network Site, click Add and then check COMPUTE.

5. To associate an IP subnet with this logical network, click Insert row and enter 192.168.30.0/24 for the IP subnet. Click Next and click Finish.

6. Close the Jobs window.

Configure the Management Logical Network

While the Hyper-V Manager can create a Logical Network, the definition is not complete, and you must add the site information. To complete the Logical Network definition for the Management Logical Network, complete these steps:

1. Right-click Management Logical Network and click Properties.

2. To add a Network Site, click Network Site, click Add, and then check All Hosts.

3. To associate an IP subnet with this logical network, click Insert row and enter 192.168.0.0/24 for the IP subnet. Click OK.

Define IP Address Pools

In order for VMM to check compliance for a routed network, such as the Management Logical Network, you need to define the IP Address Pool. Recall that you created the Management Logical Network in Chapter 2. Figure 4.6 shows a completed Name page. You enter a descriptive Name. The Description is optional. To select a logical network to associate with this IP pool, click the Logical network chevron and select the logical network.

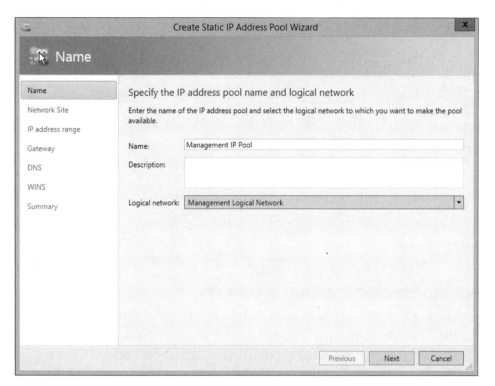

Figure 4.6
Create Static IP Address Pool Wizard Name page.
Source: VMM Administrator Console/Windows Server 2012 R2.

1. To start the Create Static IP Address Pool Wizard, right-click Management Logical Network and then click Create IP Pool.

2. Enter Management IP Pool for the Name.

3. If necessary, click the Logical network chevron and select Management Logical Network.

4. Click Next.

Identify the Network Site

The next page is the Network Site page. See Figure 4.7 for a completed page. On this page, you see the Management Logical Network and 192.168.10.0/24 IP subnet entered for the Create Logical Network Wizard. If you continue with the Create Static IP Address Pool

Wizard after using the Create Logical Network Wizard for the same logical network, the entries should be correct. Otherwise, click the Network site chevron and select the correct logical network. Likewise, select the correct IP subnet.

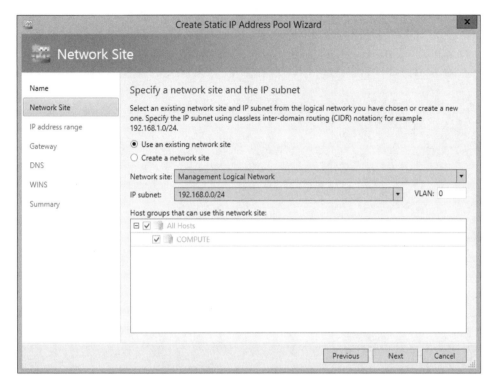

Figure 4.7
Create Static IP Address Pool Wizard Network Site page.
Source: VMM Administrator Console/Windows Server 2012 R2.

1. If necessary, click the Network site chevron and select Management Logical Network.

2. If necessary, click the IP subnet chevron and select 192.168.0.0.

3. Review the Network Site information and click Next.

Specify the IP Address Range

The IP address range page is next, as shown in Figure 4.8. On this page, you are specifying the IP address range for the Static IP address allocators. VMM can allocate Static IP addresses to future host computers. By specifying a Static IP address range for host computers, you facilitate VMM IP address compliance for host computers.

For the indicated subnet, a default range is entered for you. It is a best practice to accept the default range. For IP address ranges managed by another device, such as a home router, you exclude these IP addresses (for example, 192.168.0.1–192.168.0.99). Also, you need to exclude a range of IP addresses that you assign as static IP addresses for preexisting host computers and virtual machines (192.168.0.100–192.168.0.125).

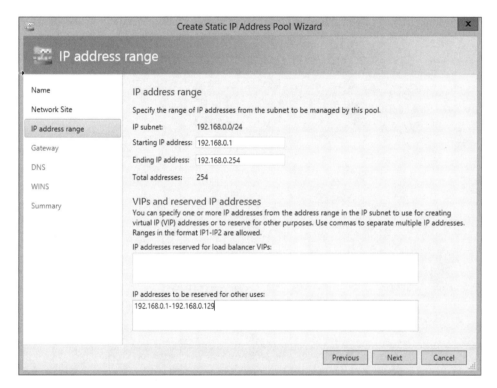

Figure 4.8
Create Static IP Address Pool Wizard IP address range page.
Source: VMM Administrator Console/Windows Server 2012 R2.

1. Review the IP Subnet settings and correct as necessary.

2. Enter 192.168.0.1–192.168.0.129 for the IP addresses to be reserved for other uses.

3. Click Next.

Alternate IP Addresses May Be Needed

For your network, you may need to exclude alternative IP address ranges. The 192.168.0.1–192.168.0.99 is allocated by the home Internet router. The 192.168.0.100–192.168.0.129 is reserved for static IP address assignments for servers on the Management network.

Specify the Gateway

You can specify the Gateway for networks that are routed to other networks. On the next page, see Figure 4.9, enter the address for the router. By convention, this IP address is the first device IP address on the network. For unrouted networks, leave this field blank.

Figure 4.9
Create Static IP Address Pool Wizard Gateway page.
Source: VMM Administrator Console/Windows Server 2012 R2.

1. Click Insert, double-click Enter gateway address and then enter 192.168.0.1 for the Gateway Address.

2. Click Next.

Configure Host Name Resolution

The next task is to enter DNS information for this network, Figure 4.10 shows a completed page. In Chapter 2, you created the Active Directory Domain Services. As a part of this exercise, the DNS role was added. To enter the IP address for DNS, which is the same as AD DS, click Insert and enter the IP address for the DNS server. Enter the Connection specific DNS suffix test.local. By doing this, you permit the DNS IP configuration to be used for logical network compliance.

Since you will not be using NetBIOS name resolution, you may skip the WINS page.

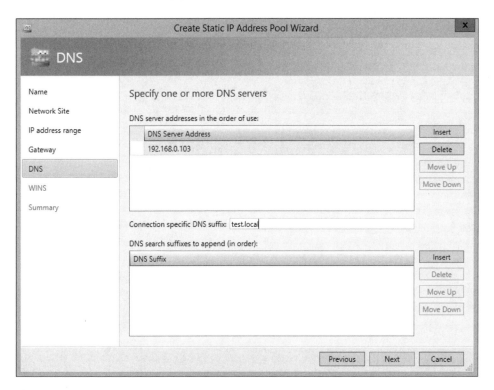

Figure 4.10
Create Static IP Address Pool Wizard DNS page.
Source: VMM Administrator Console/Windows Server 2012 R2.

1. Click Insert and then enter 192.168.0.103 for the DNS Server Address.

2. Enter test.local over Enter DNS suffix.

3. Click Next twice.

Review Summary Page

The last page is the Summary, where you can go to previous pages to correct errors. Figure 4.11 shows this Summary. You can view the PowerShell script in Notepad.

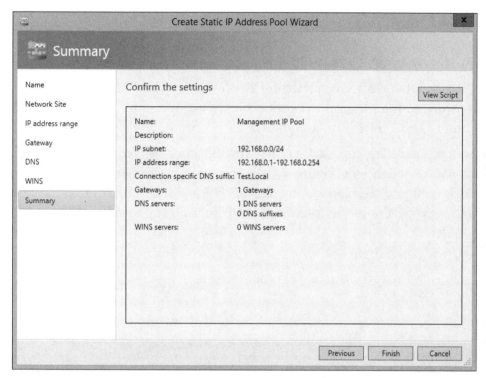

Figure 4.11
Create Static IP Address Pool Wizard Summary page.
Source: VMM Administrator Console/Windows Server 2012 R2.

1. To view the script, click View Script. Scroll the Notepad window. Close the Notepad window.

2. Click Finish.

3. Close the Jobs window.

Define IP Address Pool for Service Logical Network

To define the IP address pool to the Service Logical Network, complete these steps:

1. To start the Create Static IP Address Pool Wizard, click Service Logical Network, click Create on the ribbon, and then click Create IP Pool.

2. Enter Service IP Pool for the Name. Click the Logical network chevron and then select Service Logical Network.

3. Click Next until the Summary appears and then click Finish.

4. Close the Jobs window.

Map Logical Networks to COMPUTE Hosts

A quick review: Logical networks were created for the four networks. The next task is to map the logical network to the physical network represented by the physical adapters in the COMPUTE1 and COMPUTE2 host computers.

To locate the hosts to associate to the Logical network, click Servers and then click COMPUTE. Click the Host tab (see Figure 4.12). To open the Properties for the first host computer, click compute1.test.local and then click Properties on the ribbon. You can't get the hardware properties by right-clicking the compute1.test.local.

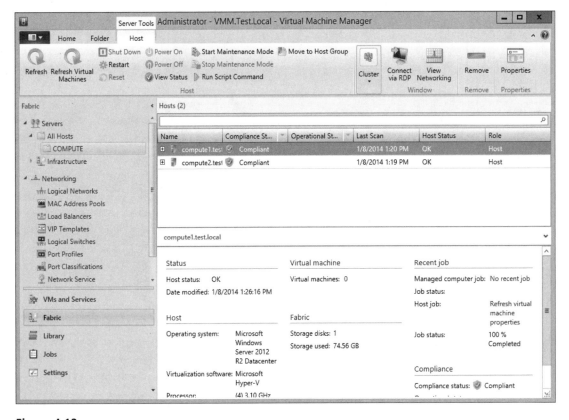

Figure 4.12
VMM showing Host tab for Servers.
Source: VMM Administrator Console/Windows Server 2012 R2.

1. To locate the hosts to associate to the Logical network, click Servers and then click COMPUTE.

2. Click the Host tab.

When the properties for compute1.test.local appear, you click Hardware. Figure 4.13 shows the completed pane. If more logical networks were available, you would need to locate the correct logical network from the list. You need to complete these steps for any additional host computers.

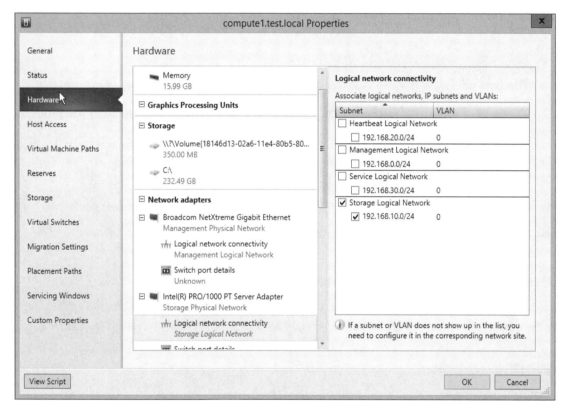

Figure 4.13
VMM Hardware properties for host computer.
Source: VMM Administrator Console/Windows Server 2012 R2.

1. To open the Properties, click compute1.test.local and click Properties on the ribbon.

2. Click Hardware and expand Network Adapters. Scroll and locate the Storage Physical Network adapter. Click Logical network connectivity and then check Storage Logical Network.

3. Click OK.

4. Repeat steps 1 through 3 for compute2.test.local.

Map Heartbeat Logical Network to Physical Hosts

To map the Heartbeat Logical Network to the physical hosts, you complete these steps.

1. To open the Properties, click compute1.test.local and click Properties on the ribbon.

2. Click Hardware and expand Network Adapters. Scroll and locate the Heartbeat Physical Network adapter. Click Logical network connectivity and then Check Heartbeat Logical Network.

3. Click OK.

4. Repeat steps 1 through 3 for compute2.test.local.

Map Service Logical Network to Physical Hosts

To map the Service Logical Network to the physical hosts, you complete these steps.

1. To open the Properties, click compute1.test.local and click Properties on the ribbon.

2. Click Hardware and expand Network Adapters. Scroll and locate the Service Physical Network adapter. Click Logical network connectivity and then Check Service Logical Network.

3. Click OK.

4. Repeat steps 1 through 3 for compute2.test.local.

Creating Virtual Machine Networks

In this section, you will learn about the creation of virtual machine networks. With network isolation, you can restrict network access to the proper sets of virtual machines.

Network Isolation

You could create a private cloud where all virtual machines were on the same virtual machine network, as shown in Figure 4.14. Each of the virtual machines communicates with each other and other network resources. There is a 1:1 mapping between the IP addresses on the physical network and the IP addresses on the VM network. With this configuration, you have a VM network tied to a logical network, which maps to a physical network.

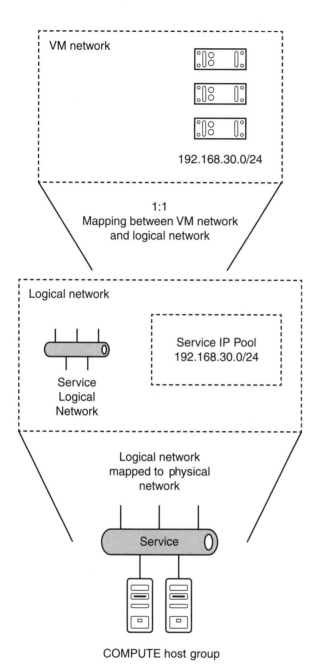

Figure 4.14
VMM maps logical networks to VM networks.

Consider this scenario where your IT department treats internal business units as tenants (or customers) of the IT department. For example, you might need a VM network for Finance, Sales, Engineering, or so on. As your private cloud grows, for performance or security, you need to isolate sets of virtual machines for these tenants on new VM networks

To add a new VM network with its logical network, you need another physical network, which would work until you ran out of network adapters on your servers.

Another approach is to incorporate a Virtual LAN (VLAN) for each tenant's virtual machines. Figure 4.15 shows two VM networks isolated by VLANs. Each VM network that you create is mapped to one VLAN. There is a single VM network for VLAN 10 and another for VLAN 20. In this example, you can accommodate two tenants. To add an additional tenant, you map a VLAN to a new VM network. However, you can only have as many VM networks as you have VLANs on the physical network. And each additional VLAN requires configuration on one or more physical switches. This is hardware defined networking.

Microsoft offers a software-defined solution for network isolation. This new approach is called Hyper-V Network Virtualization (HNV). HNV is based on the general concept of Software Defined Networking (SDN). The goal of SDN is to virtualize the network without the limitations of hardware devices.

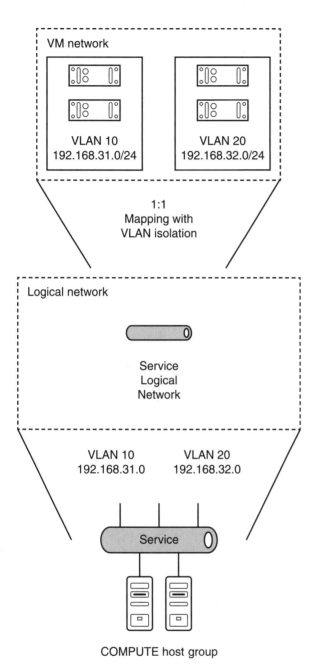

Figure 4.15
VMM maps VLANS to VM networks.

Here are some advantages for adopting HNV over VLANS:

- **Virtual networks are defined in software:** This provides administrators with the flexibility and simplicity to manage many VM networks.

- **Scalability:** Virtual networks (up to 4,000 or more virtualized networks) scale better than VLANS (switches typically permit 1,000 VLANs).

- **Isolation:** HNV provides needed isolation to tenants by default.

- **Multi-tenancy with overlapping IP address ranges:** Tenants can choose their own IP address ranges. In fact, each tenant can use the same IP address range.

HNV provides the ability to create multiple VM networks on a single shared physical network. With this approach, each tenant gets a complete VM network, which provides support for multiple virtual subnets, as shown in Figure 4.16. The Finance and Sales tenants have individual VM networks. The VM network Finance has two virtual subnets.

HNV uses Generic Routing Encapsulation (GRE), which works by encapsulating the IP packet from a virtual machine on one host with a header providing instructions to deliver the IP packet to a virtual machine on the destination host. When the encapsulated packet is received on the destination host, the header is removed before passing the IP packet to the virtual machine. GRE is implemented in the Hyper-V extensible switch on each Hyper-V host computer.

HNV abstracts IP address ranges. This is done by using two types of IP addresses:

- **Consumer Address (CA):** These are the IP addresses that the tenant uses in his virtual network.

- **Provider Address (PA):** This IP address is assigned to NIC of the virtual switch network, which allows virtual machines to talk to the physical adapter.

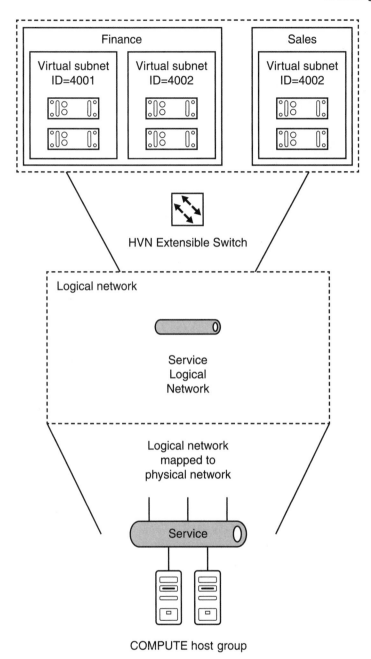

Figure 4.16
Multitenant VM networks supported by HVN routing.
© 2014 Cengage Learning®.

HNV works with GRE to associate the CA and PA addresses. A single PA is assigned to the host, and VM network packets are encapsulated (see Figure 4.17). Two tenants reside on the same cloud where each tenant has an assigned VM network. FINANCE1 and SALES1 have the same IP address of 172.16.0.10. This presents no problem because the two virtual machines are on separate VM networks. Tenant network isolation segregates these virtual machines

If SALES1 needs to communicate with SALES2, COMPUTE1 encapsulates the packet from the CA of SALES1. COMPUTE1 uses a lookup table to discover on which host computer SALES2 resides. (SALES2 is on COMPUTE2.) COMPUTE1 will send the encapsulated packet from COMPUTE1 to COMPUTE2 where the packet is stripped and passed on to SALES2.

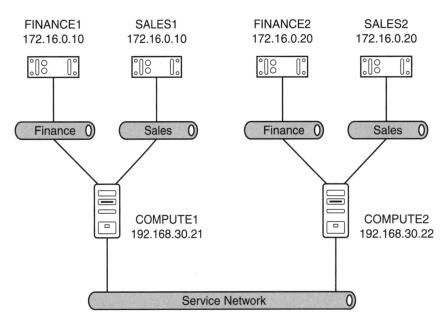

Figure 4.17
An example of HNV and GRE routing.

When creating a Logical Network that supports Network Virtualization, you check one additional box. Figure 4.18 shows this checkbox, which indicates that you are allowing new VM networks created on this logical network to use network virtualization. Since you are deploying Hyper-V Network Virtualization, the default technology for this virtualization is OK.

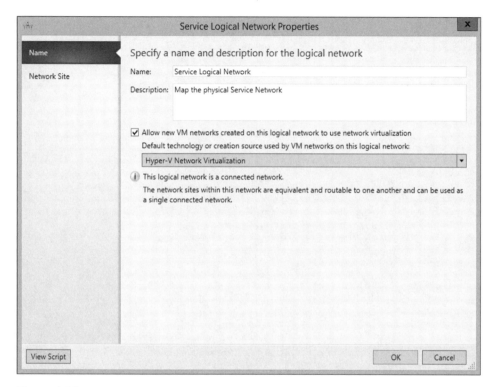

Figure 4.18
Service Logical Network Properties showing network virtualization option.
Source: VMM Administrator Console/Windows Server 2012 R2.

Create VM Network

To get started with the creation of a new VM Network, click the VMs and Services view.

1. Click the VM and Services view.

2. To start the Create VM Network Wizard, click VM Networks and click Create VM Network.

Connect to Service Logical Network

On the next page, enter the Name for the VM network and an optional description. To connect to the Service Logical Network, click the Logical network chevron and select Service Logical Network, as shown in Figure 4.19.

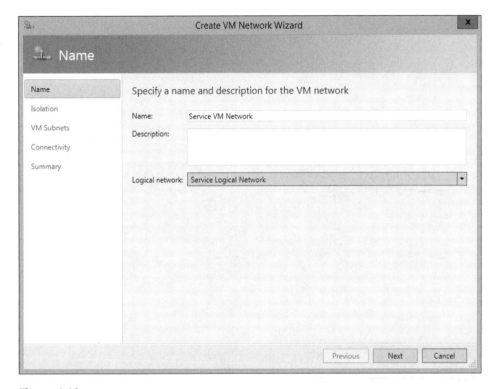

Figure 4.19
Create VM Network Wizard Name page.

Source: VMM Administrator Console/Windows Server 2012 R2.

1. Enter Service VM Network for the Name.

2. To connect to the Service Logical Network, click the Logical network chevron and select Service Logical Network.

3. Click Next.

Specify Network Isolation

The Isolation page is next (see Figure 4.20). Review the defaults. Since you are using Hyper-V network virtualization, this default will be OK. You can use IPv4 or IPv6, but not both. The default of IPv4 matches the IP addresses you are using.

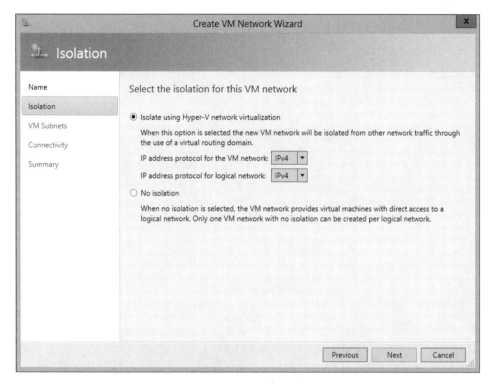

Figure 4.20
Create VM Network Wizard Isolation page.
Source: VMM Administrator Console/Windows Server 2012 R2.

1. Review the Isolation.

2. Click Next.

Specify Tenant IP Addresses

The next task is to specify the VM subnet that the tenant (or customer) will use. Figure 4.21 shows the completed entry of these customer addresses. To enter the VM subnet, click Add and enter the Name and Subnet. This example shows a private class B subnet with a network of 16 bits.

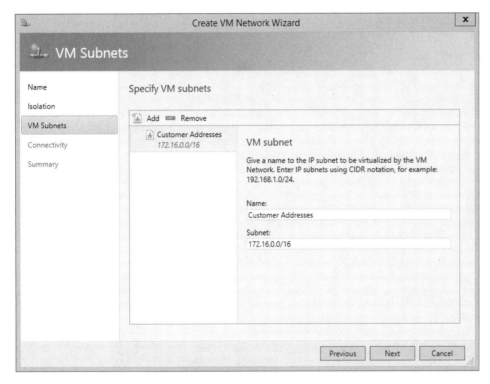

Figure 4.21
Create VM Network Wizard VM Subnets page.
Source: VMM Administrator Console/Windows Server 2012 R2.

1. To enter the Customer Addresses, click Add.

2. Enter Customer Addresses for the Name.

3. Enter 172.16.0.0/16 for the Subnet.

4. Click Next.

Specify Connectivity to Other Sites

On the next page, the Connectivity is specified, as shown in Figure 4.22. In the network design, customers will access the Service network directly, and a gateway router is not needed. If you decided to allow users to access the Service network from another network, such as the Internet, a gateway router would be needed.

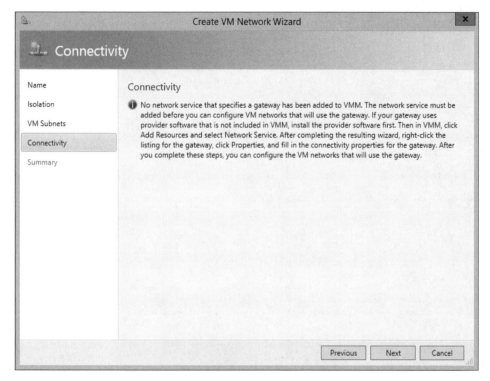

Figure 4.22
Create VM Network Wizard Connectivity page.
Source: VMM Administrator Console/Windows Server 2012 R2.

1. Review the Connectivity (optional).

2. Click Next.

Review Summary

Figure 4.23 shows the Summary page. If needed, make corrections. Click Finish to run the PowerShell script.

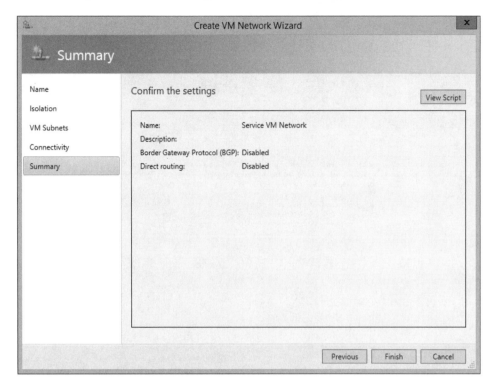

Figure 4.23
Create VM Network Wizard Summary page.
Source: VMM Administrator Console/Windows Server 2012 R2.

1. Review the Summary.

2. To view the PowerShell script, click View Script.

3. Close the Notepad window and then click Finish.

4. Close the Jobs window.

Create IP Address Pool

The next task is to create a Static IP Address pool for the VM network. From this pool, VMM assigns IP addresses for virtual machines running on the VM network.

Enter a name for the IP address pool. The wizard, see Figure 4.24, fills in the VM network and VM subnet. These will work just great.

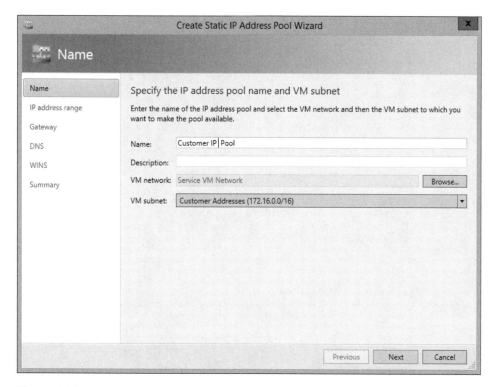

Figure 4.24
Create Static IP Address Pool Wizard Name page.
Source: VMM Administrator Console/Windows Server 2012 R2.

1. To start the Create Static IP Address Pool Wizard, right-click Service VM Network and then click Create IP Pool.

2. Enter Customer IP Pool for the Name.

3. Click Next.

Specify IP Address Range

See Figure 4.25 for the IP address range. The values filled in by the wizard meet the requirements.

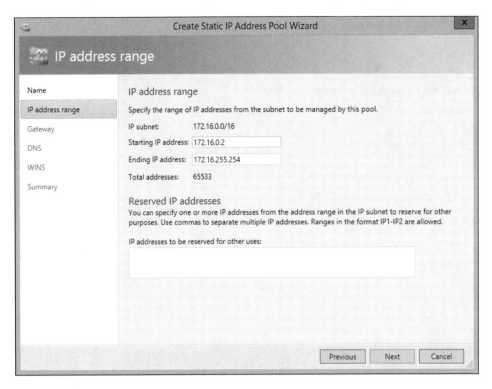

Figure 4.25
Create Static IP Address Pool Wizard IP address range page.
Source: VMM Administrator Console/Windows Server 2012 R2.

1. Review the IP address range.

2. Click Next.

Specify Gateway Address

On the next page, you must enter the IP address for the gateway. By Microsoft's convention, this must be the first IP address on the subnet. For the 172.16.0.0 network, you can enter 172.6.0.1 (see Figure 4.26).

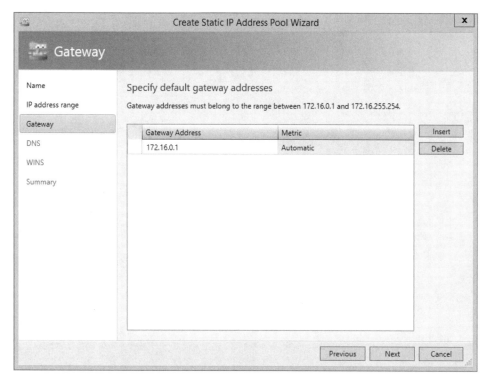

Figure 4.26
Create Static IP Address Pool Wizard Gateway page.

Source: VMM Administrator Console/Windows Server 2012 R2.

1. To specify the default IP gateway IP address, click Insert, double-click Enter gateway address, and enter 172.16.0.1.

2. Click Next.

Specify Name Resolution

The DNS server IP address is entered on the next page, as shown in Figure 4.27. Click Insert and enter an anticipated IP address for the DNS server. When future virtual machines are deployed, this IP address could be assigned to this future DNS server.

Since you are not using NetBIOS to resolve IP addresses, you can skip the WINS page.

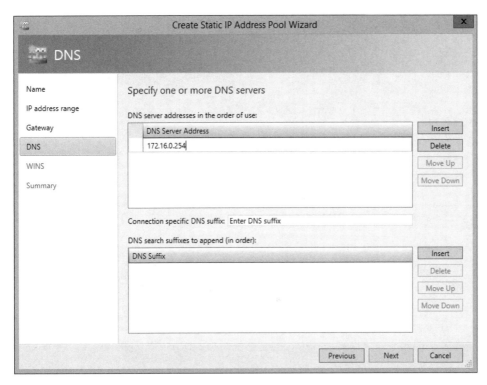

Figure 4.27
Create Static IP Address Pool Wizard DNS page.

Source: VMM Administrator Console/Windows Server 2012 R2.

1. To specify the DNS Server Address, click Insert and enter 172.16.0.254.

2. Click Next twice.

Review Summary Page

Figure 4.28 shows the Summary page. If this looks good, click Finish to run the Power-Shell script.

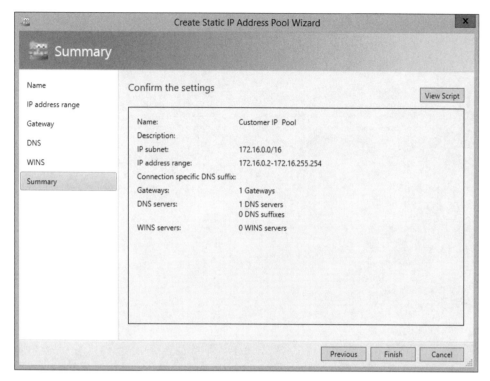

Figure 4.28
Create Static IP Address Pool Wizard Summary page.
Source: VMM Administrator Console/Windows Server 2012 R2.

1. Review the Summary page and then click Finish.
2. After the script runs, close the Jobs window.

Review VM Network

After the script runs, close the Jobs window. The VM Networks node displays the created VM Network, as shown in Figure 4.29. To see additional details or make changes, right-click the VM network name and select Properties.

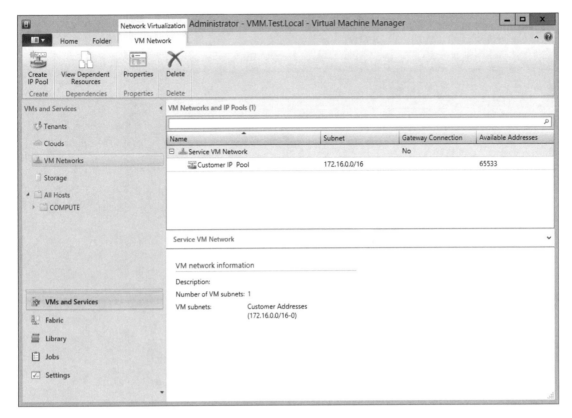

Figure 4.29
VM Network showing created Service VM Network.
Source: VMM Administrator Console/Windows Server 2012 R2.

1. To see additional details or make changes, right-click Service VM Network and then select Properties.

2. Close the Properties page.

CREATING PORT PROFILES AND LOGICAL SWITCHES

You can consistently configure identical settings for network adapters for your host computers by using port profiles and logical switches. By doing this, you no longer have to configure these settings for the network adapters on each host computer in the COMPUTE resource.

Figure 4.30 provides an example of the configuration of a logical switch. In the Uplink profile (left side of drawing), you specify the site where the network resides, and optionally, indicate network virtualization. In the Hyper-V profile, you indicate the configuration choices for the available physical properties of the network adapter, such as the offload settings. With the port classifications, you match the network to a set of Microsoft predefined port settings.

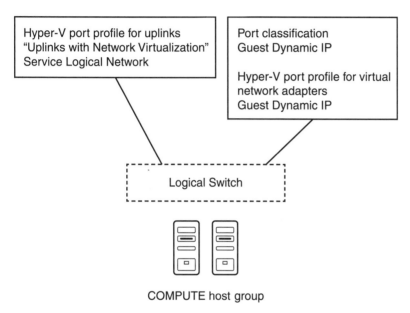

Figure 4.30
Port profiles and logical switches.
© 2014 Cengage Learning®.

Create a Native Port Profile

To create a Native Port Profile, click on Port Profiles within the Networking node. Next, click Create in the ribbon. When the create group is shown, click Hyper-V Port Profile.

Create Uplink Port Profile

On the General page, as shown in Figure 4.31, enter the name for the Hyper-V port profile. Since this is an Uplink port profile, click Uplink port profile. The defaults are OK.

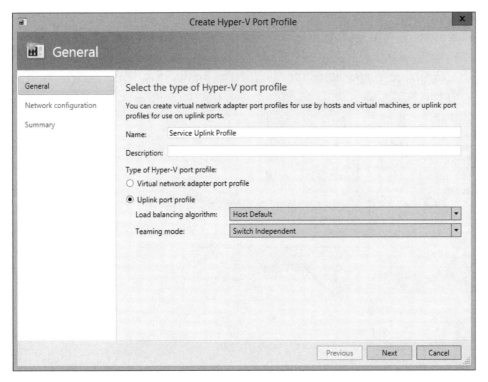

Figure 4.31
Create Hyper-V Port Profile Wizard General page.
Source: VMM Administrator Console/Windows Server 2012 R2.

1. To create the Uplink profile, click on Fabric and click on Port Profiles within the Networking node. Click Create in the ribbon.

2. When the create group is shown, click Hyper-V Port Profile.

3. Enter Service Uplink Profile for the Name.

4. Click Uplink port profile.

5. Click Next.

Tie Native Port Profile to Service Logical Network

On the next page, you tie the Native Port Profile to the network. Since this is the Service Network, you select Service Logical Network_0 and then you check Enable Hyper-V Network Virtualization. This is shown in Figure 4.32.

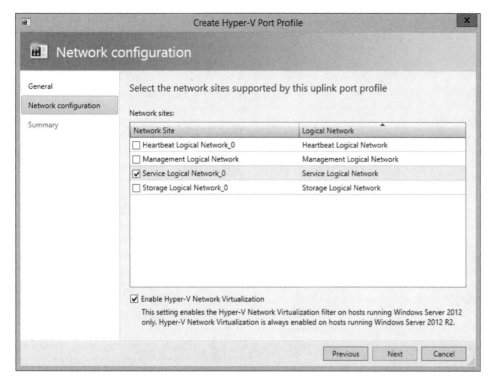

Figure 4.32
Create Hyper-V Port Profile Wizard Network configuration page.

Source: VMM Administrator Console/Windows Server 2012 R2.

1. Click Service Logical Network_0.

2. Click Enable Hyper-V Network Virtualization.

3. Click Next.

Review Summary Page

Figure 4.33 shows the Summary page. Of course, you can go to a previous page and make corrections.

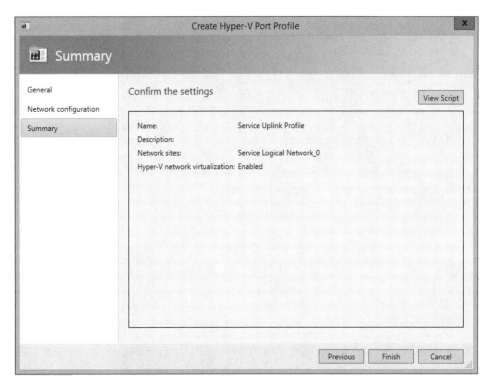

Figure 4.33
Create Hyper-V Port Profile Wizard Summary page.
Source: VMM Administrator Console/Windows Server 2012 R2.

1. Review the Summary page and return to a previous page to make corrections.

2. When finished with corrections, click Finish.

3. Close the Jobs window.

Create Hyper-V Port Profile

To create a Hyper-V port profile, click on Port Profiles within the Networking node.

On the General page, enter a name and optional description. Retain the Virtual network adapter port profile (see Figure 4.34).

Figure 4.34
Create Hyper-V Port Profile Wizard General page.
Source: VMM Administrator Console/Windows Server 2012 R2.

1. To create an adapter port profile, click Create in the ribbon.

2. When the create group is shown, click Hyper-V Port Profile.

3. Enter Service Adapter Port Profile for the Name.

4. Click Next.

Specify Offload Settings

By employing offload capabilities, you move processing to the network adapters from the computer's CPU. Your network adapters must have these hardware capabilities. The following list of options provides details about these offload capabilities:

- **Enable virtual machine queue:** Packets that are destined for a virtual network adapter are delivered directly to a queue for that adapter, and they do not have to be copied from the management operating system to the virtual machine.

- **Enable IPsec task offloading:** Some or all of the computational work that IPsec requires is shifted to a dedicated processor on the network adapter.

- **Enable Single-root I/O virtualization:** A network adapter can be assigned directly to a virtual machine.

1. When the Offload Settings page appears, select the Offload Settings that are available on your physical network adapters.

2. Click Next.

Specify Security Settings

On the Security Settings page, you can set a number of optional security settings from this list:

- **Allow MAC spoofing:** Permits a virtual machine to change the source MAC address in outgoing packets. For example, a load-balancer virtual appliance might require this setting to be enabled.

- **Enable DHCP guard:** Protects against a malicious virtual machine that represents itself as a DHCP server for man-in-the-middle attacks.

- **Allow router guard:** Protects against advertisement and redirection messages that are sent by an unauthorized virtual machine that represents itself as a router.

- **Allow guest teaming:** Permits a virtual network adapter to team with other network adapters that are connected to the same switch.

- **Allow IEEE priority tagging:** Permits priority tags for Quality of Service (QoS) to prioritize traffic.

The last option, Allow guest specified IP addresses (only available for virtual machines on Windows Server 2012 R2), allows virtual machines to add and remove IP addresses on this virtual network adapter. You need this option to simplify the process of managing virtual machine settings. The IP address that a guest adds must be within an existing IP subnet in the VM network.

1. On the Security Settings page, optionally select one or more security settings.

2. Retain the Allow guest specified IP addresses (only available for virtual machines on Windows Server 2012 R2) option.

3. Click Next.

Specify Bandwidth Settings

On the next page, you set the bandwidth settings to specify the minimum and maximum bandwidth that are available to the network adapter (see Figure 4.35). The minimum bandwidth can be expressed as megabits per second (Mbps). A value of 0 Mbps means the maximum bandwidth is not configured. Another way to specify the minimum bandwidth is to use a weighted value (from 0 to 100) that controls how much bandwidth the virtual network adapter can use in relation to other virtual network adapters.

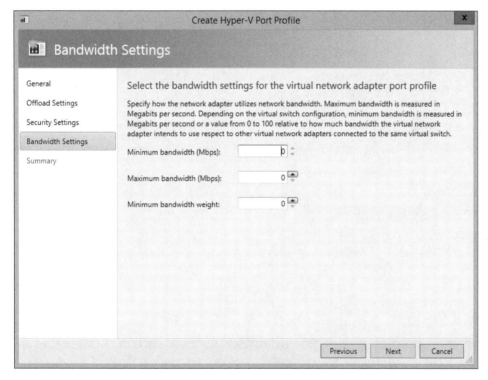

Figure 4.35
Create Hyper-V Port Profile Wizard Bandwidth Settings page.
Source: VMM Administrator Console/Windows Server 2012 R2.

1. Review the bandwidth settings.

2. Click Next.

3. Figure 4.36 shows the Summary page. If needed, make changes. Click Finish to run the PowerShell script.

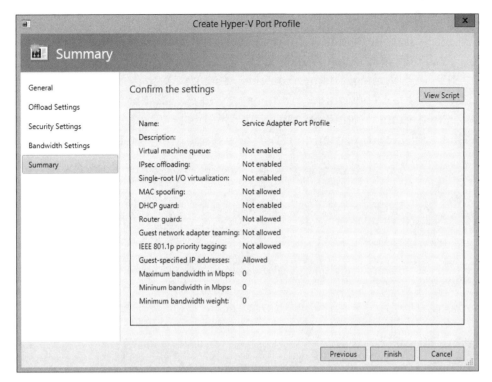

Figure 4.36
Create Hyper-V Port Profile Wizard Summary page.
Source: VMM Administrator Console/Windows Server 2012 R2.

Create a Logical Switch

A logical switch brings port profiles, port classifications, and switch extensions together so that you can apply them consistently to network adapters on the COMPUTE resource. After completing the two port profiles, you need to create the accompanying logical switch.

The setup is similar to the steps to create the port profile. After navigating to Create group, click Create Logical Switch to start the Create Logical Switch Wizard.

You will want to review the information about logical switches and then continue to the next page. You need an Uplink Profile and a Hyper-V Profile prior to creating a logical switch.

1. To create a Logical Switch, right-click Logical Switches and click Create Logical Switch.

2. Review the Getting started with a logical switch information.

3. Click Next.

Name Logical Switch

On the next page (see Figure 4.37), you can name the logical switch and provide an optional description.

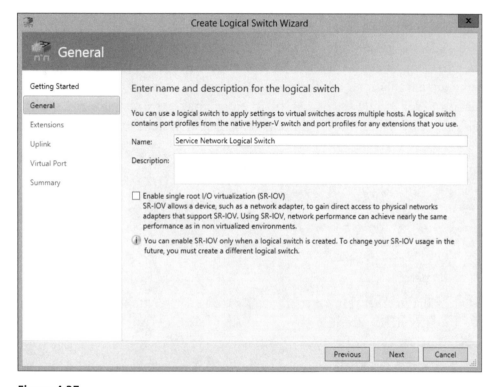

Figure 4.37
Create Logical Switch Wizard General page.
Source: VMM Administrator Console/Windows Server 2012 R2.

1. Enter Service Network Logical Switch for the name.

2. Click Next.

Specify Switch Extensions

With switch extensions, you can expand the capabilities of a logical switch (see Figure 4.38). Four types of switch extensions are supported:

- **Monitoring extensions:** Monitor and report on network traffic.

- **Capturing extensions:** Inspect and sample traffic.

- **Filtering extensions:** Block, modify, or defragment packets. They can also block ports.

- **Forwarding extensions:** Direct traffic by defining destinations, and they can capture and filter traffic.

The Microsoft NDIS Packet Capture Filter Driver allows you to configure logical switches to behave as if port mirroring were in effect. With this feature in place, you can use a protocol analyzer on one virtual machine to capture network traffic from another. The Windows Filtering Platform (WFP) allows a filter to intercept packets and perform packet inspection or modification by using the WFP management and system functions.

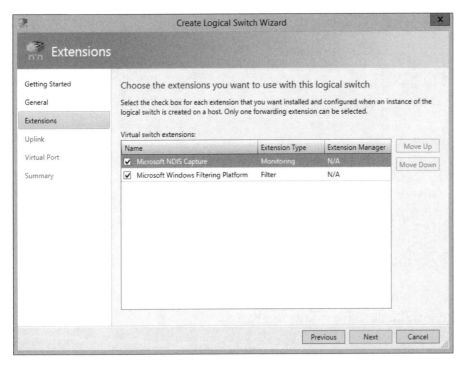

Figure 4.38
Create Logical Switch Wizard Extensions page.
Source: VMM Administrator Console/Windows Server 2012 R2.

1. To enable the monitoring of packets, check Microsoft NDIS Capture.

2. Retain Microsoft Windows Filtering Platform.

3. Click Next.

Add Uplink Port Profile

To select the Uplink port profile, click Add. Figure 4.39 shows the Add Uplink Port Profile pop-up.

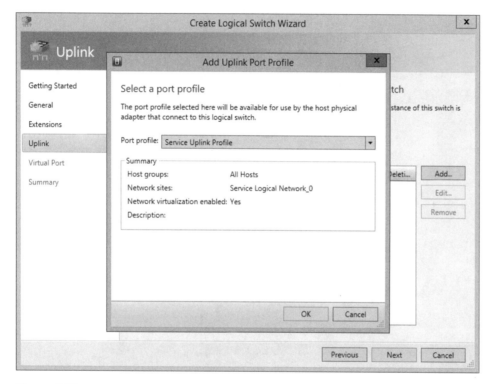

Figure 4.39
Create Logical Switch Wizard Uplink page.
Source: VMM Administrator Console/Windows Server 2012 R2..

1. To select the Service Uplink Profile, click Add and then click OK.

2. Click Next.

Add Port Classification

To add the single Port Classification, click Add. The Add Virtual Port page is displayed. You can browse the Port Profile Classifications, which are shown in Figure 4.40. Since the Service Network exists to run virtual machines, you select Medium Bandwidth.

Figure 4.40
Create Logical Switch Select a Port Profile Classification page.
Source: VMM Administrator Console/Windows Server 2012 R2.

1. To add the single Port Classification, click Add.

2. Click Browse and select Medium Bandwidth.

3. Click OK.

Add Virtual Network Adapter Port Profile

Click Include a virtual network adapter port profile in this virtual port and select the pre-viously created Service Adapter Port Profile, as shown in Figure 4.41.

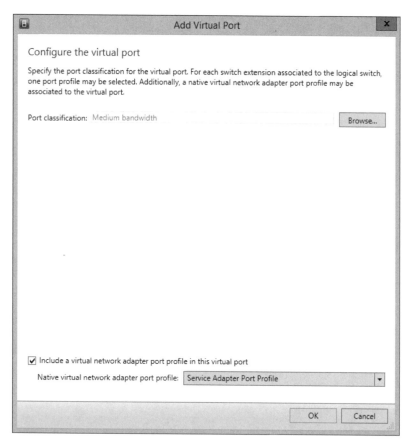

Figure 4.41
Create Logical Switch Wizard Completed Add Virtual Port page.
Source: VMM Administrator Console/Windows Server 2012 R2.

1. Click Include a virtual network adapter port profile in this virtual port.

2. Click the Native virtual network adapter port profile chevron and then select Service Adapter Port Profile.

3. Click OK.

Set Default Port Classification

You are returned to the Create Logical Switch Wizard Virtual Port page. This is the location where you set Medium Bandwidth as the Default, as shown in Figure 4.42.

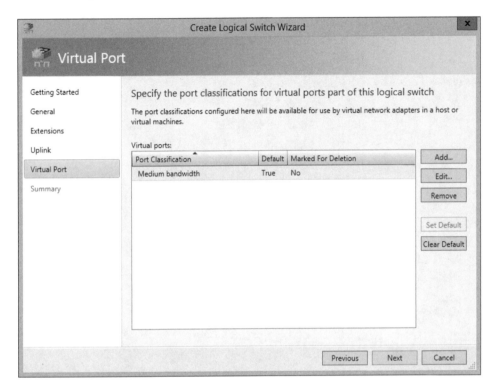

Figure 4.42
Create Logical Switch Wizard Virtual Port page.
Source: VMM Administrator Console/Windows Server 2012 R2.

1. To set the default port classification, click Medium Bandwidth and click Set Default.

2. Click Next.

Figure 4.43 shows the Summary page. If needed, make changes. Click Finish to run the PowerShell script.

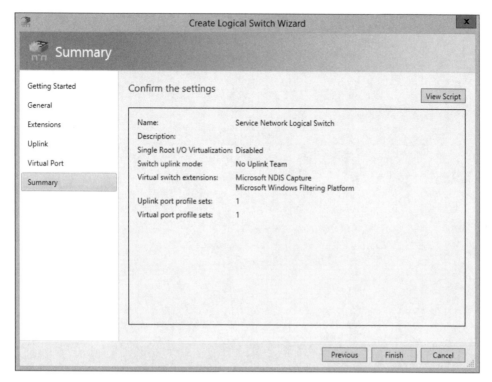

Figure 4.43
Create Logical Switch Wizard Summary page.

Source: VMM Administrator Console/Windows Server 2012 R2.

1. Review the Summary page.

2. Click Finish.

3. Close the Jobs window.

Figure 4.44 shows that the Service Network Logical Switch is added to Logical Switches. To review the Properties, right-click the Service Network Logical Switch and select Properties. You can add or remove extensions, as well as add, edit, or remove the Uplink profile and the Port Classifications.

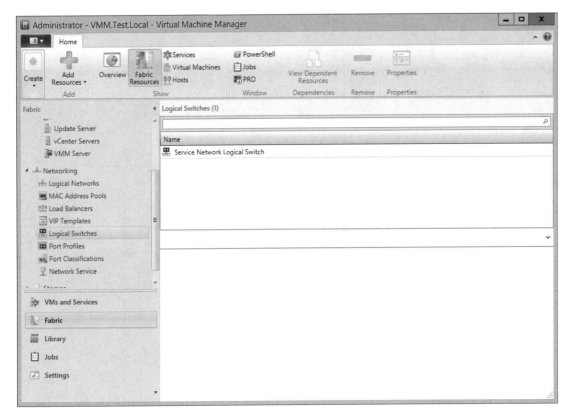

Figure 4.44
Service Network Logical Switch in Logical Switches.
Source: VMM Administrator Console/Windows Server 2012 R2.

Apply Logical Switch to COMPUTE Host Computers

You bring together the network settings that you configured in port profiles and logical switches by applying them to the physical network adapters. The network adapters are virtual network adapters on the COMPUTE host computers. The host property through which you apply port profiles and logical switches is called a *virtual switch*. Figure 4.45 shows a completed Virtual Switch for the Service Physical Network adapter.

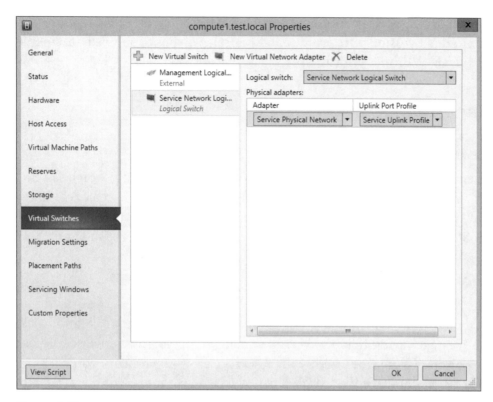

Figure 4.45
Service Network Logical Switch in Virtual Switches.
Source: VMM Administrator Console/Windows Server 2012 R2.

1. Click COMPUTE, and click the Host tab,

2. To apply a logical switch, click compute1.test.local and then click Properties.

3. Click the Virtual Switches tab, click New Virtual Switch, click New Logical Switch, click the Adapter chevron, and select Service Physical Network. Click OK twice.

4. Repeat step 2 and step 3 for compute2.test.local.

SUMMARY

- You learned how to map logical networks to physical networks, which ensures consistent network settings.

- Network isolation restricts network access to the proper sets of virtual machines. Microsoft recommends the software Network Virtualization approach.

- You learned how to consistently configure identical settings for network adapters for your host computers by using port profiles and logical switches. You need an Uplink Profile and a Hyper-V Profile prior to creating a logical switch.

CASE PROJECTS

Case 4-1: Researching VLANS

This chapter concentrated on the Microsoft Virtual Networking approach, which is relevant to the size of the private cloud being created and does not require specialized hardware. So you now feel the need to learn more about VLAN switching as applied to network isolation. Start your research with this search string: vlan network isolation.

Case 4-2: Removing Logical Networks

After creating the mapping of a logical network to a physical network, you want to remove the logical network. When you right-click on the logical network and click Remove, you get a message saying that VMM cannot remove the logical network because it is used by other objects. To continue with your research into this problem, you click on View Dependent Resources and see the list of dependencies that must be undone. Search the Web to learn how to remove these Dependent resources.

Case 4-3: Researching Network Adapter Offloads

Your have the same vendor and model network adapters in COMPUTE1 and COMPUTE2 host servers. You are considering configuring the offload setting for your Hyper-V Port Profile and want to see these settings. To see the offload settings, you right-click the Network icon on the taskbar, click the Open Network and Sharing Center, click Change Adapter Settings, right-click the Service network, click Properties, and then click Configure. Click the Advanced tab and scroll the Properties for offload properties.

What offload settings are available for your network adapters? Using the offload settings that you are considering, search the Web for information about these particular offload settings.

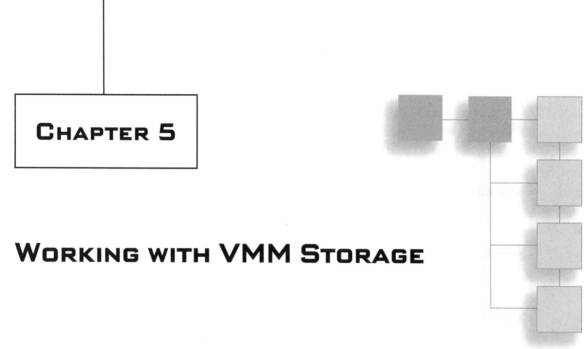

CHAPTER 5

WORKING WITH VMM STORAGE

After reading this chapter and completing the exercises, you will be able to do the following:

- Describe available storage technologies.
- Install the iSCSI Target Server.
- Manage Storage in the Fabric.
- Provide Storage to COMPUTE servers.

In this chapter, you'll learn how VMM implements storage. First, you'll review the available storage technologies available in VMM. Then you'll install the Microsoft iSCSI Target Server to support a Storage Area Network (SAN), which provides storage for the COMPUTE resource in your private cloud. You will learn to use VMM to manage the Storage resource and provide storage for the COMPUTE host computers for your private cloud.

DESCRIBING AVAILABLE STORAGE TECHNOLOGIES

In this section, you will investigate the available storage technologies that VMM supports. VMM supports the use of block-level storage, which includes Fibre Channel, iSCSI, and Serial Attached SCSI (SAS). Also supported is a new storage called the *Scale-Out File Server (SOFS)* introduced by Microsoft. All of these technologies provide storage devices consisting of multiple redundant hard drives, such as redundant array of independent disks (RAID).

The disk controller in your host computer uses block-level access to read and write to the disks that are attached internally within the computer. The host computers, such as COMPUTE1, access the storage device with a logical unit, which is a unique identifier used to designate a unit of storage. Figure 5.1 shows a host computer that uses storage disk E. When connected with the storage protocol, this disk appears to the operating system as resident (installed locally) to the computer, with read/write access at the block level. These storage devices can be partitioned and formatted with Windows Server 2012 R2 tools. In the Computer Management window, the host computer sees a local disk drive, storage disk E. On the storage server, this logical unit was defined as a unit of storage, as represented by the black block.

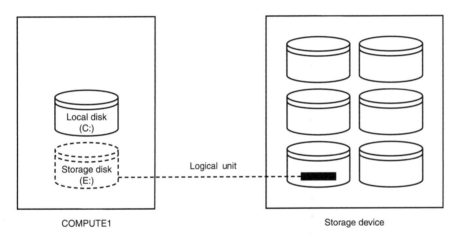

Figure 5.1
Logical unit access between host computer and storage device.
© 2014 Cengage Learning®.

Fibre Channel (pronounced fiber channel) technology provides high-performance disk storage for many corporate networks. The original version of Fibre Channel used the more expensive fiber optic cables, which reached to 10 kilometers. Fibre Channel can utilize copper wiring; however, copper limits Fibre Channel to a maximum recommended reach of 30 meters.

Fibre Channel is frequently deployed where devices are connected to each other through one or more Fibre Channel switches, as shown in Figure 5.2. With the Switched Fabric, all devices are connected to Fibre Channel switches, which is similar to modern Ethernet implementations.

The traffic between two device ports flows through the switches only, it is not transmitted to any other port. While this topology offers scalability and redundancy, it requires costly optical switches. Copper connectivity could be used to reduce the cost of connectivity. Multiple switches in a fabric usually form a mesh network with devices being on the edges of the mesh. The two fabrics share the devices, but are otherwise unconnected. One of the advantages of such a setup is the capability of failover, meaning that in case one link breaks, datagrams can be sent via the second fabric.

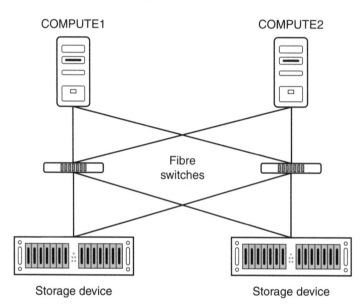

Figure 5.2
Fibre Channel.
© 2014 Cengage Learning®.

Compared to Fibre Channel, Internet SCSI is an economical solution for storage in a private cloud environment. iSCSI is Internet SCSI (Small Computer System Interface), an Internet Protocol (IP)-based storage networking standard for linking data storage facilities. Figure 5.3 shows an iSCSI Storage Area Network (SAN). The design deploys a redundant network with two network adapters in each device and a pair of Ethernet switches.

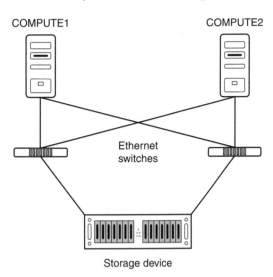

Figure 5.3
iSCSI SAN.
© 2014 Cengage Learning®.

Shared serial-attached SCSI (SAS) is an option for smaller companies that are looking for some of the benefits of a storage area network (SAN) without the costs associated with iSCSI or Fibre Channel. SAS is an interface for attaching storage to servers. Also, SAS is a type of disk drive. Shared SAS is a way to attach a storage array to two or more servers, as shown in Figure 5.4. It's best used to support servers in a single rack.

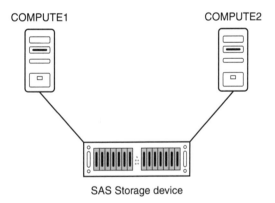

Figure 5.4
Serial-attached SCSI (SAS).
© 2014 Cengage Learning®.

Microsoft has built upon the technologies of SAS, direct attached sets of disk drives, to provide the Scale-Out File Servers (SOFS), as shown in Figure 5.5. One way of describing these sets of drives is just a bunch of disks (JBOD). These disks are aggregated into a storage pool from which virtual disks are created. Fault tolerance is provided by placing these virtual disks across multiple disk trays. Any brand of Ethernet switch can be used. The latest version of System Message Block (SMB) 3.0 is used as the communication protocol between the SOFS and the COMPUTE servers. Microsoft claims that SMB 3.0 is a better alternative than iSCSI or Fibre Channel storage protocols due to its simplicity of implementation.

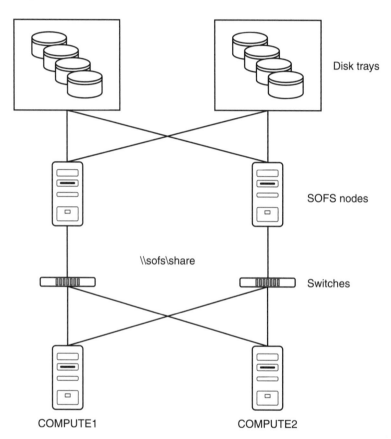

Figure 5.5
Scale-Out File Servers.
© 2014 Cengage Learning®.

The SOFS servers play the role of a SAN controller. Each of the SOFS servers is directly connected to the JBOD trays. Two to eight servers are clustered to provide redundancy and failover. A single share, in this case \\sofs\share, is used to access the storage.

Microsoft provides a software alternative to these hardware centric approaches. The iSCSI Target Server is a Microsoft solution for shared storage. From this point, it will simply be called the Target Server. The Target Server creates a virtual SAN environment running on the Windows Server 2012 R2 platform. You save money by using a server's internal hard drive. The Target Server is ideally suited for development and training environments.

The iSCSI protocol allows clients, called *initiators*, to send iSCSI commands to the target iSCSI storage device (see Figure 5.6). Targets execute the command and return the data to the clients. The iSCSI protocol encapsulates SCSI commands in TCP/IP packets. An encapsulated packet is called a protocol data unit (PDU); it contains a header, the command, and a data segment. The iSCSI initiator/target pair manages communications between the host computer and the storage device.

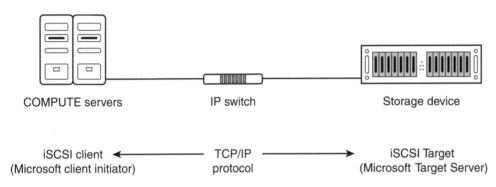

COMPUTE servers   IP switch   Storage device

iSCSI client ◄———————— TCP/IP ————————► iSCSI Target
(Microsoft client initiator)   protocol   (Microsoft Target Server)

Figure 5.6
iSCSI protocol.
© 2014 Cengage Learning®.

INSTALLING THE TARGET SERVER

In this section, you install the Target Server and then implement iSCSI Storage. First, you create a virtual machine, called TARGET, running Windows Standard Server 2012 R2. Next, you add the iSCSI Target Server role.

Once the Windows Standard Server 2012 R2 operating system is installed on the virtual machine, special consideration is required when placing the attached SCSI hard disk on the virtual machine. The pass-through disk allows the virtual machine to manage the physical hard disk; using this disk is better for the virtual machine's performance than placing virtual hard drives directly on the host computer. Also, using this disk means that you can avoid placing the Target Server's virtual hard disks in the virtual machine's hard disk files, which results in poor performance.

On the MANAGE server, you implement the Target Server in a virtual machine called TARGET (see Figure 5.7). Windows Server 2012 R2 provides the Target Server as a

Server Role. The TARGET virtual machine enables storage for the COMPUTE1 and COMPUTE2 host servers through the Storage logical switch for the Storage Network (shown as dashed lines). Virtual hard disk files for the logical units of storage reside on the block-level pass-through disk. VMM and TARGET communicate through the Management logical switch. After you install the Target Server, VMM manages TARGET with a link from the Target Server to the Storage node under Fabric.

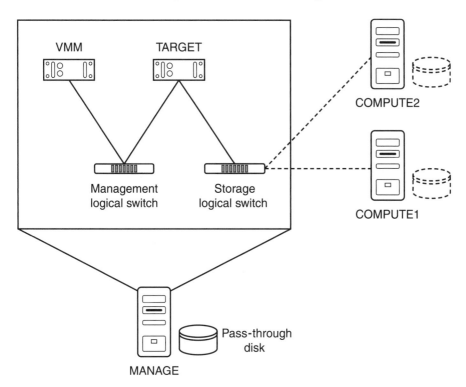

Figure 5.7
Storage Network.
© 2014 Cengage Learning®.

Install the TARGET Server Virtual Machine

You need the Windows Server 2012 R2 Standard .iso file and one standard license. Also, you need an internal disk drive with a minimum of 1TB, on the MANAGE server. To install the TARGET virtual machine, complete these steps:

1. Using Chapter 1 as a guideline, launch the New Virtual Machine Wizard and create a virtual machine conforming to the suggestions in Table 5.1.

Table 5.1   Suggested Settings for TARGET Virtual Machine Installation

Item	Suggested Setting
Name	TARGET
Generation	Generation 1
Start-up memory	1024
Use Dynamic Memory for this virtual machine	Selected
Connection	Management Logical Network
Virtual hard disk	TARGET.vhdx
Install an operating system from a bootable CD/DVD	Selected
Image files (.iso)	C:\ISOFiles\ Windows Server 2012 R2 .iso

© 2014 Cengage Learning®.

2. Using the Installing the Operating System on Host Computers guide in Chapter 1 as a guideline, start the TARGET virtual machine and install the OS in the TARGET virtual machine with the suggested settings in Table 5.2.

Table 5.2   Suggested Settings for TARGET Virtual Machine

Item	Suggested Setting
Password	Pa$$w0rd
IPV4 Address	192.168.0.107
Subnet Mask	255.255.255.0
Default Gateway	192.168.0.1
IPv4 DNS Server	192.168.0.103
Computer name	TARGET
Domain name	Test.Local

© 2014 Cengage Learning®.

3. After the reboot of the virtual machine, click the Action menu, point to DVD Drive, and click Eject.

4. To log on, click the Action menu, click Ctrl+Alt+Delete, and then enter Pa$$w0rd.

5. Continue with steps in Chapter 1 using the suggested settings in Table 5.2.

6. Wait for the install to complete the configuration of the TARGET virtual machine.

7. Click the IE Enhanced Security Configuration link and select Off for Administrators.

8. To join the domain, from the Server Manager, click the Workgroup link. Click Change, click Domain, and enter Test.Local. Log in as the Administrator with Pa$$w0rd. Wait for the Welcome to the Test domain message and restart the machine.

9. To change to the domain administrator account, click the Action menu, click Ctrl+Alt+Delete, click the back arrow, and click Other user. Enter test\administrator and Pa$$w0rd.

10. To shut down the TARGET virtual machine, click the Action menu and then select Shut Down twice.

11. Return to the Server Manager on the MANAGE server.

12. To open the Disk Management server, click Tools, click Computer Management, expand Storage, and click Disk Management.

13. To partition and format Disk 1, right-click in the unallocated area, click New Simple Volume, click Next three times, enter pass-through for the Volume label, click Next, and then click Finish.

14. To take the pass-through disk offline, right-click the Disk 1 icon and then click Offline.

15. To open the Network Connections window, right-click the Network icon on the Taskbar, click Open Network and Sharing Center, and then click Change adapter settings.

16. Record the physical adapter name for the Storage Physical Adapter.

17. Return to the Hyper-V Manager.

18. To create the Storage virtual network, click Virtual Switch Manager, click Create Virtual Switch, enter Storage Logical Network for the Name, click the External network chevron, and then select the physical adapter name recorded in step 16. Uncheck the Allow management operating system to share this network adapter and then click OK. Click Yes.

19. To view the hardware settings for the TARGET virtual machine, right-click TARGET and then click Settings.

20. To add the Storage network adapter, click Network Adapter, click Add, click the Virtual switch chevron, and then select Storage Logical Network. Click Apply.

21. To add the pass-through disk, click SCSI Controller, click Add, click Physical hard disk, click Disk 1, and then click Apply.

22. To configure Start Up settings, scroll and click Automatic Start Action, click Always start this virtual machine automatically, and enter 15 for the Startup delay. Click Apply.

23. To configure Shutdown settings, scroll and click Automatic Stop Action and then click Shut down the guest operating system. Click OK.

24. Connect and start the TARGET virtual machine. Log on to TARGET as the Test\Administrator with Pa$$w0rd.

25. To open the Network Connections window, right-click the Network icon on the Taskbar, click Open Network and Sharing Center, and then click Change adapter settings.

26. To name the Storage adapter, right-click the unidentified network, click Rename, and enter Storage.

27. To specify the IP configuration, right-click Storage, click Properties, clear the Internet Protocol Version 6 (IPv6) check box, click Internet Protocol Version 4 (IPv4), and then click Properties. Click Use the Following IP address. Enter 192.168.10.100 for the IP Address, press the Tab key, and then click OK. Click Close. Close the open windows.

28. To ready the pass-through disk, click Tools, click Computer Management, click Disk Management, right-click Disk 1, and then click Online. Close the Computer Management window.

Storage Management Initiative Specification

The Target Server uses Storage Management Initiative Specification (SMI-S), which is a storage standard developed and maintained by the Storage Networking Industry Association (SNIA). The SMI-S provider is installed when the Target Server role is added. Figure 5.8 shows how the SMI-S provider interacts with other components, such as the iSCSI Target WMI provider and the Microsoft Standard-based Management Service. Windows Management Instrumentation (WMI) is an implementation of Web-Based Enterprise Management (WBEM), which is a set of systems management technologies developed for distributed computing.

As an example of this interaction, consider that VMM needs to determine which devices the Target Server provides. This request is passed down the Management Server path (right side of diagram), and a WMI command request is created and then passed to the SMI-S provider. The information request is passed to the iSCSI Target WMI provider, which creates the request to the iSCSI Target Server. The requested information returns by the return path.

By following standard protocols, you could use a storage device from another vendor. For example, you could replace the iSCSI Target Server with a Dell EqualLogic PS Series storage array. Dell provides a WMI provider to replace the iSCSI Target WMI provider. The standard protocols make this a simple change to VMM.

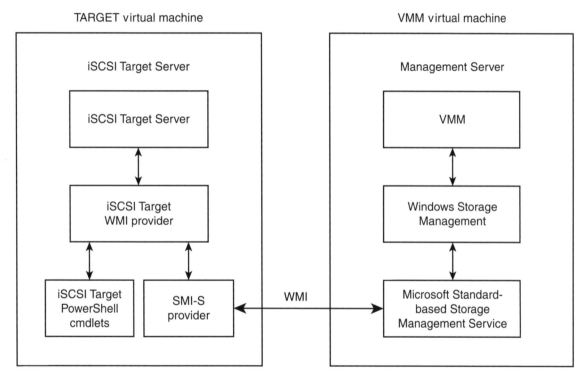

Figure 5.8
SMI-S provider interactions.
© 2014 Cengage Learning®.

Install Target Server

You can install the Target Server with the Add Roles and Features Wizard. Figure 5.9 shows the location of this role.

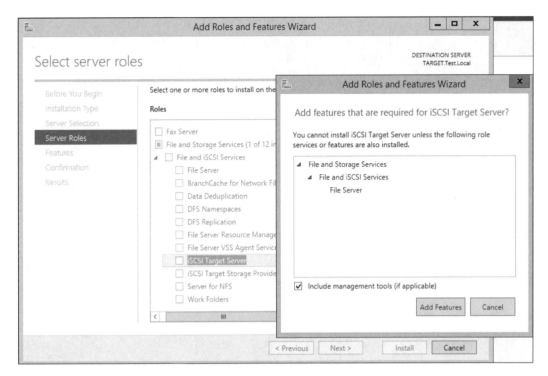

Figure 5.9
Location of the iSCSI Target Server role.
Source: Windows Server 2012 R2.

1. To add the iSCSI Target Server role, click Manage, click Add Roles and features, and click Next three times.

2. Expand File and Storage Services, expand File and iSCSI Services, scroll and check iSCSI Target Server, and click Add Features.

3. Click Next two times and then click Install.

4. Wait for the installation to complete and then click Close.

MANAGING STORAGE IN THE FABRIC

In this section, you will configure the Fabric to manage the iSCSI storage provided by the iSCSI Target Server.

Your first task is to link VMM to the iSCSI Target Server. This process follows the general scheme that you used to connect other resources. With the SMI-S provider, VMM can discover the Target Server.

Select Provider Type

You can start the Add Storage Device Wizard by clicking Storage, clicking Add Resources, and then selecting Storage Devices. See Figure 5.10 for a selected storage provider type.

Microsoft supports four provider types:

- **Windows-based file server:** SOFS server running SMB 3.0 and providing a file share.

- **SAN and NAS devices discovered and managed by a SMI-S provider:** Storage Area Network devices and Network Attached Storage devices with SMI-S providers.

- **SAN devices managed by a native SMP provider:** Storage Area Network devices managed by the Serial Management Protocol (SMP).

- **Fibre Channel fabric discovered and managed by a SMI-S provider:** Fibre Channel fabric with SMI-S provider.

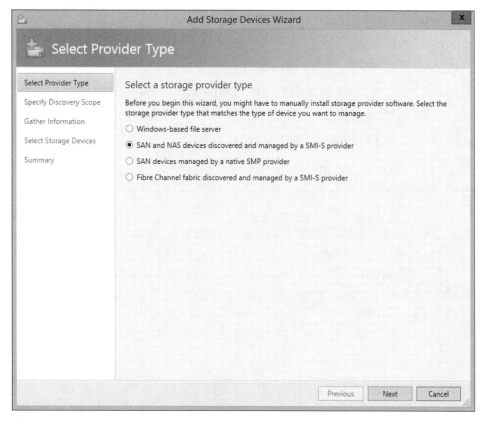

Figure 5.10
Add Storage Devices Wizard Select Provider Type page.
Source: VMM Administrator Console/Windows Server 2012 R2.

1. Return to the VMM Console.

2. To select a storage provider, click Fabric, scroll and click Storage, click Add Resources, and then click Storage Devices.

3. To select the provider, click SAN and NAS devices discovered and managed by a SMI-S provider.

4. Click Next.

Specify Discovery Scope

On the next page, you will specify the Discovery Scope to locate the SMI-S provider located on the TARGET virtual machine. Figure 5.11 shows a completed page with the discovery scope settings.

You have two choices for the communication protocol that the SMI-S provider uses:

- **SMI-S CIMXML:** Common Information Model (CIM) is an open standard that defines managed elements, which are coded with the Extensible Markup Language (XML) markup language.

- **SMI-S WMI:** Windows Management Instrumentation implementation of Web-based Enterprise Management.

For the iSCSI SMS-I provider, choose SMI-S WMI.

You should have a DNS entry for the Target Server, and target.test.local is OK. If the discovery does not locate the Target Server, use the assigned IP address. Retain the default TCP/IP port.

You need a Run As account for VMM to manage the Target Server. You create this Run As account as you have done previously. You start with a user account, such as VMMStore, created in Active Directory Users and Computers and made a member of the Domain Admins group. As a part of the discovery settings, you link this existing user account, as a Run As account. To do this, you click the Browse menu and from a pop-up page, not shown in the completed figure, you create a Run As account for this user account.

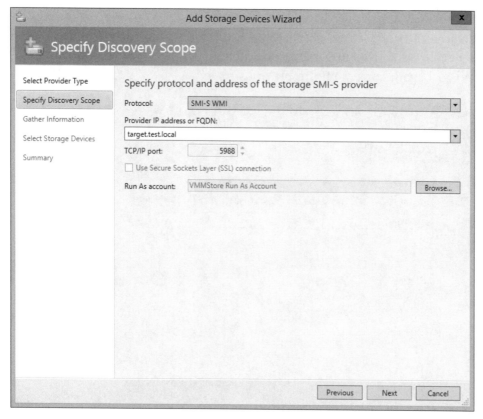

Figure 5.11
Add Storage Devices Wizard Specify Discovery Scope page.
Source: VMM Administrator Console/Windows Server 2012 R2.

1. Click the Protocol chevron and select SMS-S WMI.

2. To identify the iSCSI provider, enter target.test.local for the Provide IP address or FQDN.

3. To set up the Run As account, click Browse, click Create Run As Account, enter VMMStore Run As Account for the Name, enter test\VMMStore for the User name, enter Pa$$w0rd for the Password, and Confirm password. Click OK twice.

4. Click Next.

Locate Storage Device

The discovery runs to locate the iSCSI Target Server. On the next page, you should see the TARGET storage device, as shown in Figure 5.12. If not, you will need to run the Add Storage Devices Wizard again correcting the previous mistake.

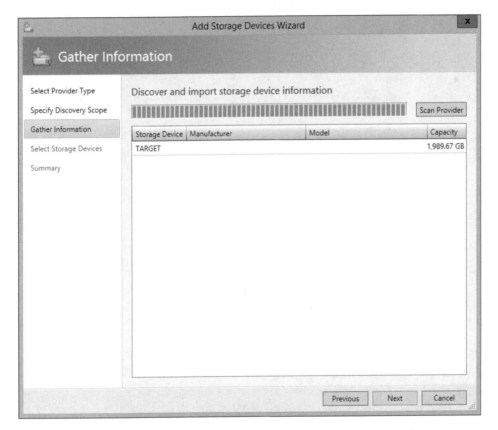

Figure 5.12
Add Storage Devices Wizard Gather Information page.
Source: VMM Administrator Console/Windows Server 2012 R2.

1. Wait for the Storage Device to appear and then click Next.

2. If you do not get a response within five minutes, click Cancel and click Yes. Return to Specify Discovery Scope and correct your mistakes.

Select Storage Device

The next task is to select the Storage Device and create a storage classification. You are presented with a list of physical devices (see Figure 5.13). In this case, it is the two drives on the MANAGE server. Pick the drive that matches the pass-through disk. Before leaving the page, you need to create a classification for this storage when the pop-up appears to name the storage classification. This classification is entirely arbitrary. Your IT group could classify storage, as Fast, Faster, Fastest, or some other scheme.

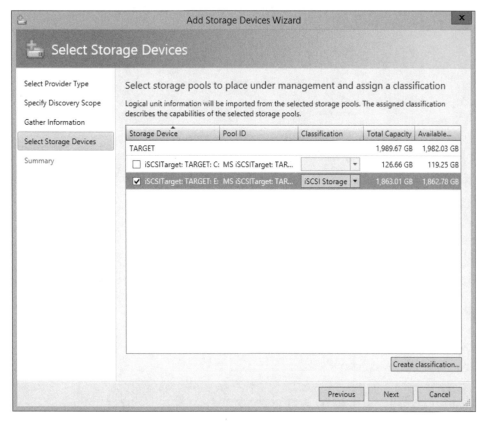

Figure 5.13
Add Storage Devices Wizard Select Storage Devices page.
Source: VMM Administrator Console/Windows Server 2012 R2.

1. To select the pass-through disk, click the iSCSITarget: TARGET: E: check box.

2. Click Create classification, enter iSCSI Storage for the Name, and then click Add.

3. Click the Classification chevron for iSCSITarget: TARGET: E: and then select iSCSI Storage. Click Next.

Review Summary

You are almost done. Review the Summary, as shown in Figure 5.14.

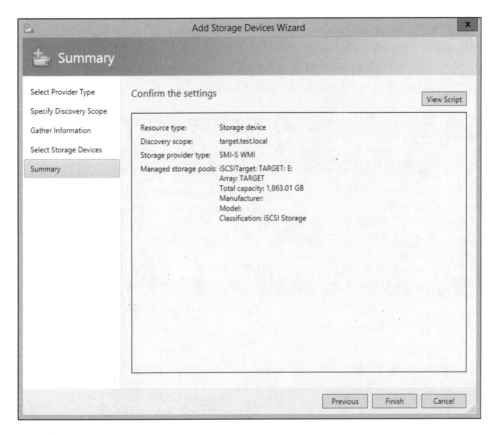

Figure 5.14
Add Storage Devices Wizard Summary page.
Source: VMM Administrator Console/Windows Server 2012 R2.

1. Review the Summary. Click Previous and correct mistakes.

2. When corrected, click Finish.

3. Wait for the script to complete. Close the Jobs window.

View Storage Pool

From Storage in the Fabric, you can see the results of your efforts. Figure 5.15 shows the Classifications and Storage Pools. You have one classification—iSCSI Storage.

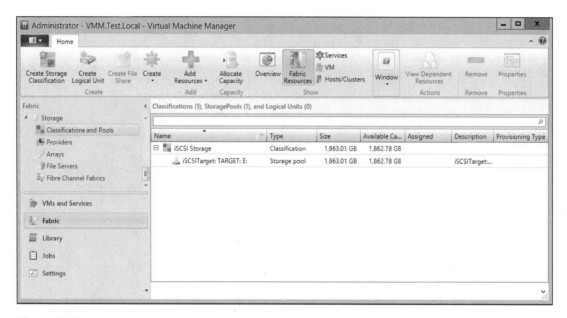

Figure 5.15
Storage showing Classifications and Pools.
Source: VMM Administrator Console/Windows Server 2012 R2.

1. To view the storage pool entries, return to Fabric and click Classifications and Pools.

2. Click the Classification Type entry. Click the Storage Pool Type entry.

Verify Providers

You can check on the health of the TARGET Server from VMM. To do this, select Providers. Along with information about this server, the key thing to check is the Status. You want to see a green check with the word Responding (see Figure 5.16).

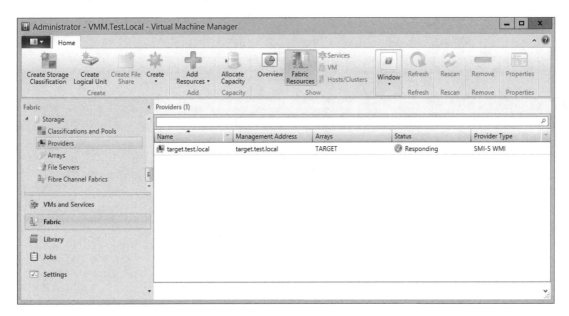

Figure 5.16
Storage showing Providers.

Source: VMM Administrator Console/Windows Server 2012 R2.

1. To verify that VMM and Target Server are communicating, click Providers.

2. Click target.test.local.

View Summary Information

The Arrays node reveals summary information, see Figure 5.17, which you need to manage your storage. This is the place to go when you need to know how much space remains. The Logical unit information provides the count of logical units you have created, assigned to COMPUTE, and created but not assigned.

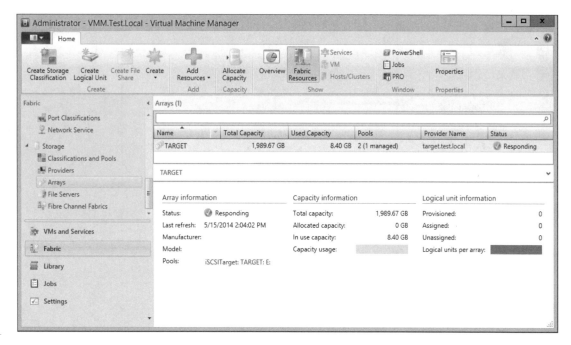

Figure 5.17
Storage showing Arrays.

Source: VMM Administrator Console/Windows Server 2012 R2.

1. To see counts for storage allocations, click Arrays.

2. Click the TARGET entry.

PROVIDING STORAGE TO HOST COMPUTERS

In this section, you will configure the Fabric to manage the iSCSI storage provided by the Target Server. From a storage pool, you can create and assign logical units.

Figure 5.18 shows the relationship between the iSCSI Initiator and the iSCSI Target. The iSCSI Initiator is running on the host computers in the COMPUTE resource. The iSCSI Target responds to the commands sent from the iSCSI Initiator.

You create a single storage pool for the iSCSI array. You allocate logical units, which are made available to the iSCSI Initiator. A Session connects the logical unit in the iSCSI Target to the logical unit in the iSCSI Initiator. The host computer sees the disk drive, which is a virtual hard disk in the iSCSI array, as a local disk drive.

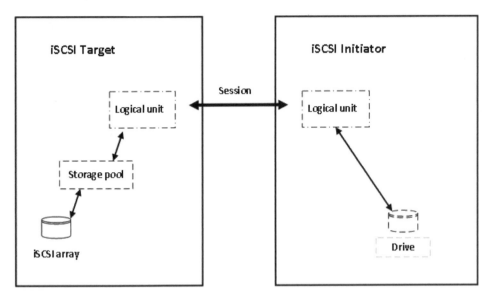

Figure 5.18
iSCSI Initiator-iSCSI Target relationship.
Source: VMM Administrator Console/Windows Server 2012 R2.

Before providing storage, you need to take care of two configuration issues to permit communication between the iSCSI Target and the iSCSI Initiator. Start the Microsoft iSCSI Initiator Service on the host computers in the COMPUTE resource. To do this, click Tools in the Server Manager console and select Services. Locate the Microsoft iSCSI Initiator Service and set the Startup type to Automatic and then start the service.

Microsoft designed Multipath I/O (MPIO) to mitigate the effects of a network adapter failure by providing an alternate data path between storage devices and the host computers. While you do not have an alternative network adapter for storage, this feature is still required. You added this feature to the COMPUTE host computers in Chapter 1.

Allocate Storage to COMPUTE

The first task is to allocate storage to the COMPUTE resource from the storage pool. To do this, from Storage, link the COMPUTE resource. Next, add the iSCSI Target pool to the COMPUTE resource. Figure 5.19 shows this allocation.

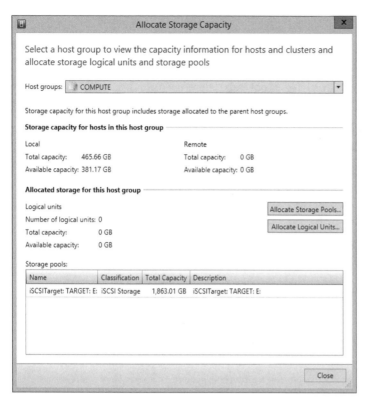

Figure 5.19
Allocate Storage Capacity Page with an allocation.
Source: VMM Administrator Console/Windows Server 2012 R2.

1. Return to COMPUTE1.

2. To start the Microsoft iSCSI Initiator, click Tools in the Server Manager console and then select Services.

3. Locate and right-click the Microsoft iSCSI Initiator Service. Click Properties, click the Startup type chevron, and select Automatic. Click Start and click OK. Close the Services window.

4. Complete steps 1 through 3 for COMPUTE2.

5. Return to the VMM console on the VMM virtual machine.

6. Click Fabric. Click Storage and Allocate Capacity. Click the Host groups chevron and select COMPUTE.

7. Click Allocate Storage Pools and click iSCSITarget: TARGET: E: Click Add and click OK. Click Close.

Add iSCSI Array

The next task is to add the iSCSI array and create an iSCSI session on each host computer in the COMPUTE resource. To add the iSCSI array, return to host group under Servers and then select the host computer. Click the Host tab, click Properties, and then select the Storage tab on the left. Click iSCSI Arrays, click Add, and then click Add iSCSI Array. Click the Array chevron and select your Array (TARGET). To create an iSCSI session, click Create New iSCSI Session (TARGET is shown as the Array) and then click Create. Figure 5.20 shows the added iSCSI array.

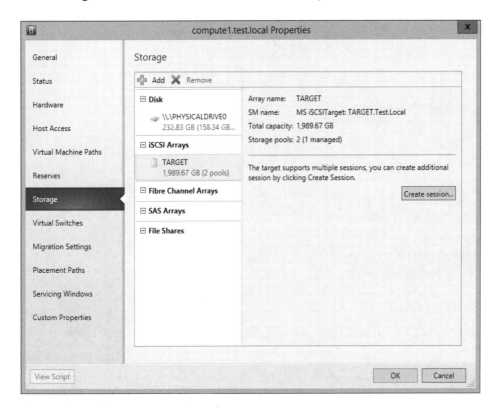

Figure 5.20
TARGET iSCSI Array added.

Source: VMM Administrator Console/Windows Server 2012 R2.

1. Return to the COMPUTE host group under Servers. Click Fabric and click Servers.

2. To add the iSCSI array, click compute1.test.local. Click the Host tab and click Properties. Select the Storage tab on the left. Click iSCSI Arrays, click Add, and then click Add iSCSI Array. Click the Array chevron and select TARGET.

3. Click the Create New iSCSI Session and then click Create. Click OK.

4. Repeat steps 1 through 3 for COMPUTE2.

Two Ways to Create a Logical Unit

There are two methods to create a logical unit from storage: Create the logical unit and then assign the logical unit to the host computer; or start with the host computer and create the logical unit.

Create Logical Unit from VMM Console

For the first method, you start from the Storage node in the VMM console. Click Create Logical Unit to create the logical unit. A pop-up appears where you enter the name and size, as shown in Figure 5.21. This creates a virtual hard disk called COMPUTE1TEMP that starts with a minimal capacity and grows to 50GB.

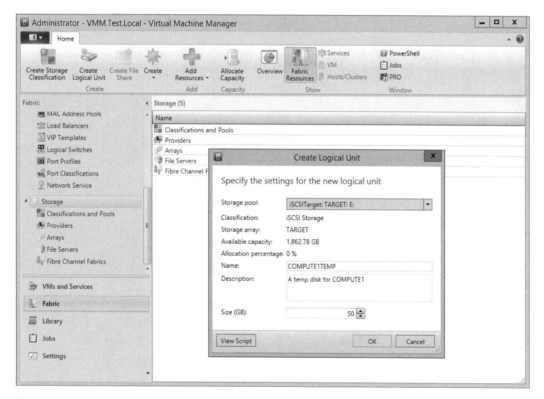

Figure 5.21
Completed Create Logical Unit pop-up.
Source: VMM Administrator Console/Windows Server 2012 R2.

1. Return to the Storage node in the VMM console.

2. To create the logical unit, click Create Logical Unit, enter COMPUTE1TEMP for the Name, and enter 50 for the Size (GB).

3. To view the script, click View Script. Close the Notepad window. Click OK.

Figure 5.22 shows the created logical unit in the Storage Pool. Your logical units are allocated from this storage pool.

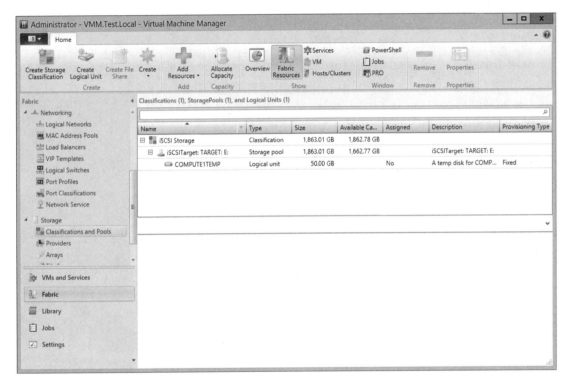

Figure 5.22
COMPUTE1TEMP Logical unit in the Storage Pool.
Source: VMM Administrator Console/Windows Server 2012 R2.

1. To see the Storage Pool, click Classifications and Pools.

2. Expand iSCSITarget: TARGET: E:

Assign Logical Unit

To assign the logical unit, start with Allocate Capacity. Select the host group. Click Allocate Logical Units. Click the logical unit you created (COMPUTE1TEMP) in the Logical Unit column and then click Add (see Figure 5.23).

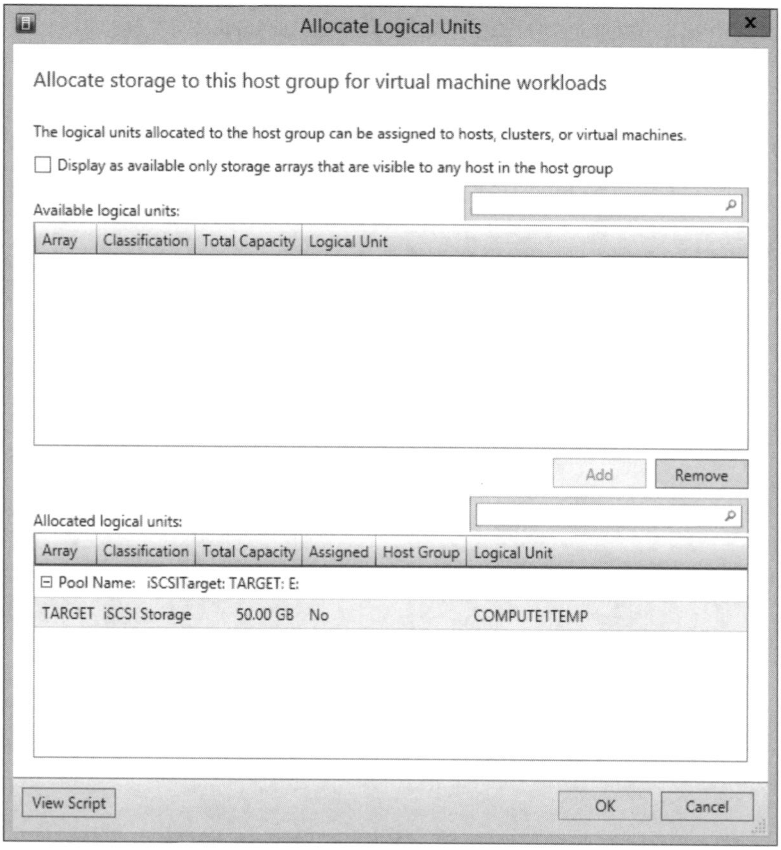

Figure 5.23
COMPUTE1TEMP assigned to the COMPUTE host group.
Source: VMM Administrator Console/Windows Server 2012 R2.

1. To assign the logical unit, click Allocate Capacity. Click the Host group's chevron and then select COMPUTE. Click Allocate Logical Units.

2. Click COMPUTE1TEMP in the Logical Unit column and then click Add. Click OK. Close the window.

Add Logical Unit to Host Computer

To add the logical unit to the host computer, select host group. Click the host computer. Click the Host tab and click Properties. Click Storage and click the Array, click Add, and then click Add Disk. Click the Logical unit chevron and select the logical unit. Figure 5.24 shows the completed page. You need to specify the Volume label, such as TEMP, and assign a drive letter. Click OK to format the virtual hard disk and assign it to the host computer.

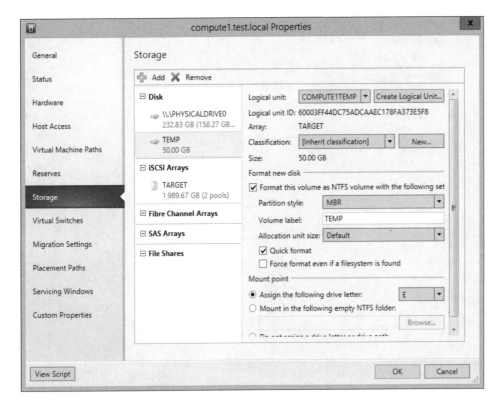

Figure 5.24
Logical unit added to the COMPUTE host computer.
Source: VMM Administrator Console/Windows Server 2012 R2.

1. Return to the COMPUTE host group under Servers.

2. Click the Host tab and then click Properties.

3. To add the logical unit to the host computer, click compute1.test.local. Click the Host tab and click Properties. Click Storage and click TARGET. Click Add and then click Add Disk.

4. If necessary, click the Logical unit chevron and select COMPUTE1TEMP.

5. Enter TEMP for the Volume label. Click OK.

Check for Drive on the Host Computer

To check on the volume on the host computer, open Disk Management, as shown in Figure 5.25. Again, the host computer sees the storage as the locally attached hard drive.

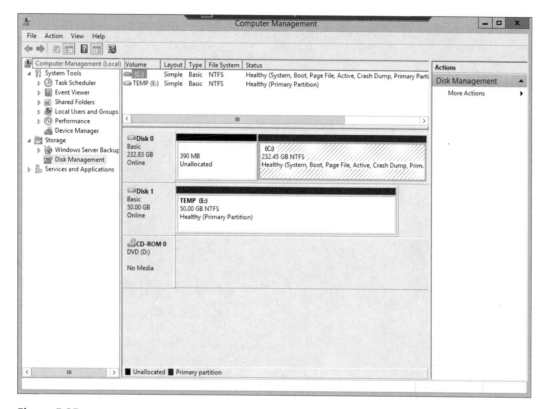

Figure 5.25
Disk Management showing TEMP.
Source: VMM Administrator Console/Windows Server 2012 R2.

1. Go to COMPUTE1.

2. Click Tools and click Computer Management.

3. To check the volume on the host computer, open Disk Management.

4. You should see an E drive.

5. Repeat the steps starting with Create Logical Unit from VMM Console for COMPUTE2.

Allocate from Host Computer

For the second method, start with the host computer and create the logical unit. Starting with the host computer's property page, click Add and Add disk. By selecting Create Logical Unit, you can name the Logical unit (FROMTEMP1) and allocate disk space in the pop-up. You are returned to the Properties page. You should see the logical unit that you named. Next, you provide a volume label, assign a drive letter, and format the volume as you did before. Figure 5.26 shows the completed logical unit.

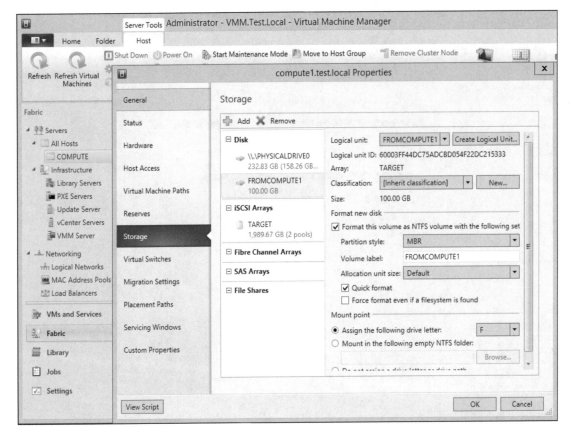

Figure 5.26
Create logical unit on host computer.

Source: VMM Administrator Console/Windows Server 2012 R2.

1. Return to the VMM console.

2. Click compute1.test.local.

3. Click the Host tab and click Properties.

4. Select the Storage tab. Click Add and Add disk.

5. To add a logical unit starting from the host computer, click Create Logical Unit.

6. Enter FROMCOMPUTE1 for the Name and enter 100 for the Size (GB). Click OK.

7. Enter FROMCOMPUTE1 for the Volume label.

8. Click Assign the following drive letter and select F. Click OK.

9. Return to COMPUTE1.

10. To check the volume on the host computer, open Disk Management. You should see an E and F drive.

11. Complete steps 2 through 10 for COMPUTE2.

Remove a Logical Unit

To remove a logical unit, you work backward. First, remove the disk from the host computer. Then in Classifications and Pools, remove the logical unit. Recall that \\.\PHYSI-CALDRIVE0 is your C drive with the operating system.

To do this, complete these steps:

1. Return to the VMM console.

2. Click compute1.test.local.

3. Click the Host tab and click Properties.

4. Select the Storage tab.

Drag Bar to View Disk Information

To make it easier to view the disk details, grab the vertical separator bar and drag it to the right.

5. Highlight the disk to remove it.

6. Verify that this is the proper disk and click Remove.

7. Click Yes to confirm removal.

8. Repeat steps 5 through 7 for the remaining disks.

9. Repeat steps 2 through 8 for compute2.test.local.

10. Return to the Storage node.

11. Click Classifications and Pools.

12. Right-click on the first Logical Unit with NO in the Assigned column.

13. Click Remove.

14. Click OK to confirm the removal.

15. Wait for the Logical Unit to be removed.

16. Repeat steps 12 through 15 for the remaining Logical Units.

SUMMARY

- You reviewed the available storage technologies available in VMM, which included Fibre Channel, iSCSI, Shared serial-attached SCSI, and Scale-Out File Server.

- You installed the Microsoft iSCSI Target Server to support a storage area network (SAN) to provide storage for the COMPUTE resource in your private cloud.

- You learned to use VMM to manage the Storage resource and provide storage for the COMPUTE host computers.

CASE PROJECTS

Case 5-1: Researching SAN Hardware Offerings

In this chapter, you worked with the Microsoft iSCSI Target Server. While this choice was economical and the only cost was for a 2TB hard drive, you are interested in other possible hardware iSCSI offerings.

At the low end of the scale, consider the NetGear ReadyNAS. Other possible offerings, increasing in relative price, are the Drobo SAN for Business series, the HP Modular Smart Array series, and the Dell EqualLogic PS Series. This is just a sample of the many excellent iSCSI SAN products on the market.

Case 5-2: Researching Storage Networking Industry Association Certification

You are interested in learning about possible certification offers in storage technologies. The Storage Networking Certification Program (SNCP) offers the SNIA Certified Storage Engineer (SCSE) certificate, which requires two exams: CompTIA Storage+ (SGO-001) and Storage Networking Management and Administration S10–210. Search the Web for SGO-001 and S10-210.

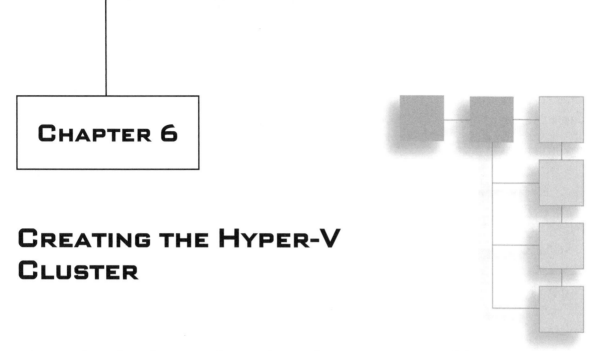

CHAPTER 6

CREATING THE HYPER-V CLUSTER

After reading this chapter and completing the exercises, you will be able to do the following:

- Describe the Hyper-V cluster.
- Build a Hyper-V cluster.
- Test live migration and failover clusters.

In this chapter, you will learn to describe the concepts related to the Hyper-V cluster. One of the benefits of Hyper-V is the Hyper-V cluster, which supports high availability by creating failover clusters out of separate physical computers. First, you will learn to build the Hyper-V cluster. Then to test it, you'll perform a live migration and simulate a failover.

DESCRIBING THE HYPER-V CLUSTER

In this section, you'll learn to describe the technological concepts related to working with a Hyper-V cluster. With a Hyper-V cluster, your host computers appear as one computer, which provides the opportunity for expansion of your private cloud as it grows in size to meet increased demands for additional computing power. Redundancy and failover are key pieces in the creation of the Microsoft Private Cloud. Microsoft developed the Cluster Shared Volume (CSV) to make it easier for you to move virtual machines from one host computer to another within the cluster.

Clustering Servers

Clustering means connecting multiple servers to make them work as a unified system, as shown in Figure 6.1.

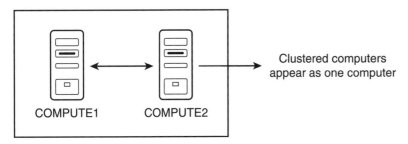

Figure 6.1
Clustered servers.
© 2014 Cengage Learning®.

Clustering increases the private cloud's load balancing and redundancy.

- Load balancing distributes processing across multiple servers, which is important when you do not know how many requests to expect for a group of servers or when the requests will arrive. Load balancing might allocate incoming requests evenly to all servers, or it might send requests to the next available server.

- Redundancy is the ability of a cluster to respond gracefully to an unexpected hardware or software failure. Failover is the capability to switch to a redundant or standby server automatically when the active server fails.

Redundancy and failover keep your system running smoothly when one of the components fails. Failover automation occurs using a "heartbeat" network of two host computers. Essentially, the second server monitors the first host computer and will immediately begin executing the functions of the first computer if it detects a failure.

When the Hyper-V cluster begins providing service to the user in the example shown in Figure 6.2, COMPUTE1 is running the virtual machine with the user application. This figure shows one virtual machine, but in reality, numerous virtual machines could be involved in this scenario. The host computers exchange heartbeat pulses and are aware of each other.

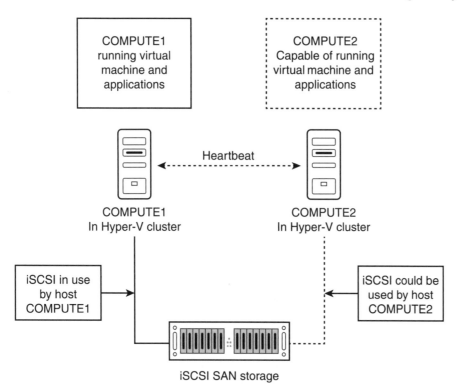

Figure 6.2
Host computers exchange heartbeat pulses.
© 2014 Cengage Learning®.

At some point, COMPUTE1 has developed difficulties and has almost stopped functioning. COMPUTE1 stops sending regular heartbeat signals across the network to COMPUTE2. Figure 6.3 shows what happens in the brief interval just after COMPUTE1 stops sending signals.

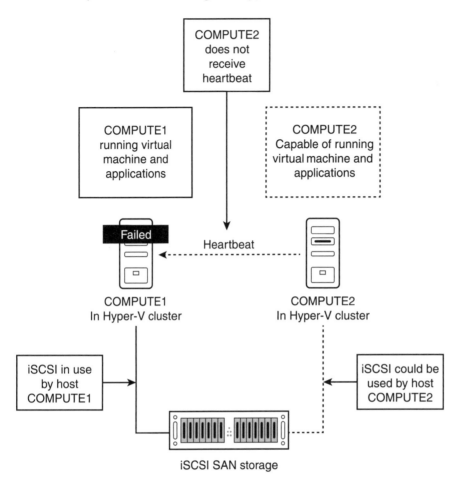

Figure 6.3
Host COMPUTE2 does not receive the heartbeat pulse.
© 2014 Cengage Learning®.

Shortly after the heartbeat signals stop arriving from COMPUTE1, COMPUTE2 begins taking over the functions of the virtual machine, as shown in Figure 6.4. Service is interrupted only for a short time and is not noticed by most users.

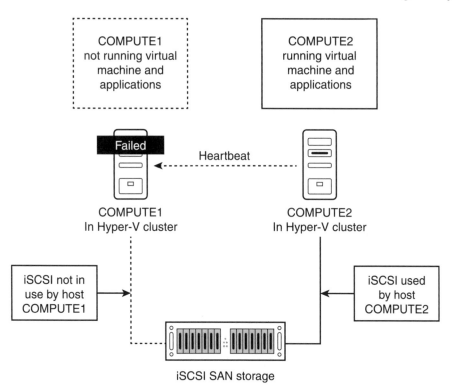

Figure 6.4
Host COMPUTE2 takes over.
© 2014 Cengage Learning®.

You can use a similar process for scheduled downtime. For example, if a host computer is running correctly and is the current owner of the virtual machines, but software updates need to be applied to the host computer, you can move the virtual machines to another host computer so that the updates can be applied.

Cluster Shared Volumes

One requirement of the Hyper-V cluster is that virtual machines must be stored on local hard drives. Virtual machines cannot be started from network storage because the storage driver used on Windows operating systems during initial OS loading can only access local storage. iSCSI storage meets this requirement because the operating system perceives that the storage is local.

A second requirement is that each host computer must use a unique logical unit, as shown in Figure 6.5. This requirement makes it difficult to move a virtual machine among host computers. For example, moving a virtual machine between logical units requires a migration from one logical unit to the other. The time lapse for this move would prohibit failover within clustered hosts.

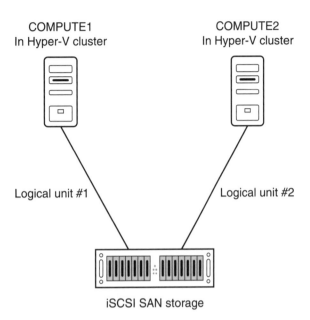

Figure 6.5
One logical unit per host computer.
© 2014 Cengage Learning®.

The Microsoft solution to this predicament is called the *cluster shared volume*. A volume configured as a CSV can be accessed by all the host computers of a Hyper-V cluster. Each host computer can access and manage files on the volume. Therefore, different host computers can host different virtual machines that all have virtual hard disk files on the same volume. Figure 6.6 shows a single LUN shared by two host computers in the Hyper-V cluster.

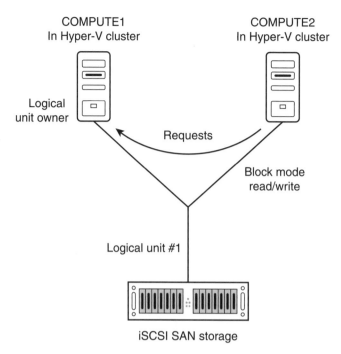

Figure 6.6
Logical unit shared by two host computers.
© 2014 Cengage Learning®.

With a CSV, the path appears to be on the system drive of the host computer as the C:\ClusterStorage folder. However, the contents are the same when viewed from any host computer in the Hyper-V cluster. The volume is owned by one host computer. Some operations, such as opening a file, can be performed only by the volume owner. To enable this type of access, a request for the operation is communicated to the owning host computer. Block mode data read/writes can be performed by any host computer in the cluster, which provides common storage for virtual machines. Common storage is a requirement for high availability when a virtual machine may be placed on any host computer or migrated to any host.

Live Migration

Live migration moves running virtual machines from one host computer to another. You use live migration to balance loads between host computers or to move a virtual machine off a host computer when you perform maintenance on the host. Figure 6.7 shows a live migration in which the cluster copies the memory being used by the virtual machine from the current host computer to another host. When the transition to the other host computer occurs, the memory and state information is already in place for the virtual machine. The transition is usually fast enough that a client using the virtual machine does not lose the network connection.

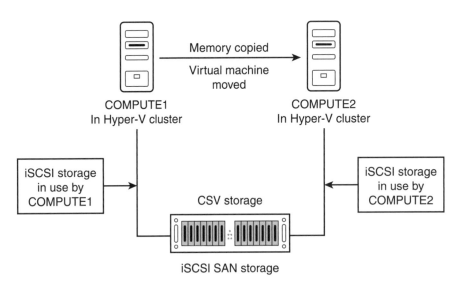

Figure 6.7
Live migration within a Hyper-V cluster.
© 2014 Cengage Learning®.

Configuring Failover Clustering

In "Describing the Hyper-V Cluster," you learned that a heartbeat is used to determine when a virtual machine failover occurs from one host computer to a second host. The concept of a quorum is related to failover.

If you have been an officer in a club or a professional organization, you know that a certain percentage of voting members must be present to conduct business. This percentage is known as a quorum. In the failover cluster, a quorum must be present for the cluster to function. Each host computer in the cluster that communicates with other host computers has a vote.

By default, Windows Server 2012 R2 uses a dynamic quorum. The vote of the quorum witness is dynamically adjusted based on the number of voting nodes in the cluster. If there is an odd number of votes, the quorum witness does not have a vote. If there is an even number of votes, the quorum witness has a vote. The quorum witness vote is also dynamically adjusted based on the state of the witness resource. If the witness disk is offline or failed, the cluster sets the witness vote to "0."

BUILDING A HYPER-V FAILOVER CLUSTER

You might think that the creation of a Hyper-V cluster would be difficult. VMM provides the Create Hyper-V Wizard to create the failover cluster for your private cloud. When using the wizard, you will bring together the components created in previous chapters:

- The COMPUTE servers and VMM library from Chapter 3, "Configuring the Fabric Resources."

- The logical and VM networks in Chapter 4, "Working with Networks Using VMM."

- You will create two new logical units for your private cloud as you learned about logical units for storage in Chapter 5, "Working with VMM Storage."

Create Logical Units for Cluster

Prior to starting the Create Hyper-V Wizard, you must configure two logical units for your private cloud implementation:

- **Witness:** A special disk used to make decisions if host computers lose communication with each other.

- **VMStorage:** Shared storage for all virtual machines deployed to the two host computers in the cluster.

You can set the size of the Witness disk to be as small as 1 gigabyte (GB). The remaining disk space is allocated for the virtual machines and future expansion. If needed, refer to Chapter 5, "Working with VMM Storage," for information about creating these storage allocations. To create storage for your private cloud, complete these steps:

1. Return to the VMM console.

2. Click Fabric and expand Storage. Click Classifications and Pools.

3. To add the Witness Disk, click Create a Logical Unit. Enter Witness for the Name, enter 1 for the Size, and then click OK.

4. Repeat step 3 for VMStorage with a size of 500.

5. To allocate the logical units to the COMPUTE host group, click Allocate Capacity, click Allocate Logical Units, click VMStorage, and click Add. Click Witness and click Add. Click OK and then Close.

Create Cluster

Prior to starting the creation of the Hyper-V cluster, you must configure your host computers to use unencrypted BITS file transfers. This will reduce the time required to deploy future virtual machines.

To start the Create Hyper-V Wizard, from the Servers node, you click the Create icon and then select Hyper-V cluster.

On the first page, you enter the FQDN for your future cluster, as shown in Figure 6.8. You need to provide a user account for the installation. The Run As account that you used to install VMM works.

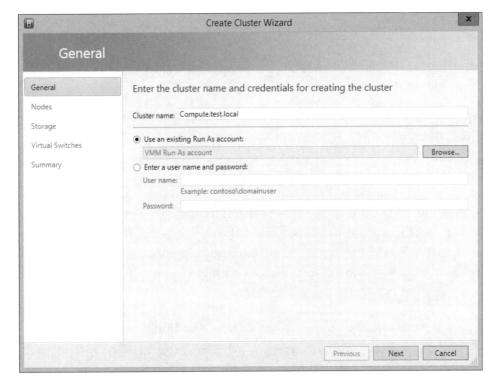

Figure 6.8
Create Cluster Wizard General page.
Source: VMM Administrator Console/Windows Server 2012 R2.

1. Return to Servers.

2. To improve performance for virtual machine deployment, right-click All Hosts, click Properties, click Allow unencrypted BITS file transfers, and then click OK.

3. To start the Create Cluster Wizard, click the Home tab, click Create, and then click Hyper-V cluster.

4. Enter Compute.test.local for the cluster name.

5. To specify the Run As account to create the cluster, click Browse, click VMM Run As account, and then click OK.

6. Click Next.

All Nodes to Cluster

On the Nodes pages, you select the host group of the host computers in the cluster. Figure 6.9 shows a complete page with the nodes added. From the Available hosts, select and add the desired host computers. Since you do not need support from Microsoft for your cluster, you can select Skip cluster validation tests. In this case, you added both of the host computers in the COMPUTE host group.

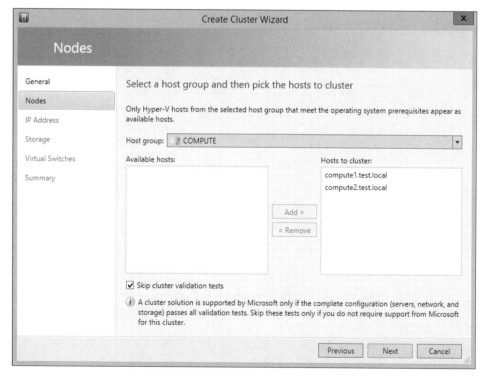

Figure 6.9
Create Cluster Wizard Nodes page.
Source: VMM Administrator Console/Windows Server 2012 R2.

1. To add the host computers to the cluster, click the Host group chevron, click COMPUTE, click compute1.test.local, and click Add.

2. Click compute2.test.local and then click Add.

3. To save time to create the cluster, click Skip cluster validation tests.

4. Read message about skipping cluster validation tests.

5. Click Next.

Provide IP Address for Cluster

The next task is to provide the IP address of the cluster. Since the two host computers act as one, you provide a new, unique IP address, as shown in Figure 6.10.

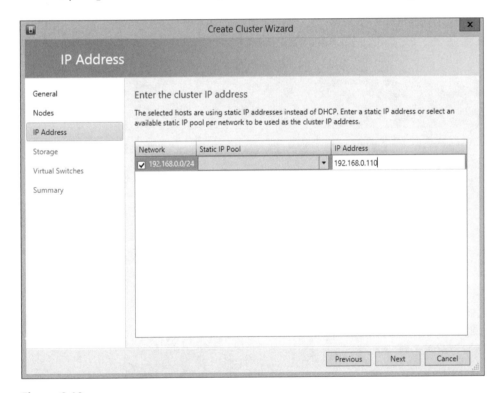

Figure 6.10
Create Cluster Wizard IP Address page.

Source: VMM Administrator Console/Windows Server 2012 R2.

1. To enter the IP Address for the cluster, check 192.168.0.0/24 and enter 192.168.0.110 for the IP Address.

2. Click Next.

Add Witness and VMStorage

Next, add the logical units for the Witness and VMStorage. You allocated these two units of storage prior to starting the Create Hyper-V Wizard. Since the assignments will be made by the PowerShell script, you do not assign the logical units to host computers. These two logical units will be available to both host computers.

The larger of the two, VMStorage, is used to store virtual machines. Working from left to right, select the storage classification (iSCSI Storage). Leave the defaults for Size, Partition Style, and File System. In the next field, enter the Volume Label. Select the Quick Format. Scroll to the right and check CSV. The Witness disk was selected by the wizard. A completed page is shown in Figure 6.11.

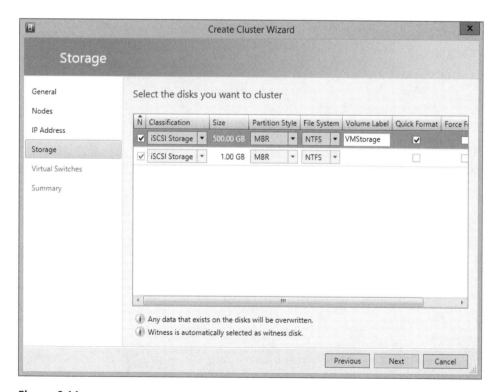

Figure 6.11
Create Cluster Wizard Storage page.
Source: VMM Administrator Console/Windows Server 2012 R2.

1. To enable the 500GB volume as a cluster shared volume, click the check box for the 500.00GB entry, enter VMStorage as the Volume Label, click Quick Format, scroll to the right, and click CSV.

2. Click Next.

Provide Names for Networks

Your host computers support four networks. Here are the four networks:

- **Management:** 192.168.0.0—manages the host computers and access to virtual machines outside of the cluster.

- **Storage:** 192.168.10.0—provides access to iSCSI storage.

- **Heartbeat:** 192.168.20.0—maintains status for the Hyper-V cluster.

- **Service:** 192.168.30.0—provides access to virtual machines.

In Chapter 4, you completed the creation of virtual switches for the Management and Service networks, which support virtual machines. The remaining networks, which are used only by the host computers, do not need virtual switches and appear on the next page.

1. Review the Virtual Switches page.

2. Click Next.

Review Summary Page

The Summary page for the Create Hyper-V Cluster Wizard appears next. Review the Summary. Correct any errors and then click Finish.

1. Review the Summary page.

2. Click Previous to correct any errors.

3. Click Finish.

Track Progress of Installation

As the PowerShell script runs, you can track the progress in the Jobs window. This install is time consuming and may take up to 30 minutes. When the wizard completes, review the job details. If a failure appears, research and correct the problem. Rerun the Create Hyper-V Cluster Wizard. Tasks that were completed successfully will not be repeated.

1. To observe progress of the installation, click Install cluster in the Jobs window and click the Details tab.

2. Verify that the job has a status of Complete.

3. If a failure appears, click the Summary tab; then research and correct the problem. Rerun the Create Cluster Wizard. Tasks that were completed successfully will not be repeated.

Troubleshoot Cluster Creation

The validation reports are available on Compute1.test.local in the C:\Windows\Cluster\Reports folder. This is an excellent source for additional information should you encounter problems with the creation of a Hyper-V cluster.

View Host System Status

After the cluster is created, you can view the status for the Hyper-V cluster. From the Compute cluster node, you can view the status of each host node. Figure 6.12 shows the status for the compute1.test.local host computer.

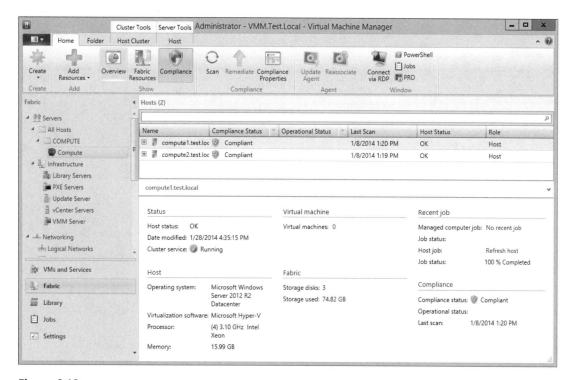

Figure 6.12
Cluster node showing status of COMPUTE1.
Source: VMM Administrator Console/Windows Server 2012 R2.

1. To view the cluster status and information on each host in the cluster, click Compute (gray icon) and then click compute1.test.local.

2. Review the information and then click compute2.test.local.

View Networking Configuration

Figure 6.13 shows the networking configuration for the Compute cluster. To view this, click View Networking icon. You use this for a quick overview of the four networks in the cluster.

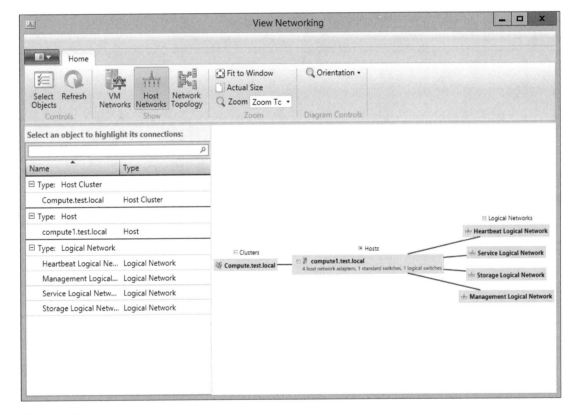

Figure 6.13
Networking configuration for Compute cluster.
Source: VMM Administrator Console/Windows Server 2012 R2.

1. To view the networking configuration for COMPUTE, right-click compute1.test.local, click View Networking, and expand compute1.test.local.

2. Repeat step 1 for compute2.test.local.

Track Usage of VMStorage

You will want to track the usage of storage for your virtual machines. To do this, you click Classifications and Pools and then click VMStorage (see Figure 6.14). With the 500GB of storage allocated, you should be able to store at least 25-30 virtual machines. The 1GB of storage is adequate for quorum in the cluster.

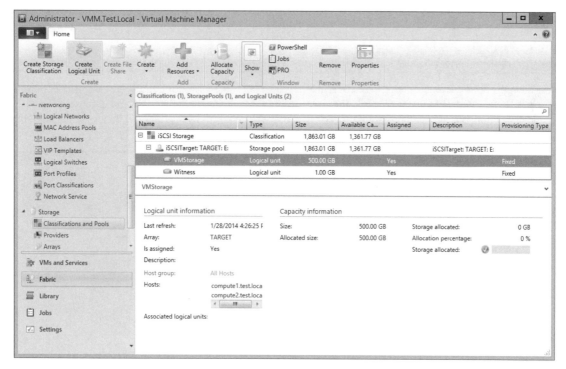

Figure 6.14
Status of VMStorage.

Source: VMM Administrator Console/Windows Server 2012 R2.

1. To view the Storage logical unit information, click Classifications and Pools, and then click VMStorage.

2. Review the information and then click Witness.

TESTING LIVE MIGRATION AND CLUSTER FAILOVER

In this section, you'll learn to perform live migration and to test the cluster failover. First, you deploy a virtual machine. Consider these steps to create a virtual machine as a preview of the deployment of virtual machines that you will learn in detail in Chapter 8.

After deploying the virtual machine, you can perform live migration and test cluster failover.

Building a Virtual Machine

To create a virtual machine, you use the Create Virtual Machine Wizard. You may need to refer to the Create and Configure a Virtual Machine section in Chapter 1, "Introduction to the Private Cloud."

Create Virtual Machine Wizard in VMM

You have previously created the ADDS, CLIENT, SQL, TARGET, and VMM virtual machines using the Hyper-V Manager's New Virtual Machine Wizard. The Create Virtual Machine Wizard in VMM adds pages needed to place the virtual machine in the cloud. These new pages will be shown in this section as you build the TestMigration virtual machine.

To create this virtual machine complete these steps:

1. Return to VMM and the Fabric.

2. Click the VMs and Services view. Expand and click the Compute node.

3. To start the Create Virtual Machine Wizard, click Create Virtual Machine twice.

4. Click Create the new virtual machine with a blank hard disk.

5. Click Next.

6. Enter TestMigration for the Virtual machine name.

7. Click Next.

8. To use the existing hardware profile, click the Hardware Profile chevron.

9. Select HP-1NET-1VHD-512MB.

10. To attach the Windows Server 2012 R2 iso, scroll and click Virtual DVD drive, and then click Existing ISO image.

11. Click Browse, click the Windows Server 2012 R2 iso, and then click OK.

Connect to VM Network

To connect to the VM network that you created in Chapter 4, you click Connected to a VM network in the Connectivity section, as shown in Figure 6.15. The only choice,

Service VM Network, is grayed out and will be used. Click the VM subnet chevron and select Customer Addresses, which will place the virtual machine on the 172.16.0.0 network. In the IP address section, retain the IPv4. In the MAC address section, keep the null static MAC address. When the virtual machine is created, a MAC address is assigned. In the Port profile section, select Medium bandwidth for the Classification.

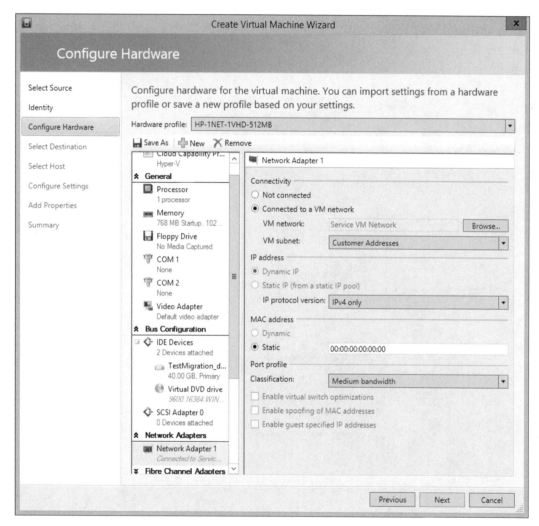

Figure 6.15
Create Virtual Machine Wizard Configure Hardware page showing network settings.
Source: VMM Administrator Console/Windows Server 2012 R2.

1. To connect to the Service network, scroll and click Network Adapter 1.

2. Click Connected to a VM Network.

3. Click Browse, click Service VM Network, and click OK.

4. Click the VM subnet chevron and select Customer Addresses.

5. Click the Classification chevron and select Medium bandwidth.

Make the Virtual Machine Highly Available

For the last Configure Hardware setting, you will indicate that the virtual machine will run in a Hyper-V cluster. Figure 6.16 shows the Make this virtual machine highly available option chosen.

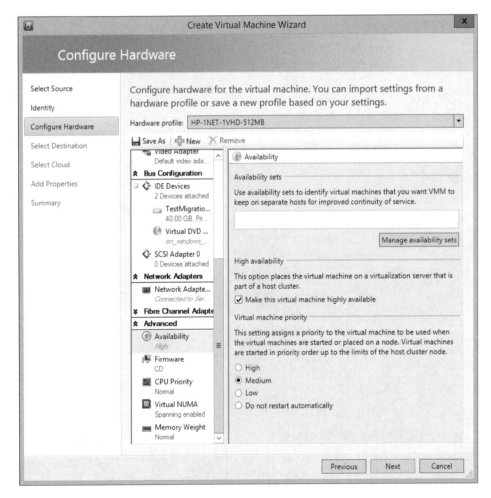

Figure 6.16
Create Virtual Machine Wizard Configure Hardware page with virtual machine highly available.
Source: VMM Administrator Console/Windows Server 2012 R2.

1. To indicate that this virtual machine will be on a Hyper-V cluster, scroll and click Availability.

2. Click Make this virtual machine highly available.

3. Review your hardware choices.

4. Click Next.

Place Virtual Machine in COMPUTE Host Group

On the next page, you place the virtual machine in the COMPUTE host group (see Figure 6.17).

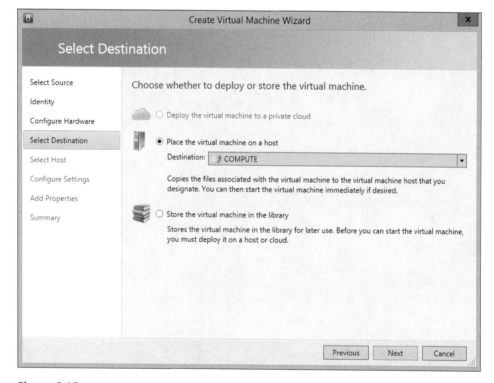

Figure 6.17
Create Virtual Machine Wizard Select Destination page.
Source: VMM Administrator Console/Windows Server 2012 R2.

1. Review the host group destination.

2. Click Next.

Place Virtual Machine on Host Computer

Within the COMPUTE host group, you can select a host computer, as shown in Figure 6.18. The star rating system was developed by Microsoft to assist with the placement of virtual machines. VMM assigns host ratings that range from zero (not suitable) to five stars (highly suitable). The rating is based on the virtual machine's resource requirements, such as processor, memory, disk, and network I/O capacity. You will learn more about the star rating system in Chapter 7.

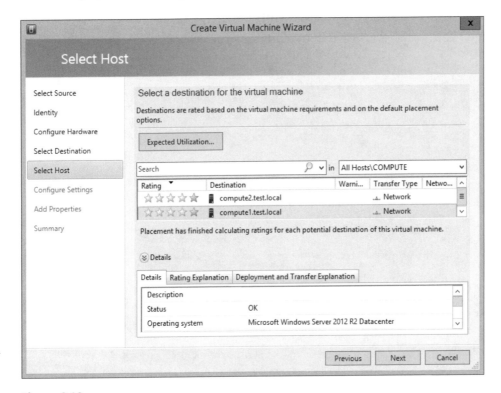

Figure 6.18
Create Virtual Machine Wizard Select Host page.
Source: VMM Administrator Console/Windows Server 2012 R2.

1. Wait for the ratings to complete.

2. To place the virtual machine on a host computer, click compute1.test.local.

3. Click Next.

Review Configure Settings

On the Configure Settings page, you can review the settings. Recall that the location path appears to be on the system drive of the host computer as the C:\ClusterStorage\Volume1\, as shown in Figure 6.19.

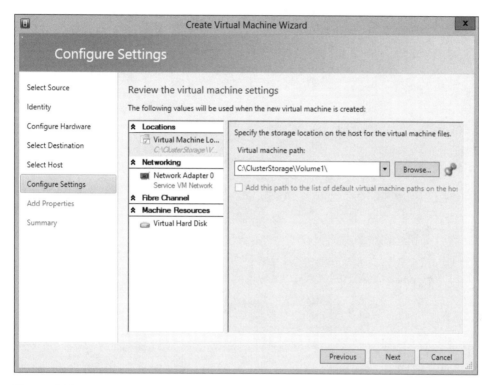

Figure 6.19
Create Virtual Machine Wizard Configure Settings page.
Source: VMM Administrator Console/Windows Server 2012 R2.

1. Review the virtual machine settings.

2. To store the virtual machine in the CSV, click Next.

Add Properties for Startup/Shutdown

Figure 6.20 shows the Automatic actions that are suitable for this virtual machine. When the host computer starts, and if the virtual machine was running at host computer shutdown, the virtual machine will be restarted automatically. Likewise, if the virtual machine was running at host computer shutdown, the virtual machine state is stored to enable a fast restart.

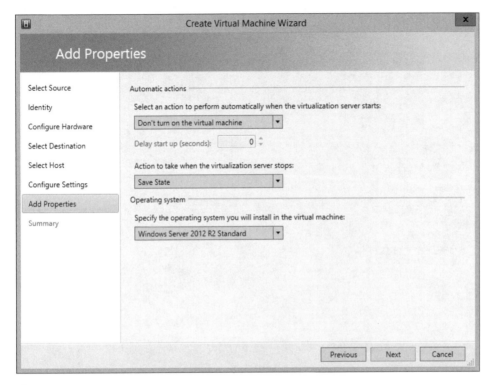

Figure 6.20
Create Virtual Machine Wizard Add Properties page.
Source: VMM Administrator Console/Windows Server 2012 R2.

1. Review the default Automatic actions and Operating system designation.

2. Click Next.

3. Review the Summary.

4. Click Start the virtual machine after deploying it.

5. Click Create.

Creation Takes Time

Wait for the virtual machine to be created and started. This process is time consuming, and it may take up to 20 minutes. You may safely ignore the message about the offload transfer.

Virtual Machine Running

Figure 6.21 shows the virtual machine running within the Compute Hyper-V cluster on the compute1.test.local host computer. To connect to the virtual machine, click the virtual machine, click the Connect or View icon, and then click Connect via Console. From this point, you can work through the server setup screens to install Windows Server 2012 R2.

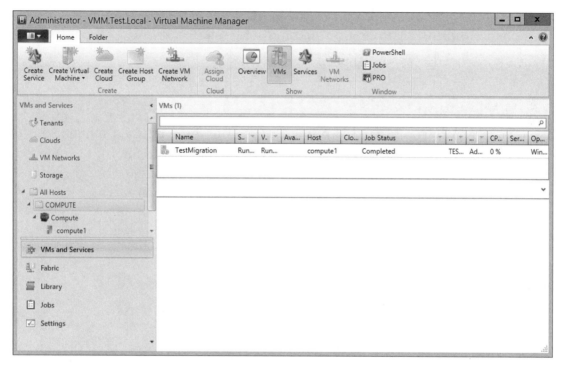

Figure 6.21
Created virtual machine running in COMPUTE Host Group.

Source: VMM Administrator Console/Windows Server 2012 R2.

1. To connect to the running virtual machine, click the VMs and Services node, Expand All Hosts, expand COMPUTE, and expand Compute.

2. Click TestMigration, click the Connect or View icon, and then click Connect via Console.

3. Review the Windows Setup and then click Next.

4. Click Install now.

5. If requested, enter the product key and click Next.

6. To select an operating system, select the Standard Server with GUI and click Next.

7. Click I accept the license terms and click Next.

8. Click Custom: Install Windows Only (advanced).

9. Click Next.

10. Wait for the files to be copied and the installation completed.

11. Enter Pa$$w0rd for Password and Reenter password. Press Enter.

12. Click Ctrl-Alt-Del on the menu.

13. Log on to the virtual machine with Administrator and Pa$$w0rd.

14. When the network's pop-up appears, click No.

Test Live Migration

To test live migration, you locate the running virtual machine on the Compute cluster node. In this case, the running virtual machine is located on the compute1 host computer, as shown in Figure 6.22. To start the live migration process with the Migrate VM Wizard, select the running virtual machine and then click the Migrate Virtual Machine icon.

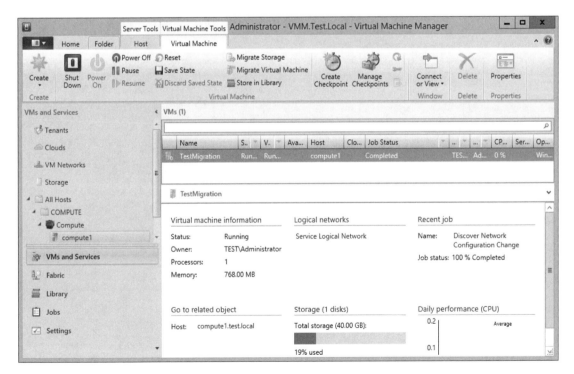

Figure 6.22
Create a virtual machine running on the compute1 host computer.

Source: VMM Administrator Console/Windows Server 2012 R2.

1. Minimize the TestMigration Virtual Machine Viewer window. Return to VMs and Servers.

2. To locate the running virtual machine, click compute1 under the Compute cluster.

3. To view details for TestMigration, click TestMigration.

Figure 6.23 shows the page where you select the destination host computer. Since there are only two host computers in the cluster and compute1.test.local is indicated as the current host, you pick compute2.test.local. If you have more than two host computers in the cluster, you can choose the host computer with the most stars.

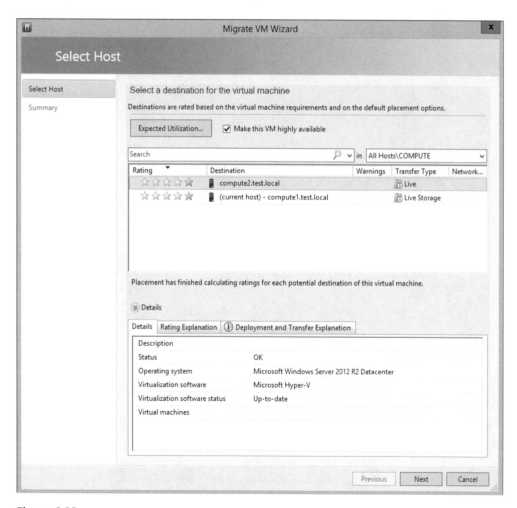

Figure 6.23
Migrate VM Wizard Select Host page.
Source: VMM Administrator Console/Windows Server 2012 R2.

1. To start live migration, click TestMigration, click Migrate Virtual Machine, and click compute2.test.local.

2. Click Next.

You can review the Summary page, shown in Figure 6.24, and click Move to start the PowerShell script.

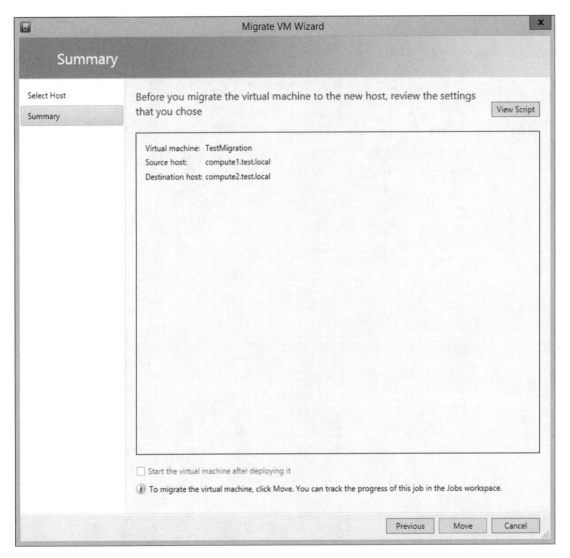

Figure 6.24
Migrate VM Wizard Summary page.
Source: VMM Administrator Console/Windows Server 2012 R2.

1. Review the Summary page.

2. Click Move.

Figure 6.25 shows the Jobs page for the executing PowerShell script to migrate the virtual machine.

Figure 6.25
Jobs page showing PowerShell script execution.
Source: VMM Administrator Console/Windows Server 2012 R2.

1. Click the Jobs node.

2. Wait for the PowerShell script to complete.

3. Close the Jobs window.

To run live migrations concurrently, you must manually start each migration. You can specify how many concurrent migrations to run. The default setting is two, which is the number of simultaneous live migrations that are enabled in Hyper-V. To live migrate more than two, change the maximum number of simultaneous live migrations (see Figure 6.26).

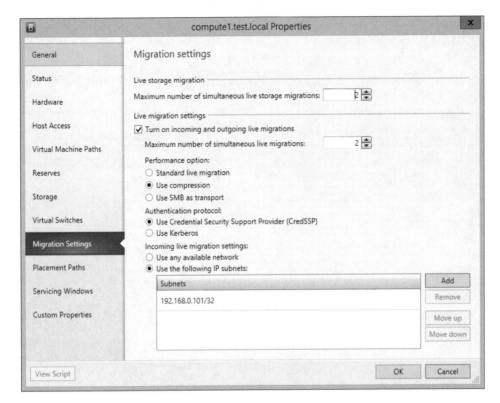

Figure 6.26
Migration settings for Compute1.
Source: VMM Administrator Console/Windows Server 2012 R2.

1. Return to VMs and Services.

2. To review Migration Settings, right-click Compute1, click Properties, and click Migration Settings.

3. Review the setting for Maximum number of simultaneous live migrations.

4. Click OK.

Test Failover

Recall that the two host computers exchange heartbeat pulses over the network. When one host computer does not receive the periodic heartbeat pulse, a failover occurs. Then the virtual machines are migrated to another running host computer.

To test the failover process, the host computer with the running virtual machines, one in this case, is placed in maintenance mode. Figure 6.27 shows the running virtual machine.

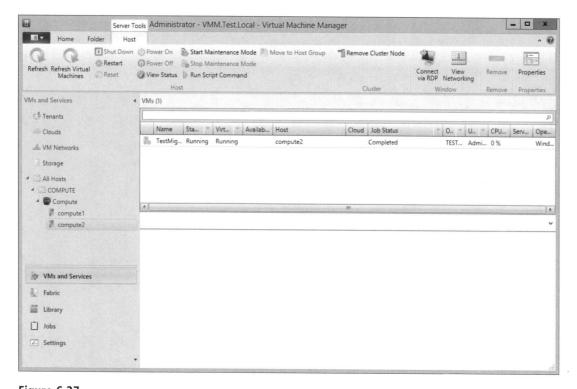

Figure 6.27
Virtual machine running on compute2.
Source: VMM Administrator Console/Windows Server 2012 R2.

1. To see the host on which TestMigration is running, click compute2.

2. To place the host computer in a state where it can no longer run virtual machines, click the Host tab and then click the Start Maintenance Mode icon.

Figure 6.28 shows the Start Maintenance Mode page, which is displayed next. You can select from two choices:

- **Move all virtual machines to other hosts in the cluster:** Service is not interrupted. Virtual machines are migrated to other host computers in the cluster using the Star system to control placement.

■ **Place all running virtual machines into a saved state:** Service is interrupted. Virtual machines are stopped and placed into a saved state. At the completion of maintenance, the virtual machines are restarted.

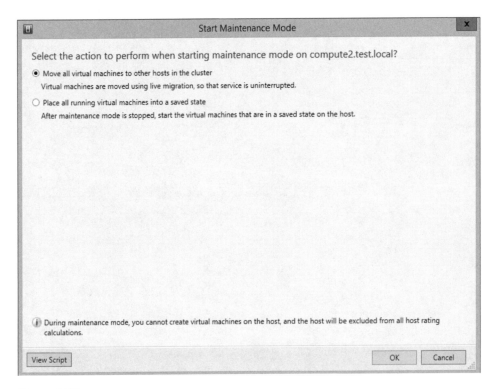

Figure 6.28
Start Maintenance Mode page.

Source: VMM Administrator Console/Windows Server 2012 R2.

Start Failover with Start Maintenance

The status of the virtual machine is changed to Under Migration. After migration is complete, the running virtual machine appears on the other host computer.

1. To locate the running virtual machine, click compute2 under the Compute cluster.

2. To simulate a failing host computer, click the Host tab and click Start Maintenance Mode.

3. Review the Start Maintenance Mode page and click OK.

4. Wait for the virtual machine to be migrated.

Verify Virtual Machine Migration

Select compute1 to see that the virtual machine was migrated and verify that it is running (see Figure 6.29). To return the compute2 computer to operational status, select Stop Maintenance Mode.

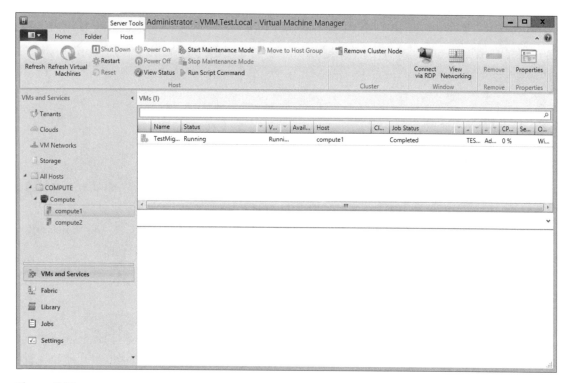

Figure 6.29
Virtual machine running on compute1.

Source: VMM Administrator Console/Windows Server 2012 R2.

1. To verify that the virtual machine is running, click compute1.

2. To bring the host computer back online, click compute2 and then click Stop Maintenance Mode.

In this instance, you used maintenance mode to simulate a failure. You can use these steps to take a host computer offline to perform maintenance. The virtual machines are migrated to other host computers. When you are ready, click Stop Maintenance to indicate that the host computer should be returned to service. Because the virtual machines are not returned automatically, you need to migrate the virtual machines back to the host computer.

Summary

- You learned to describe the technical terms within the structure of a Hyper-V cluster, such as failover clusters, clustered shared volumes, and live migration.

- You built a Hyper-V cluster to ensure redundancy and failover.

- You learned to execute live migration to move a virtual machine between hosts.

- You learned to test failover by using Maintenance Mode to take a host computer out of service.

Case Projects

Case 6-1: Time for Virtual Machine Migration

The migration of a virtual machine occurs quickly. The users of the particular virtual machine should not experience an interruption in service.

To determine the time required for a migration, click the Jobs node. Locate and click Move virtual machine TestMigration. The Duration is in the Summary tab.

Case 6-2: Microsoft Fast Track Cloud Program

You may be interested in researching hardware and software solutions to build the private cloud. One excellent place to start is the Microsoft Fast Track Cloud Program. Many major hardware firms, such as Dell and HP, are participants. Search for the string: Microsoft Fast Track Cloud.

CHAPTER 7

CREATING THE PRIVATE CLOUD

After reading this chapter and completing the exercises, you will be able to do the following:

- Prepare to create your PRIVATE Cloud.
- Create the Tenant Administrator role.
- Create your PRIVATE Cloud.

When working with the private cloud, self-service users can deploy their own virtual machines from building blocks, such as virtual hard disks and templates. These users access virtual machines from the VMM console. User roles control the actions, such as create, start, or shutdown, which self-service users can take while working with their virtual machines in a private cloud.

After completing the exercises in the previous six chapters, you already put in place the resources to create your PRIVATE Cloud.

PREPARING TO CREATE THE PRIVATE CLOUD

In this section, you'll create your PRIVATE Cloud.

First, you will take care of some last-minute details that are required for the Create Private Cloud Wizard. You'll create a VIP template for the Microsoft Network Load

Balancer. You will provide resources in the Library. Then you will create a Tenant Administrator user role.

Configuring Load Balancing

Load balancing distributes processing across multiple servers, which is important when you do not know how many requests to expect for a group of servers or when the requests will arrive. Load balancing might allocate incoming requests evenly to all servers, or it might send requests to the next available server.

VMM includes load balancing integration so that you can automatically provision load balancers for your PRIVATE Cloud. For example, you provision load balancing for your Web application severs. You can use Microsoft Network Load Balancing (NLB), or you can add supported hardware load balancers through the VMM console. NLB is included as an available load balancer when you install VMM. NLB uses round robin as the load-balancing method.

Virtual IP (VIP) is the load-balancing IP address where users point their Web browsers to access your website. A VIP will have at least one or more Web servers assigned to it. The VIP will spread traffic among them using metrics and methods.

To use the Microsoft NLB, you will configure a VIP template. There are seven pages in the Load balancer VIP template Wizard.

Enter Name for the VIP Template

On the first page, you can name the VIP template and enter the port number. You enter 80 for the port for a Web server. For a completed Name page, see Figure 7.1.

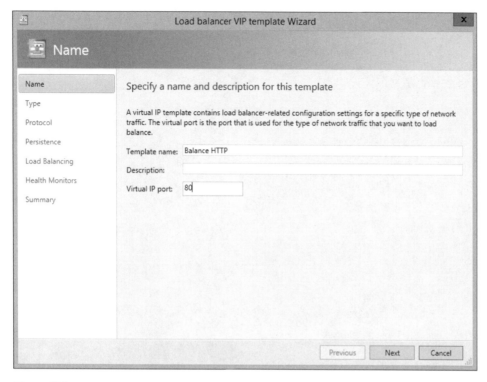

Figure 7.1
Load balancer VIP template Wizard Name page.
Source: VMM Administrator Console/Windows Server 2012 R2.

1. Return to VMM and the Fabric.

2. Expand Networking and then click VIP Templates.

3. To start the Load balancer VIP template Wizard, click Create and then click Create VIP Template.

4. Enter Balance HTTP for the Template name and then enter 80 for the Virtual IP port.

5. Click Next.

Specify Microsoft Network Load Balancing

Since you do not have a hardware network load balancer available, you can choose to use the Microsoft NLB. Figure 7.2 shows the completed selections. For a specific hardware network load balancer, follow the manufacturer's instructions.

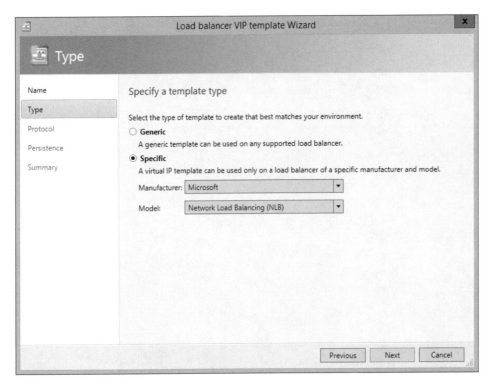

Figure 7.2
Load balancer VIP template Wizard Type page.

Source: VMM Administrator Console/Windows Server 2012 R2.

1. To specify the NLB type, click Specific, click the Manufacturer chevron, and select Microsoft. Retain the Network Load Balancing (NLB) entry.

2. Click Next.

Retain TCP Protocol

TCP is the most common transport protocol and is used by your virtual machines. See Figure 7.3, which shows TCP selected.

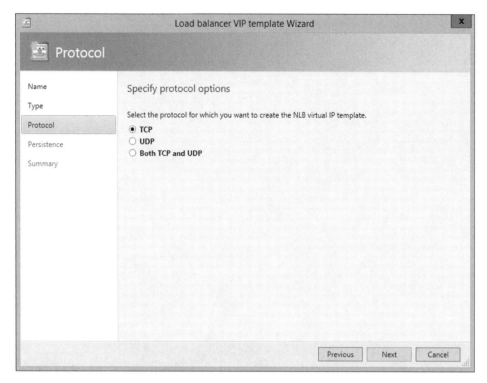

Figure 7.3
Load balancer VIP template Wizard Protocol page.
Source: VMM Administrator Console/Windows Server 2012 R2.

1. For the protocol, retain TCP.

2. Click Next.

Specify Persistence

On the Persistence page, you select the Enable persistence option to enable session persistence. See Figure 7.4 for a completed page. This means that the load balancer will always try to direct the same user to the same virtual machine that is behind the load balancer. This choice is based on the source IP address and the subnet mask. You accept the default value of Source IP in the Persistence type list. In the Subnet mask to apply list, select Single. NLB directs multiple requests from the same client IP address to the same host in the NLB cluster.

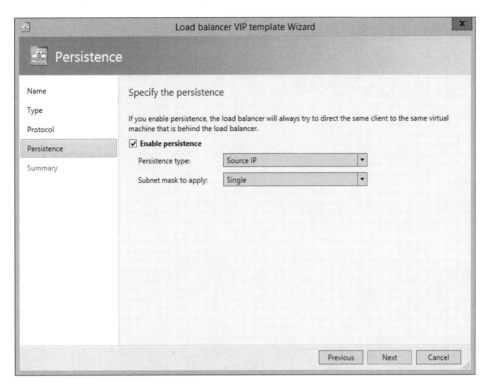

Figure 7.4
Load balancer VIP template Wizard Persistence page.
Source: VMM Administrator Console/Windows Server 2012 R2.

1. To indicate how to connect from the client to the same host, click Enable persistence.

2. Retain Source IP. Click the Subnet mask to apply the chevron and then select Single.

3. Click Next.

4. Review the Summary and then click Finish.

5. Close the Jobs window.

Providing Resources for Self-Service Users

To share physical resources with the users of your PRIVATE Cloud, you might create file folders and share these resources. These file folders contain the resources to deploy virtual machines. As an administrator, you populate the file folders with templates, ISO files, and other resources. You make these resources available by adding these file folders as read-only library shares.

Self-Service User's View of Library

The library for self-service users is structured to simplify access to library resources. While administrators see all of the library resources, these self-service users see a Cloud Libraries node, which displays physical resources for their use, as shown in Figure 7.5. In the Self-Service User Data node, self-service users see the resources that they have uploaded to the library. In addition, this a good place for administrators to place resources that are only used by self-service users. In the Templates and Profiles nodes, not shown, they can see the templates and profiles that are assigned to their self-service user role.

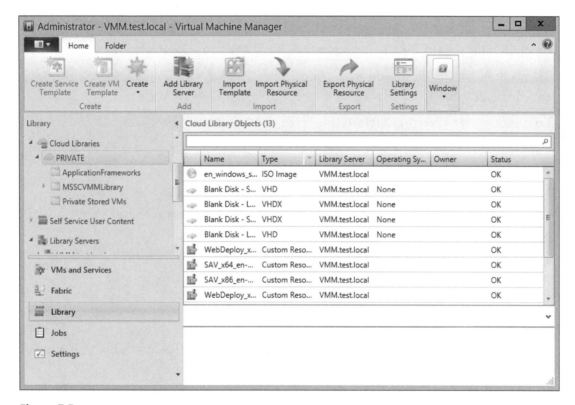

Figure 7.5
Self-Service user view of Library.
Source: VMM Administrator Console/Windows Server 2012 R2.

Create Security Groups

In your scenario, you can create security groups in Active Directory Users and Computers for the private cloud. VMM uses these security permissions to control what self-service users can view in the library.

To create security groups, complete the following steps:

1. Return to the ADDS virtual machine.

2. In the Server Manager, click Local Server, click Tasks, and then click Active Directory Users and Computers. Expand test.local and click Users.

3. To create a global security group, click Action, point to New, and select Group.

4. Enter Private for the Group name and then click OK.

5. To create a domain local security group, click Action, point to New, and select Group.

6. Enter Private_Cloud for the Group name, click Domain Local, and then click OK.

7. Right-click Private, click Add to a group, enter Private_Cloud, click Check Names, and then click OK twice.

8. To create a user account, click Action, point to New, and select User.

9. Enter Peter for the First name, enter Cloud for the Last name, enter PCloud for the User logon name, and then click Next.

10. Enter Pa$$w0rd for the Password and Confirm password. Clear the User must change password at next logon option, and then click Password never expires. Click Next. Click Finish.

11. Right-click Peter Cloud, click Add to a group, enter Private, click Check Names, click Private, and then click OK three times.

Create Shares for Read-Only Resources

To store resources for your self-service users, you create shared folders. These folders will include read-only library shares for their private clouds and user data paths.

To create the two required shared folders and copy the Application Frameworks, complete the following steps:

1. Return to the VMM virtual machine.

2. Open the Windows Explorer and navigate to the root of the C: drive.

3. To create the C:\ Cloud Resources folder, right-click in the whitespace, point to New, and click Folder. Enter Cloud Resources and press Enter.

Do Not Nest Shared Folders

Do not add a folder for a new library share in the path of an existing library share, such as MSSCVMMLibrary or another share you created.

4. To create the Private Cloud Resources subfolder, double-click Cloud Resources, right-click in the whitespace of the Cloud Resources folder, point to New, and click Folder. Enter Private Cloud Resources and press Enter.

5. To share the folder, right-click Private Cloud Resources, click Properties, click the Sharing tab, click Advanced Sharing, click Share this folder, click Permissions, click Allow - Full Control, and then click OK twice.

6. To apply security for the Private Cloud Resources folder, click the Security tab. Click Edit, click Add, enter Private_Cloud, click Check Names, and click OK. Click Allow - Modify and click OK. Click close.

7. To create the ApplicationFrameworks subfolder, right-click in the whitespace of the Cloud Resources folder, point to New, and click Folder, Enter ApplicationFrameworks, and then press Enter.

8. To share the folder, right-click ApplicationFrameworks, click Properties, click the Sharing tab, click Advanced Sharing, click Share this folder, click Permissions, click Allow - Full Control, and then click OK twice.

9. To apply security for the ApplicationFrameworks folder, click the Security tab. Click Edit, click Add, enter Private_Cloud, click Check Names, click OK. Click Allow - Modify, click OK. Click Close.

10. Return to the Library Servers node in VMM Manager.

11. Expand Library Servers, expand vmm.test.local, and expand the MSSCVMMLibrary. Right-click ApplicationFrameworks and then click Explore.

12. Select the four folders, right-click the selected folders, and then click Copy. Close the ApplicationFrameworks window.

13. Return to the Windows Explorer and navigate to the ApplicationFrameworks folder. Click Paste. Close the ApplicationFrameworks window.

Select Shared Folders

After you complete the previous steps, you are ready to add these shared folders as library shares. You can do this with the Add Library Shares Wizard. Select the share names for the folders as shown in Figure 7.6.

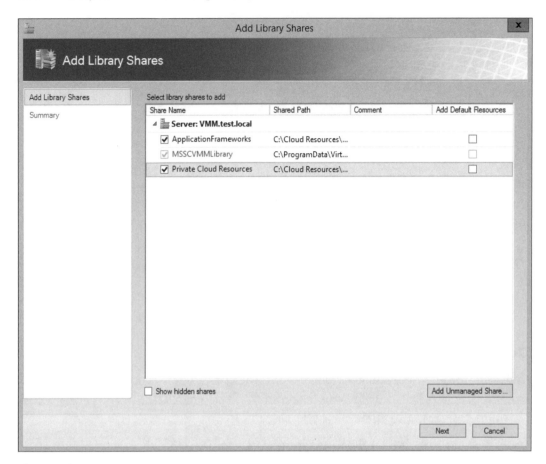

Figure 7.6
Add Library Shares.
Source: VMM Administrator Console/Windows Server 2012 R2.

1. Return to the VMM console, click the Library node.

2. Expand the Library Servers tab, right-click vmm.test.local, and click Add Library Shares.

3. Select each of the shares and click Next.

Check Library Share Names

Once added, library shares can't be removed by VMM, so be sure this is what you want before clicking Add Library Shares.

4. Review the Summary and then click Add Library Shares. When completed, close the Jobs screen.

CREATING THE TENANT ADMINISTRATOR USER ROLE

You create a Tenant Administrator user role in VMM to define the scope of management operations for this administrator. Members of the Tenant Administrator role can create, deploy, and manage their own virtual machines by using the VMM console.

Tenant Administrators are one of four profiles that are available. The user profiles are the following:

- **Fabric Administrator (Delegated Administrator):** Performs all administrative tasks within their assigned host groups, clouds, and library servers.

- **Read-Only Administrator:** Views properties, status, and job status of objects within their assigned host groups, clouds, and library servers.

- **Tenant Administrator:** Creates, deploys, and manages their own virtual machines by using the VMM console or a Web portal. They can also specify which tasks the self-service users can perform on their virtual machines. Tenant Administrators can place quotas on computing resources and virtual machines.

- **Application Administrator (Self-Service User):** Creates, deploys, and manages their own virtual machines by using the VMM console or a Web portal.

Create Security Groups

Before creating a Tenant Administrator user role, you need to create security groups and user run accounts. Complete these steps:

1. Return to the ADDS virtual machine on MANAGE.

2. Create a Domain Local security group: PrivateTenantAdmins.

3. To make Peter Cloud a Tenant Administrator, right-click Peter Cloud, click Add to a group, click Advanced, enter Private for Starts with, click Find Now, click PrivateTenantAdmins, and then click OK three times.

4. Create the user account PrivateRun. Use Pa$$w0rd as the password and set Password never expires.

5. Add the PrivateRun account to Private_Cloud.

Name User Role

You use the Create User Role Wizard to create the Tenant Administrators. There are seven pages in this wizard. As with other wizards, on the first page you will name the object.

1. Return to VMM and Expand VMs and Services.

2. To start the Create User Role Wizard, right-click Tenants and then click Create User Role.

3. Enter PrivateTenantAdmin for the name.

4. Click Next.

Select User Profile Role

Figure 7.7 shows the Tenant Administrator user profile role selected. Your Tenant Administrator creates, deploys, and manages virtual machines by using the VMM console.

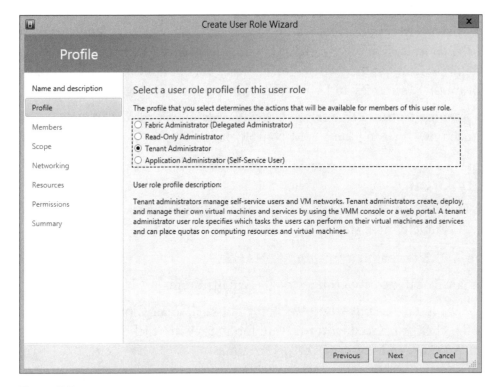

Figure 7.7
Create User Role Wizard Tenant Administrator selected.
Source: VMM Administrator Console/Windows Server 2012 R2.

1. Click Tenant Administrator.

2. Review the User role profile description.

3. Click Next.

Select Security Group

On the next page, you can add the security groups that will serve as Tenant Administrators. You add the domain local security group PrivateTenantAdmins (see Figure 7.8).

Figure 7.8
Create User Role Wizard Security Group for Tenant Administrator.
Source: VMM Administrator Console/Windows Server 2012 R2.

1. Click Add, click Advanced, enter Private for Starts with, click Find Now, and then select PrivateTenantAdmins. Click OK twice.

2. Click Next.

Delay Cloud Assignment

Since you will be creating the cloud that this Tenant Administrator will administer in a later exercise, you can elect to delay the assignment of the cloud.

1. To delay the assignment of a cloud, click Next.

Add Service VM Network

Your users will need a VM network for their virtual machines. You can add the Service VM Network that you created in Chapter 4.

1. To add a VM Network, click Add and then click Service VM Network.

2. Click OK.

3. Click Next.

Specify Resources

Your Tenant Administrator will need some basic profiles and VM templates to get started building virtual machines. Also, he will need a folder in the library for resources that he uploads, as shown in Figure 7.9.

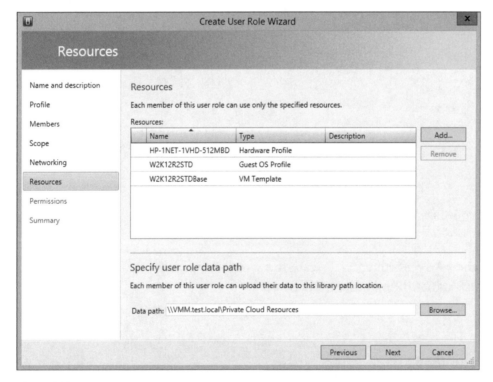

Figure 7.9
Create User Role Wizard available resources added.
Source: VMM Administrator Console/Windows Server 2012 R2.

1. To see the available resources, click Add. Click the first resource and then click OK.

2. Repeat step 1 for the additional resources.

3. To add the Private Cloud Resources upload folder, click Browse, click Private Cloud Resources, and then click OK.

4. Click Next.

Provide Permissions

The Tenant Administrator needs to be able to manage the PRIVATE Cloud. To ensure that he can, you select all of the permissions.

1. For permissions, check Select all.

2. Click Next.

Limit VM Networks

You decide not to limit the number of VM networks to the initial VM network, and retain the defaults.

1. Review Limit the number of VM networks for roles and Limit the number of VM networks for users.

2. Click Next.

Provide Run As Account

Your self-service users need a Run As account to use the templates and profiles that they use to create virtual machines and services. To specify the Run As account, you complete the next page, as shown in Figure 7.10.

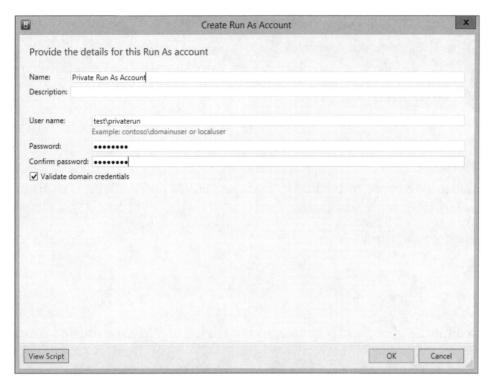

Figure 7.10
Create User Role Wizard Private Run As Account.

Source: VMM Administrator Console/Windows Server 2012 R2.

1. Click Add. Click Create Run As Account, enter Private Run As Account for the Name, enter test\privaterun as the User name, and use Pa$$w0rd as the password. Click OK.

2. Select Private Run As Account and click OK. Click Next.

3. Review the Summary and click Finish.

CREATING THE PRIVATE CLOUD

After completing numerous exercises, you are ready to create your private cloud. First, you will complete a minor detail and create an additional library share to store virtual machines. You will use the Create Cloud Wizard to create the private cloud.

Cloud Capacity Settings

The private cloud capacity equals the capacity of the underlying fabric. You can configure these quotas for your private cloud:

- **Virtual CPUs:** Sets the limits of the number of available virtual CPUs. The number of virtual CPUs is equal to the number of cores in available processors.

- **Memory:** Sets a quota on memory (in gigabytes) that is available for virtual machines that are deployed on the private cloud. This is the total memory of host computers in the COMPUTE host group.

- **Storage:** Sets a quota on storage capacity (in gigabytes) that is available to virtual machines that are deployed on the private cloud. This is the amount of iSCSI storage available.

- **Custom Quota points:** Sets a limit for virtual machines that are deployed on the private cloud based on total quota points that are assigned to the virtual machines through their virtual machine templates. Quota points are an arbitrary value that can be assigned to a virtual machine template based on the anticipated size of the virtual machine.

- **Virtual machines:** Limits the total number of virtual machines that can be deployed on the private cloud.

Create Stored VMs Library Shares

Here are the steps to create the library share to store virtual machines for future deployment.

1. Open the Windows Explorer and navigate to of the C:\Cloud Resources folder.

2. To create the C:\ Private Stored VMs subfolder, right-click in the whitespace of the Cloud Resources folder, point to New, and click Folder. Enter Private Stored VMs and press Enter.

3. To share the folder, right-click Private Stored VMs, click Properties, click the Sharing tab, click Advanced Sharing, click Share this folder, click Permissions, click Allow - Full Control, and then click OK twice.

4. To set security for the Private Stored VMs folder, click the Security tab, click Edit, click Add, enter Private_Cloud, click Check Names, and then click OK. Click Allow - Modify and then click OK. Click close.

5. Return to the Library node in VMM Manager.

6. Click Library Servers, right-click vmm.test.local, and then click Add Library Shares.

7. Select Private Stored VMs and click Next.

8. Review the Summary and then click Add Library Shares.

9. Wait for the script to complete and close the Jobs window.

Create Your PRIVATE Cloud

This is the big event that you have been working toward—your private cloud. All of the previously created resources are required for your private cloud. You use the Create Cloud Wizard to create a private cloud. There are 12 pages in the Create Cloud Wizard.

Name the Private Cloud

In the first page for the Create Cloud Wizard, you name the cloud, as you have done when working with previous wizards.

1. Return to VMM and the Fabric node.

2. Click VMs and Servers. Click Clouds.

3. To start the Create Cloud Wizard, click Create Cloud.

4. Enter PRIVATE for the name. Click Next.

Select Host Group

Next, you identify the host group that will run your virtual machines. Figure 7.11 shows the COMPUTE host group selected.

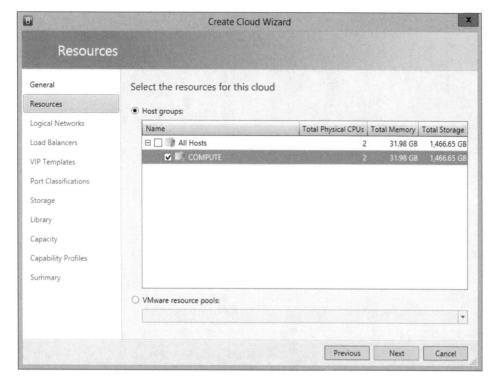

Figure 7.11
Create Cloud Wizard COMPUTE Host group selected.
Source: VMM Administrator Console/Windows Server 2012 R2.

1. To specify the host group, click COMPUTE.

2. Click Next.

Identify Logical Resources

Your cloud needs networking resources. You can select each of the logical networks that you created in the previous exercises, as shown in Figure 7.12.

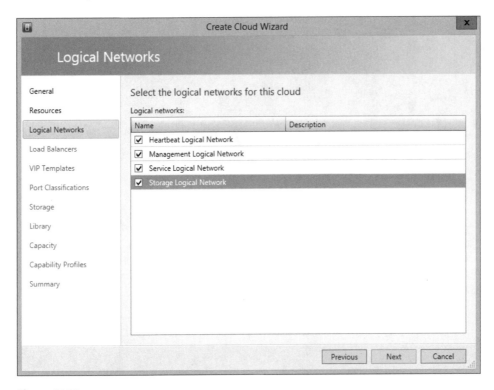

Figure 7.12
Create Cloud Wizard networks added.
Source: VMM Administrator Console/Windows Server 2012 R2.

1. To identify the logical networks for the cloud, click each of the four entries.
2. Click Next.

Add a Load Balancer

Your self-service users may deploy Web servers that require load balancing for effective processing of HTML activity. You select Microsoft Network Load Balancing (see Figure 7.13).

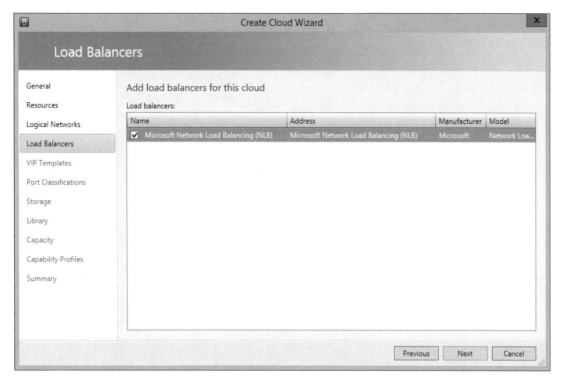

Figure 7.13
Create Cloud Wizard Microsoft Network Load Balancing selected.

Source: VMM Administrator Console/Windows Server 2012 R2.

1. For the Load balancer, select the default Microsoft Network Load Balancing (NLB).

2. Click Next.

Identify the VIP Template

Figure 7.14 shows the identified VIP template to configure Microsoft Network Load Balancing.

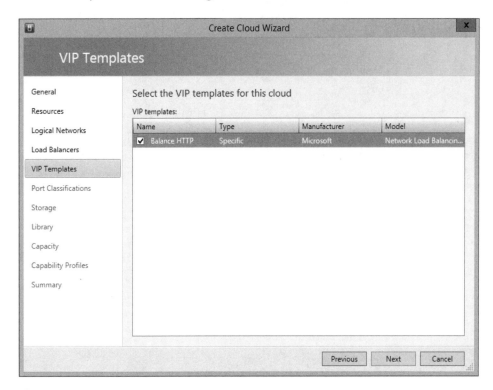

Figure 7.14
Create Cloud Wizard VIP Template to configure the load balancer.
Source: VMM Administrator Console/Windows Server 2012 R2.

1. For the VIP Template, click the Balance HTTP entry.

2. Click Next.

Specify Port Classifications

Figure 7.15 shows the selected port classification. You created a port classification in Chapter 4, "Working with Networks Using VMM," to identify the virtual network adapter port profile. These port classifications provide information about the bandwidth available for a given logical network.

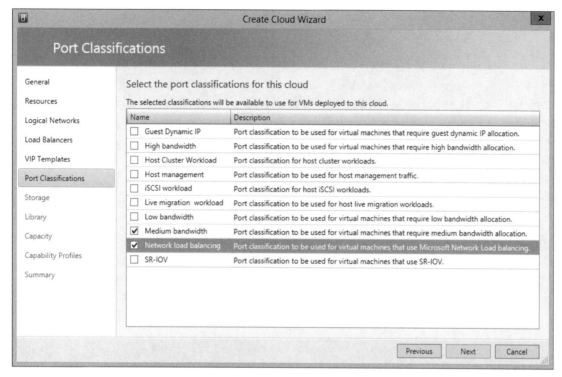

Figure 7.15
Create Cloud Wizard port classifications specified.
Source: VMM Administrator Console/Windows Server 2012 R2.

1. For the port classifications to be available to virtual machines in the cloud, click Medium bandwidth and then click Network load balancing.

2. Click Next.

Select iSCSI Storage

In Chapter 5, "Working with VMM Storage," you created the Microsoft iSCSI Target Server to provide storage for virtual machines. Figure 7.16 shows iSCSI Storage selected for virtual machine storage.

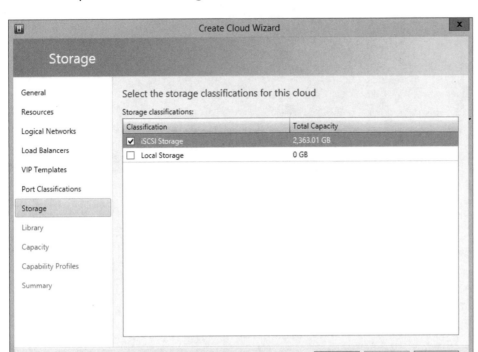

Figure 7.16
Create Cloud Wizard iSCSI Storage selected.
Source: VMM Administrator Console/Windows Server 2012 R2.

1. For Storage, click iSCSI Storage.

2. Click Next.

Indicate Library Resources

Your cloud users will need access for Library resources. To store virtual machines in a private library, you can select Private Stored VMs. For the Library resources to build and deploy virtual machines, you select MSSCVMMLIBRARY and ApplicationFrameworks (see Figure 7.17).

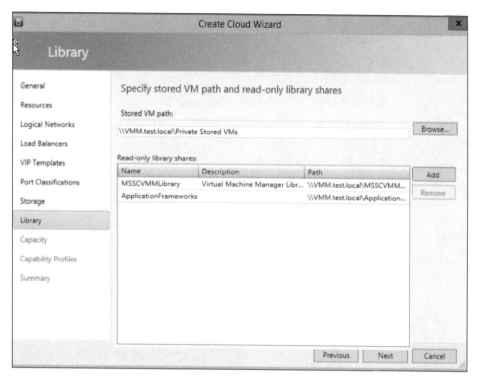

Figure 7.17
Create Cloud Wizard Library resources specified.
Source: VMM Administrator Console/Windows Server 2012 R2.

1. Click Browse and select Private Stored VMs. Click OK.

2. To add the Library components, click Add, select MSSCVMMLIBRARY, and select ApplicationFrameworks. Click OK.

3. Click Next.

Set Cloud Capacity

On the next page, you will set capacity limits for the PRIVATE Cloud. For the definitions of these capacity terms, refer to the section on "Cloud Capacity Settings" in this chapter. Figure 7.18 shows the capacity settings.

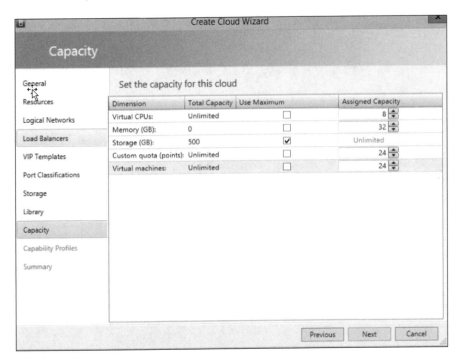

Figure 7.18
Create Cloud Wizard cloud capacity settings.

Source: VMM Administrator Console/Windows Server 2012.

1. Using Table 7.1 as a guide, complete the entries for the Capacity page. You may need to adjust these capacities to align with your particular host servers in the COMPUTE group.

Table 7.1   Cloud Capacity Suggested Entries

Dimension	Total Capacity	Use Maximum	Assigned Capacity
Virtual CPUs	Unlimited	No	8
Memory (GB)	0	No	32
Storage (GB)	500	Yes	
Custom quota (points)	Unlimited	No	24
Virtual machines	Unlimited	No	24

© 2014 Cengage Learning®.

2. After completing capacity settings, click Next.

Add Capability Profile

Because you are running the Hyper-V hypervisor, you can select Hyper-V, as shown in Figure 7.19.

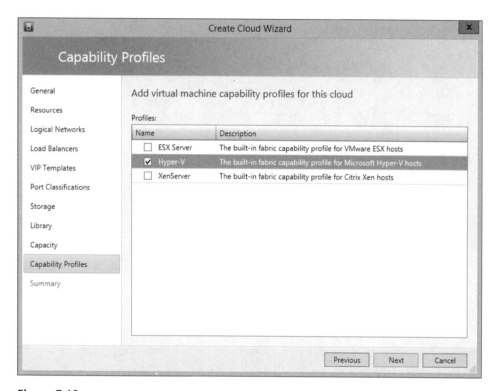

Figure 7.19
Create Cloud Wizard Capability Profiles.
Source: VMM Administrator Console/Windows Server 2012.

1. To set the Hyper-V capability, click Hyper-V.

2. Click Next.

Review Summary

Figure 7.20 shows the Summary. If you see problems, click Previous and correct the mistake.

Figure 7.20
Create Cloud Wizard Summary.
Source: VMM Administrator Console/Windows Server 2012.

1. Review the Summary and then click Finish.

2. Wait for the job to complete. Close the Jobs window.

Assign Tenant Administrator to Cloud

You need to assign the Tenant Administrator, as shown in Figure 7.21. He can create, deploy, and manage his own virtual machines. He can also specify which tasks the self-service users can perform on their virtual machines and services.

Figure 7.21
Assign Tenant Administrator to Cloud.
Source: VMM Administrator Console/Windows Server 2012.

1. Expand Clouds and click cloud PRIVATE. Click the Assign Cloud icon in Create group.

2. Click the chevron and select PrivateTenantAdmin. Click OK twice.

Install VMM Console

You created the CLIENT virtual machine in Chapter 1. To access VMM, you install the VMM console by completing these steps.

1. Restore the CLIENT virtual machine.

2. Log on to the CLIENT virtual machine as Administrator with Pa$$w0rd.

3. When the Server Manager window appears, click Local Server.

4. To change the IP address of the DNS server, click the 192.168.0.109 link, right-click Ethernet, click Properties, click Internet Protocol Version 4 (TCP/IPv4), click Properties, and change the Preferred DNS server to 192.168.0.103. Click OK and click Close. Close the Network Connections window.

5. To join the domain, from the Server Manager, click the Workgroup link. Click Change, click Domain, and enter test.local. Log in as test\administrator with Pa$$w0rd.

6. Wait for the Welcome to the Test domain message and restart the machine.

7. Click Action and then click Ctrl+Alt+Delete. Click Switch User. Click Other Users. Log on as test\PCloud with Pa$$w0rd.

8. Click Media, point to DVD Drive, and click Capture D:.

Steps for VMM 2012 R2 Evaluation

If you are using the SCVMM 2012 R2 evaluation software, replace steps 9 through 12 with these steps:

1. To copy the SC2012_R2_SCVMM file, click This Pc, double-click DVD Drive (D:), right-click SC2012_R2_SCVMM, and click Copy.

2. To paste the VMM file, right-click Local Disk (C:) and click Paste. Click Continue. Log in as test\administrator with Pa$$w0rd. Click Yes.

3. Wait for the file copy to complete.

4. Right-click SC2012_R2_SCVMM and click Run as administrator. Log in as test\administrator with Pa$$w0rd. Click Yes.

5. When the SCVMM Setup wizard appears, click Next twice. Click Extract.

6. Wait for the extraction to complete and click Finish.

7. Navigate to the C:\VMM2012R2 folder and double-click setup. Log in as test\administrator with Pa$$w0rd. Click Yes. Click Install.

---

9. To start the VMM installation, click the Windows Explorer icon. Right-click DVD Drive (D:) SC2012R2VMM and then click Install or run the program from your media.

10. Log in as the Administrator with Pa$$w0rd. Click Yes.

11. Click Install.

12. Wait for the VMM common files to be installed and Select features to install to appear.

13. Click VMM console. Click Next.

14. Click I agree with the terms of the license. Click Next twice.

15. For Microsoft Update, click Off. Click Next twice.

16. Wait for the prerequisite check to complete.

17. Click Next and then click Install.

18. Wait for the features to be installed. Click Close.

Set Options to Run VMM Console

At the time this book was written, a problem existed within VMM regarding the use of the Virtual Machine Viewer to work with a virtual machine. The wrong credentials are passed. Here is a brief work-around to take care of this problem:

1. Return to the VMM virtual machine.

2. Click on Settings view, expand Security, and then click User Roles.

3. Right-click PrivateTenantAdmin and click Properties.

4. Click Run As accounts, click Add, Click VMMRun As Account, and then click OK twice.

Connect to VMM Server

You can use a VMM connection to work with VMM. Figure 7.22 shows these connection settings.

Figure 7.22
Connect to VMM Server.
Source: VMM Administrator Console/Windows Server 2012.

To connect to the VMM server and change to the PRIVATE Cloud, complete these steps.

1. Return to the CLIENT virtual machine.

2. Enter vmm.test.local:8100 for Server name.

3. Click Specify credentials. Enter test\vmmrun for the User name. Enter Pa$$w0rd for the Password.

4. Check Automatically connect with these settings. Click Connect.

5. Expand Clouds and click PRIVATE.

View VMM Console

The Tenant Administrator uses the VMM Console to work with virtual machines (see Figure 7.23). He can only see the resources that are provided by the user profile.

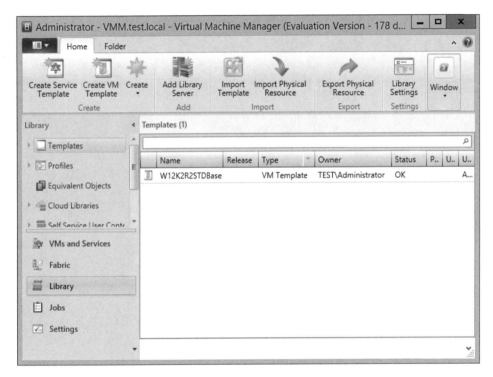

Figure 7.23
VMM Console for Tenant Administrator.
Source: VMM Administrator Console/Windows Server 2012.

1. To view the Library components that are available on the PRIVATE Cloud, click the Library view.

2. Expand Library.

Deploy a Virtual Machine

To verify that your private cloud functions correctly, you can have Peter Cloud, the Tenant Administrator, deploy a virtual machine. As you will see, the virtual machine wizard draws components from the Library to build the virtual machine. In Chapter 8, "Working with Application Self-Service Users," this virtual machine, called PrivateBase, will be used to create a virtual machine template. The virtual machine template becomes the Library component for the deployment of virtual machines by application self-service users.

Start Virtual Machine Wizard

To start the virtual machine wizard and build the PrivateBase virtual machine, complete these steps:

1. Click VMs and Services.

2. Expand Clouds. Click PRIVATE. Click Create Virtual Machine.

3. To specify the virtual hard disk, click Browse. Click Blank Disk – Small.vhdx. Click OK and then click Next.

4. Enter PrivateBase for the Virtual machine name. Click Next.

Complete Hardware Profile

As you deploy the virtual machine, you update the hardware profile for this new virtual machine.

1. Click the Hardware profile chevron and select HP-1NET-1VHD-512MBD.

2. Click Virtual DVD Drive, click Existing ISO image, click Browse, select Windows Server 2012 R2, and then click OK.

3. Scroll and click Network Adapter 1, click Connect to a VM Network, click Browse, and click Service VM Network. Click OK.

4. Click VM subnet, click Customer Addresses, click Port profile Classification chevron, and select Medium bandwidth.

5. Click Availability and then click Make this virtual machine highly available.

6. Click Next.

Select Destination

Figure 7.24 shows that the default for private cloud deployment is retained.

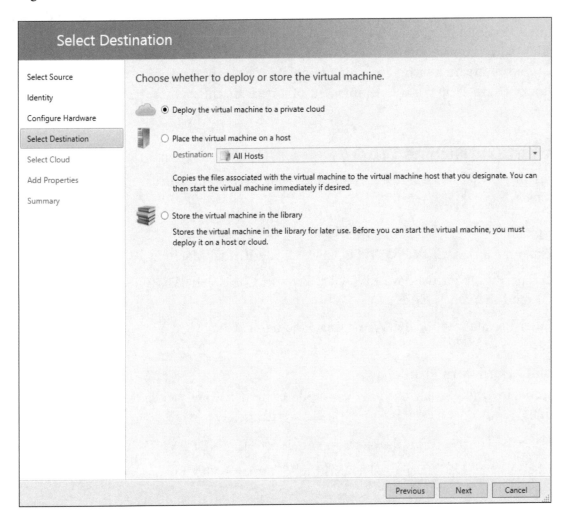

Figure 7.24
Virtual Machine Wizard Select Destination page.
Source: VMM Administrator Console/Windows Server 2012.

1. To select the destination, retain the Deploy the virtual machine to a private cloud.

2. Click Next.

Select Cloud

On the next page, you can select the host computer in the COMPUTE host group to place the virtual machine. You should select the host computer with the highest star rating (see Figure 7.25).

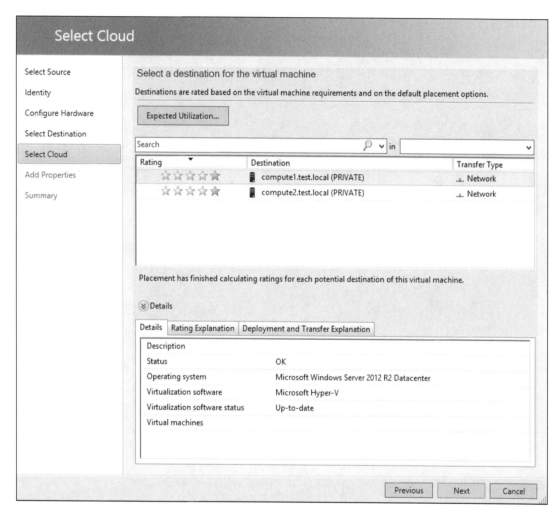

Figure 7.25
Virtual Machine Wizard Select Cloud.
Source: VMM Administrator Console/Windows Server 2012.

1. To specify the server in the cloud, click compute1.test.local(PRIVATE).
2. Click Next.

Add Properties

On the Properties page, you can specify the actions to take on start and shutdown. The defaults will work.

1. Review the Properties page.

2. Click Next.

Review Summary

See Figure 7.26 for the Summary.

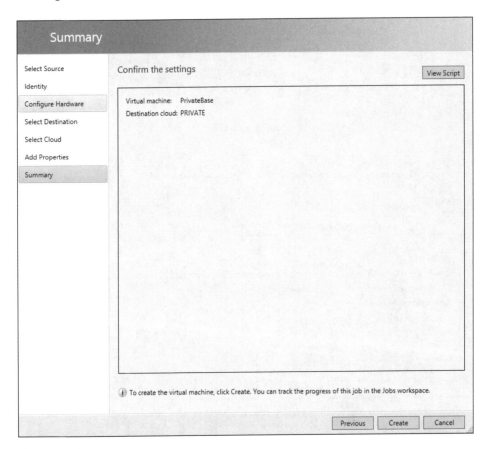

Figure 7.26
Virtual Machine Wizard Summary for review.
Source: VMM Administrator Console/Windows Server 2012.

1. Review the Summary.

2. Click Create.

3. Wait for the deployment to complete.

Script Creates Virtual Machine

In the Jobs window, you can see the progress of the script to deploy the virtual machine (see Figure 7.27). You may ignore the "VMM could not offload the transfer" message. The copy offload provides a mechanism to perform full-file copies between two host servers. In this case, the copy was between the library server and a host computer, and the copy offload could not be used.

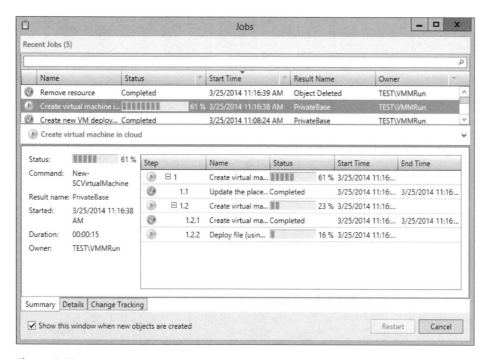

Figure 7.27
Jobs showing script executing.
Source: VMM Administrator Console/Windows Server 2012.

Virtual Machine Placed in COMPUTE

After the deployment completes, the virtual machine is placed on the host computer, as shown in Figure 7.28. Clicking on the entry provides a context menu from which you can connect to the virtual machine.

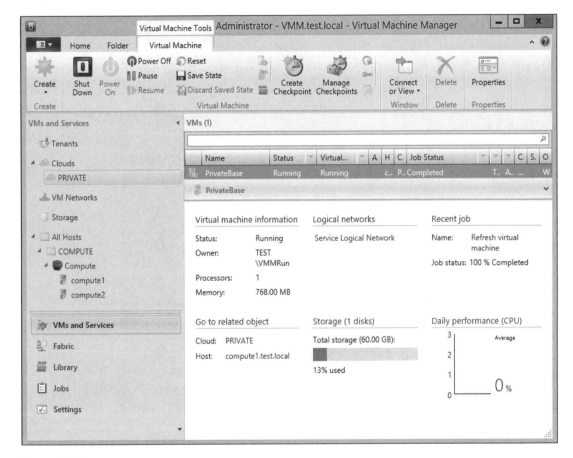

Figure 7.28
Virtual Machine placed on the host computer.
Source: VMM Administrator Console/Windows Server 2012.

1. To start the PrivateBase virtual machine, right-click the entry in PRIVATE and select Power On.

2. To connect to the PrivateBase virtual machine, right-click the entry in PRIVATE, click Connect or View, and then select Connect via console.

Complete Operating System Installation

To configure the operating system installation, complete these steps.

1. Using Chapter 1, "Introduction to the Private Cloud," as a guideline, configure the OS in the Client virtual machine using the suggested settings in Table 7.2.

Table 7.2   Suggested Settings for Client Virtual Machine Installation

Item	Suggested Setting
Password	Pa$$w0rd
IPV4 Address	Provided by Service VM Network
Computer name	PrivateBase

2. To log on, click the Action menu, click Ctrl+Alt+Delete, and then enter Pa$$w0rd.

3. Continue with the steps in Chapter 1 using the suggested settings in Table 2.6.

4. Wait for the install to complete and complete the configuration of the PrivateBase virtual machine.

5. To shut down the PrivateBase virtual machine, click Local Server, click Tasks, and then click Shut Down Local Server. Click the Chevron and select Shut down. Click the Option chevron and select Operating System: Reconfiguration (Planned). Click OK.

6. After the shutdown of the virtual machine, return to the VMM console, right-click PrivateBase, click Properties, click Hardware Configuration, click Virtual DVD Drive, and click No media. Click OK.

SUMMARY

In this chapter, you created the PRIVATE Cloud. You saw the efforts of the previous six chapters come together.

- You took care of a few incidentals in preparation for creating the PRIVATE Cloud, such as creating shared folders, updating the library, and creating security groups and user accounts.

- You created the Tenant Administrator role to manage the PRIVATE Cloud.

- With the Create Cloud Wizard, you created the PRIVATE Cloud.

- To verify that the PRIVATE Cloud worked, you deployed your first virtual machine to the cloud.

CASE PROJECTS

Case 7-1: Biggest Private Cloud

Now that you have your small private cloud running, have you ever thought about who has the "biggest" private cloud? Do a Web search for "world's largest private cloud."

Case 7-2: Impact of Private Cloud Computing

A number of research firms survey IT's interest in many topics. See if you can determine the impact of the private cloud in organizations. Try a search for "impact of private cloud computing."

CHAPTER 8

WORKING WITH APPLICATION SELF-SERVICE USERS

After reading this chapter and completing the exercises, you will be able to do the following:

- Describe the App Controller.
- Create a virtual machine template.
- Create an Application Self-Service User.
- Install the App Controller.
- Deploy virtual machines.

In the previous chapter, you built the PRIVATE Cloud and created the Tenant Administrator role. In this chapter, you will continue with the actions of the Tenant Administrator and implement the application self-service user role. A key component for the application self-service user to gain access to virtual machines is the App Controller. Microsoft provides App Controller as a product for managing applications that are deployed in private clouds. In this chapter, you will install and configure it.

DESCRIBING THE APP CONTROLLER

Microsoft states that the App Controller is a self-service portal for application owners to manage their IT services housed in private clouds. App Controller is a Silverlight-based, IIS website with a SQL Database back-end that connects directly to VMM. Microsoft

Silverlight is an application framework for running rich Internet applications, with features similar to those of Adobe Flash.

Figure 8.1 shows that the data flows between components from a client computer with a Web browser to a Web server, then to the App Controller, through the VMM server, and finally to a virtual machine. The App Controller is the key component in this communication chain.

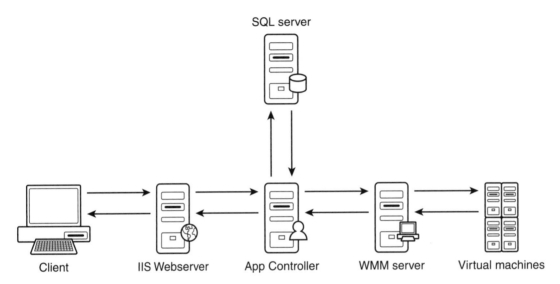

Figure 8.1
Interaction of application components.
© 2014 Cengage Learning®.

App Controller is intended to be used by application owners: the people who deploy and manage an application. You should not confuse these owners with the end users who actually use an application. End users should not be doing anything with App Controller.

An owner might be an administrator or a developer who needs a platform to test an application. The key point is self-servicing: App Controller enables application owners to deploy new instances of an application without requiring them to deal with jobs such as creating VMs, VHDs, or networks, or installing OSs. To achieve that level of automation, the administrator should do a lot of work in VMM.

App Controller can't create or manage building blocks for VMs, nor can it be used to create new objects from scratch. Anything you work with in App Controller, such as guest

OS profiles, hardware profiles, and VM networks, must be created by the administrator. As a Tenant Administrator, you create application self-service user roles and associate these roles with private clouds and quotas.

App Controller doesn't have its own security infrastructure. It relies completely on the security settings in VMM, so available options for a user in App Controller depend directly on the rights and permissions that are assigned to the self-service user in VMM. Authentication is performed by using a Web-based form.

CREATING A VM TEMPLATE USING VM ON HOST

To help your self-service users deploy virtual machines, you create a virtual machine (VM) template. For consistency, you create the template based on the PrivateBase virtual machine you created and deployed to the PRIVATE cloud in Chapter 7, "Creating the Private Cloud."

To create a VM Template, you use the Create VM Template Wizard. There are seven pages in this wizard.

Select Source

If the virtual machine that you intend to use is running, you must shut it down. Also, check to see that the DVD Drive does not have the .iso file that was used to install the operating system.

The flow of this wizard is similar to other wizards in VMM. After starting the wizard, you select the source for the VM template. Rather than selecting an object in the library, you start with an existing virtual machine previously deployed to a host computer in COMPUTE. Figure 8.2 shows the Select Source page.

You will see a warning that creating a template will destroy the existing virtual machine. This is OK, as PrivateBase was created in Chapter 7 to be used for a future VM template. Prior to moving the virtual machine to the library, SYSPREP, a Windows utility that allows a computer to be generalized, will be run on the virtual machine. Running SYSPREP allows the PC to be generalized with new, unique IDs so that you get an "Out of the Box" experience (OOBE) after the virtual machine is deployed.

Figure 8.2
Create VM Template Wizard Select Source.
Source: Windows Server 2012 R2/System Center VMM 2012 R2.

1. Return to the VMM virtual machine and the Virtual Machine Manager.

2. Click the Library view.

3. To start the Create VM Template Wizard, click Create VM Template.

4. To indicate that the source virtual machine is on a host, click From an existing virtual machine that is deployed on a host, and then click Browse.

5. Click PrivateBase and then click OK. Click Next.

6. When you see the warning message that creating a VM template will destroy the virtual machine, click Yes.

Identify Template

Figure 8.3 shows the VM template named with an identity. This is the name that the application self-service user will select when a virtual machine is deployed.

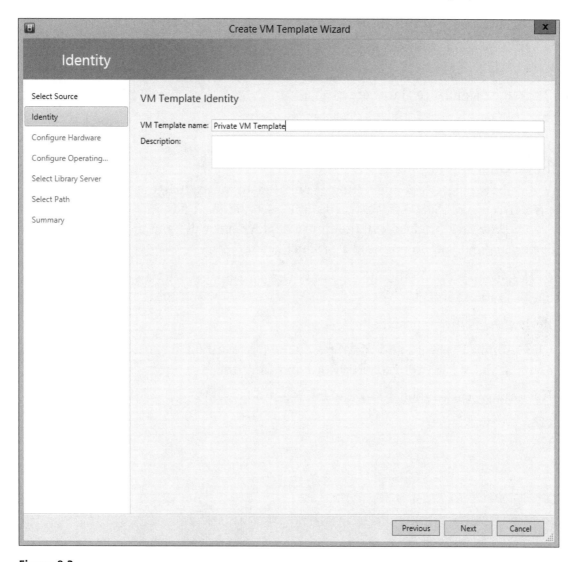

Figure 8.3
Create VM Template Wizard Identity page.
Source: Windows Server 2012 R2/System Center VMM 2012 R2.

1. Enter Private VM Template for the VM Template name.

2. Click Next.

Review Hardware Configuration

As the hardware configuration was set when PrivateBase was created, you can't change the hardware profile.

1. Review the Configure Hardware profile.

2. Click Next.

Configure Operating System

Figure 8.4 shows the OS configuration. You need to verify that the Operating System entry is correct and change it. Also, you must set the local administrator password. If you do not provide a product key, the future deployment will hang. If you are using the 180-day evaluation, you do not need a product key.

1. Click the Guest OS Profile chevron and select Create new Windows operating system customization settings.

2. Review the Software profile.

3. Click Admin Password and click Specify the password for the local administrator account. Enter Pa$$w0rd for Password and Confirm.

4. If necessary, click Product Key and enter a product key.

5. Click Next.

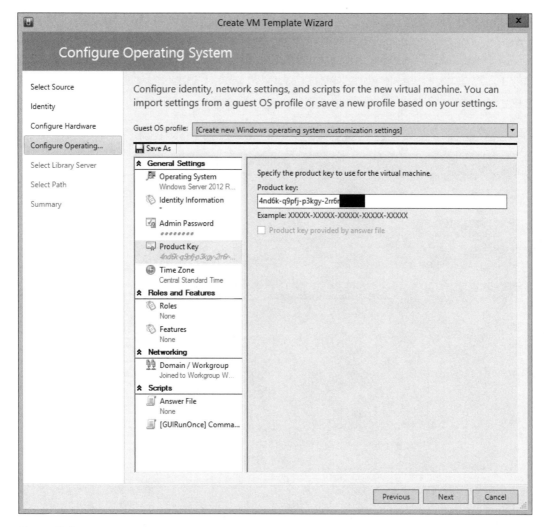

Figure 8.4
Create VM Template Wizard Configure Operating System.
Source: Windows Server 2012 R2/System Center VMM 2012 R2.

Select Library Server

Since you have only the vmm.test.local library server, the default is OK.

1. Review the Library Server.

2. Click Next.

Select Destination Folder

After browsing, you will be presented with the option to select a folder where you want to place the VM template. The best choice is to place it in the MSSCVMMLibrary where it will be easy to retrieve when creating the self-service role. Figure 8.5 shows the results of this choice.

Figure 8.5
Create VM Template Wizard Select Path.
Source: Windows Server 2012 R2/System Center VMM 2012 R2.

1. Click Browse and then select MSSCVMMLibrary. Click OK.
2. Click Next.

Review Summary

On the next page, you will review the summary,. Recall that you can return to a previous page to make a correction. It should take about five minutes to create the template.

1. Review the Summary.

2. Click Create.

Add VM Template to Tenant Administrator

For the Tenant Administrator to use this created template, you must add it to the user role. The properties for user roles are available at the Security node under Settings. The completed addition is shown in Figure 8.6.

Figure 8.6
VM template added to Resources.

Source: Windows Server 2012 R2/System Center VMM 2012 R2.

1. Click Settings view. Expand Security and then click User Roles.

2. Right-click PrivateTenantAdmin and then click Properties.

3. Click Resources, click Add, and then select Private VM Template. Click OK twice.

CREATING AN APPLICATION SELF-SERVICE USER ROLE

You created the Tenant Administrator user role in Chapter 7. The Tenant Administrator defines the objects that self-service users can manage and the management operations that these users can perform in the PRIVATE cloud.

One of the tasks for this administrator is to create the Application Self-Service User roles. Members of the Application Self-Service User role can create, deploy, and manage their own virtual machines and services by using the VMM console or a Web portal.

Create Security for User Role

By using security groups, you can control who has the permissions to use the elements within the PRIVATE cloud. To set up this security, complete these steps:

1. Return to the ADDS virtual machine.

2. In the Server Manager, click Tasks and then click Active Directory Users and Computers.

3. Create a Domain Local security group: AppSelfService.

4. Create a new user: Sarah for the First name, enter Self for the Last name, enter SSelf for the User logon name.

5. Enter Pa$$w0rd for the Password and Confirm password. Clear the User must change password at next logon option, and then click Password never expires. Click Next. Click Finish.

6. Right-click Sarah Self, click Add to a group, enter Private, click Check Names, click Private, and then click OK three times.

7. Right-click Sarah Self, click Add to a group, enter AppSelfService, click Check Names, and then click OK twice.

Create Folder for AppSelfService Users

Users of the Application Self-Service User Role may need a folder to store files as they work with their virtual machines. This requires a folder in the path of the folder assigned to the Tenant Administrator. To create this folder, complete these steps.

1. Return to the VMM virtual machine. Click the Windows Explorer icon and navigate to C:\Cloud Resources.

2. Create a new folder called AppSelfService.

3. To share the folder, right-click AppSelfService, click Properties, click the Sharing tab, click Advanced Sharing, click Share this folder, click Permissions, click Allow - Full Control, and then click OK twice.

4. To set the security, click the Security tab, click Edit, click Add, enter AppSelfService, click Check Names, and click OK. Click Allow - Modify, and then click OK twice. Click Close.

5. Return to the Virtual Machine Manager.

6. Click Library and Expand Library Servers.

7. Right-click vmm.test.local and select Add library shares.

8. Check AppSelfService, click Next, click Add Library Shares, and close the Jobs window.

9. Right-click vmm.test.local and then select Refresh.

Using the Create User Role Wizard

As the Tenant Administrator, you create an Application Self-Service User Role in VMM to define the scope of management operations for the users of the PRIVATE cloud. Members of the Application Self-Service User Role can create, deploy, and manage their own virtual machines by using the VMM console.

This role should be created by the Tenant Administrator. For this to be done properly, log on as PCloud and assume the persona of Peter Cloud on the CLIENT virtual machine.

Provide Name for Self-Service Role

After starting the Create User Role Wizard, you provide a name for the new user role.

1. Return to the Client VM.

2. Log on as Peter Cloud using PCloud and Pa$$w0rd.

3. Click the VMs and Services node.

4. Right-click Tenants and click Create User Role.

5. Enter AppSelfService for the Name and then click Next.

Select Profile

Figure 8.7 shows the Application Administrator role selected. This role allows the self-service user to create, deploy, and run virtual machines.

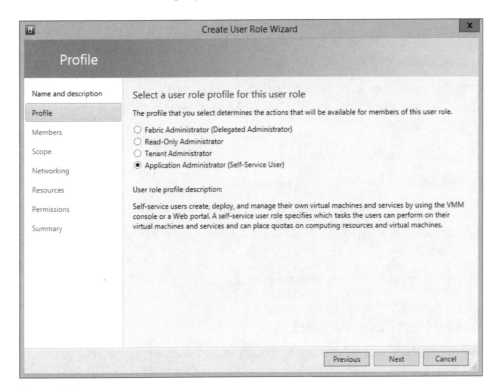

Figure 8.7
Create User Profile Wizard select profile.
Source: Windows Server 2012 R2/System Center VMM 2012 R2.

1. Click Application Administrator (Self-Service User).

2. Click Next.

Provide Members

On the next page, see Figure 8.8, you provide the security group that contains the potential users. Recall that Sarah Self (SSelf) is a member of the AppSelfService security group.

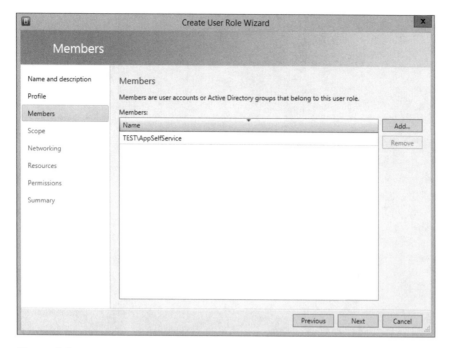

Figure 8.8
Create User Profile Wizard add AppSelfService security group.
Source: Windows Server 2012 R2/System Center VMM 2012 R2.

1. Click Add, enter AppSelfService, and click Check Names. Click OK.

2. Click Next.

Identify Cloud

After identifying the self-service users, you identify the cloud for them. The PRIVATE cloud works.

1. Click PRIVATE.

2. Click Next.

Specify Member Level Quotas

You need to ration the resources used by individual self-service users. Table 8.1 specifies the resources that an individual member uses in proportion to the capacity for the private cloud. This rations resources so that all users have a chance to run their virtual machines. For a completed page, see Figure 8.9.

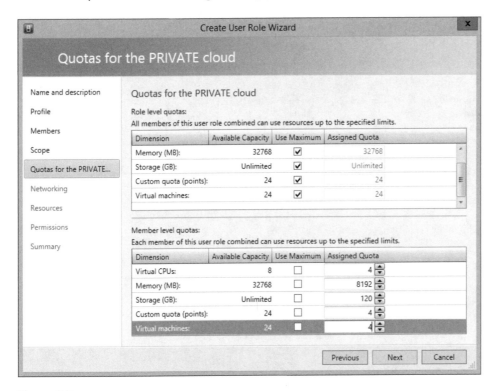

Figure 8.9
Create User Profile Wizard specify quotas.

Source: Windows Server 2012 R2/System Center VMM 2012 R2.

1. Using Table 8.1 as a guide, enter the Member level quotas.
2. Click Next.

Table 8.1   Member Level Quotas

Dimension	Assigned Quota
Virtual CPUs	4
Memory (MB)	8192
Storage (GB)	120
Custom quota (points)	4
Virtual machines	4

© 2014 Cengage Learning®.

Identify VM Network

On the next page, you identify the VM network. You created the Service VM Network in Chapter 4, "Working with Networks Using VMM," for this purpose (see Figure 8.10). The Management Network is reserved for the virtual machines running on the MANAGE server.

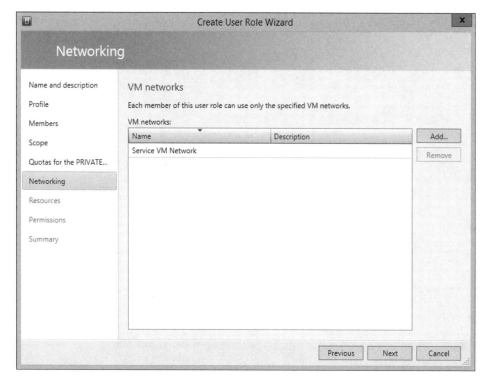

Figure 8.10
Create User Profile Wizard identify VM network.
Source: Windows Server 2012 R2/System Center VMM 2012 R2.

1. Click Add, click Service VM Network, and then click OK.
2. Click Next.

Identify Resources

Here is where you add the previously created Private VM Template. In the Create Folder for AppSelfService Users section, you created a folder called AppServiceFolder. The completed addition is shown in Figure 8.11.

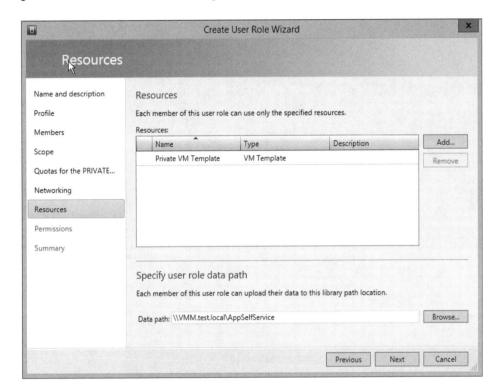

Figure 8.11
Create User Profile Wizard identify Resources.
Source: Windows Server 2012 R2/System Center VMM 2012 R2.

1. To add a template to deploy virtual machines, click Add, click Private VM Template, and then click OK.

2. To add a library folder for use by the self-service users, click Browse and select AppSelfService. Click OK.

3. Click Next.

Select Permissions

On the next page, you select the permitted actions for the AppSelfService user role. Table 8.2 shows these permitted actions. You are restricting the members to deploying virtual machines from the Private VM Template and running the deployed virtual machines (see Figure 8.12).

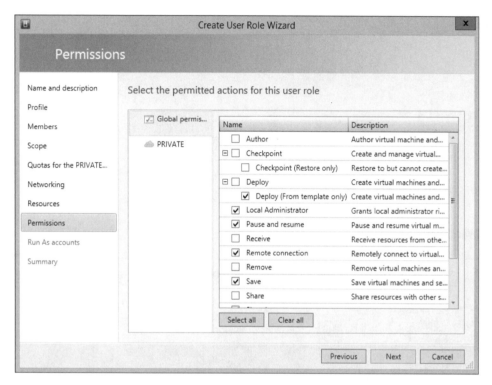

Figure 8.12
Create User Profile Wizard select Permissions.
Source: Windows Server 2012 R2/System Center VMM 2012 R2.

1. Using Table 8.2, select the indicated permissions.

2. Click Next.

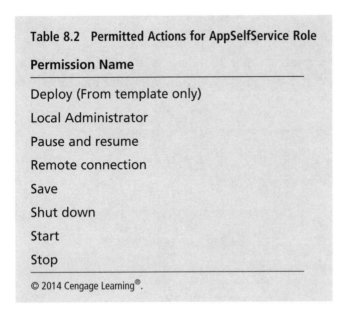

Table 8.2 **Permitted Actions for AppSelfService Role**

Permission Name
Deploy (From template only)
Local Administrator
Pause and resume
Remote connection
Save
Shut down
Start
Stop

© 2014 Cengage Learning®.

Specify Run As Accounts

You select a Run As account for the Self-Service User role to use with the templates that they use to deploy virtual machines. Figure 8.13 shows the Private Run As Account after selection.

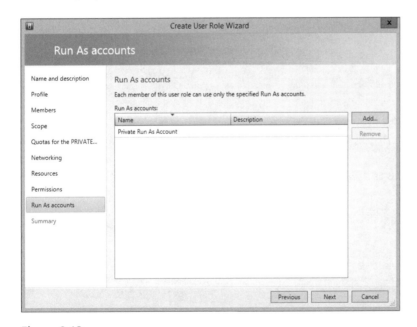

Figure 8.13
Create User Profile Wizard specify Run As account.
Source: Windows Server 2012 R2/System Center VMM 2012 R2.

1. Click Add and click Private Run As Account. Click OK.

2. Click Next.

Review Summary

On the next page, you review the summary (see Figure 8.14). To make a correction, return to a previous page.

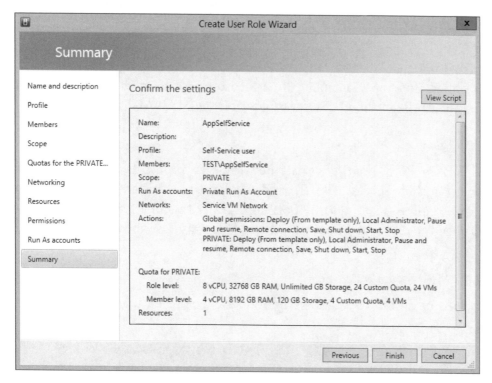

Figure 8.14
Create User Profile Wizard review Summary.
Source: Windows Server 2012 R2/System Center VMM 2012 R2.

1. Review the Summary.

2. Click Finish.

3. Wait for the script to finish.

4. Close the Jobs window.

INSTALLING APP CONTROLLER

In this section, you will install the prerequisites and then install the App Controller. You download the App Controller .iso file, resolve the BITS transfer conflict, and configure IE. Then you are ready to install the App Controller.

Installing and Configuring Prerequisites

There are a number of small tasks that need to be completed prior to installing the App Controller. Complete the following three tasks first.

Download App Controller

You will need to obtain the App Controller 2012 R2 iso and a product key. For ease of installation, place this iso file in the C:\ISOfiles folder on the MANAGE host computer.

Frozen BITS Transfer

A conflict, called *Frozen BITS Transfer*, exists between two protocols, Microsoft Background Intelligent Transfer Service (BITS) and Hypertext Transfer Protocol Secure (HTTPS), which are trying to use the same port 443. To fix this problem, move BITS to another port and open the Advanced Firewall inbound port, as described in the following steps:

1. Return to the VMM virtual machine.

2. To start the Registry Editor, press the Windows key, type regedit, and click the regedit icon.

3. To change the key, expand HKEY_LOCAL_MACHINE, expand SOFTWARE, expand Microsoft, and scroll and expand Microsoft System Center Virtual Machine Manager Server. Click Settings, right-click BITSTcpPort, click Modify, click Decimal, enter 8500, and click OK. Close the Registry Editor window.

4. To restart the System Center Virtual Machine Management service, point to Tools and click Services. Scroll and right-click System Center Virtual Machine Management and click Restart. Wait for the service to restart. Close the open windows.

5. Return to the Server Manager on the COMPUTE1 host computer.

6. To open the new port, point to Tools and click Windows Firewall with Advanced Security. Click Inbound Rules, click New Rule in the right pane, click Port, and click Next. Enter 8500, click Next, click Allow the connection, click Next twice, enter Open 8500 in the Name text box, and click Finish. Close the Windows Firewall with Advanced Security window.

7. To restart the management services, point to Tools and click Services. Scroll and right-click Windows Remote Management (WS-Management), click Restart, and click Yes. Wait for the services to restart. Close the open windows.

8. Repeat steps 5 through 7 for COMPUTE2.

Configure IE Enhanced Security Configuration

1. Go to the CLIENT virtual machine.

2. Press the Windows key, click Peter Cloud, and then click Sign Out.

3. Log on as test\administrator with Pa$$w0rd.

4. Click Local Server on Server Manager. Click IE Enhanced Security Configuration, click Users – Off, and Click OK.

5. Press the Windows key, click Administrator, and then click Sign Out.

6. Log on as test\PCloud with Pa$$w0rd.

Installing the App Controller

You install the App Controller on the VMM virtual machine by completing twelve pages in this installation.

Start App Controller Setup

You start the installation of the App Controller Server from the App Controller Setup, as shown in Figure 8.15.

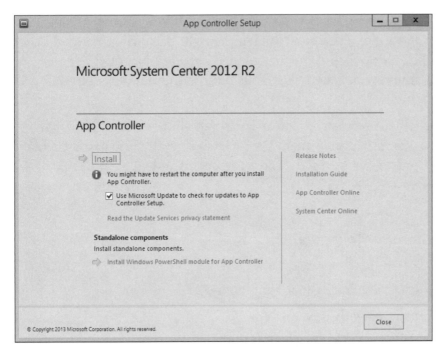

Figure 8.15
App Controller Setup App Controller install.

Source: Windows Server 2012 R2/System Center App Controller 2012 R2.

1. Return to the VMM virtual machine.

2. Click Media on the menu bar, point to DVD Drive, click Insert Disk, click the App Controller iso file, and then click Open.

3. Click the Windows Explorer icon, right-click the DVD Drive (D:) SC2012R2AC, and then select Install or run program from your media.

4. Click Install. Wait for the update check.

Steps for SCAC 2012 R2 Evaluation

If you are using the SCAC 2012 R2 evaluation software, replace steps 2 and 3 with these steps:

1. Click Media on the menu bar, point to DVD Drive, and click Capture D.

2. To extract the VMM files, click the Windows Explorer Icon, double-click DVD Drive (D:), double-click SC2012_R2_SCAC, and click Next.

3. Change D:\SC2012_R2_SCAC to C:\SC2012_R2_SCAC and click Next. Click Extract.

4. Wait for the extraction to complete. Click Finish.

5. Navigate to the C:\SC2012 R2 SCAC folder and double-click setup.

Enter Product Key

On the next page, you enter the product key. This is the same product key that you used for the VMM install. The SCAC 2012 R2 evaluation software doesn't need a product key.

1. If this is not the SCAC 2012 R2 evaluation software, enter your product key.
2. Click Next.

Review License Terms

Next, you can now review and accept the software license terms.

1. Review the license terms.
2. Click I have read, understood, and agree with the terms of the license agreement.
3. Click Next.

Check Prerequisites

In the next step, the installation checks to see if you have the proper hardware and software available. A progress bar indicates the progress. After checking, the setup proceeds on its own. Wait for the prerequisite check to complete.

Install Missing Software

After the prerequisite check, the setup displays the names of missing software, as shown in Figure 8.16. The setup can only install roles and role services.

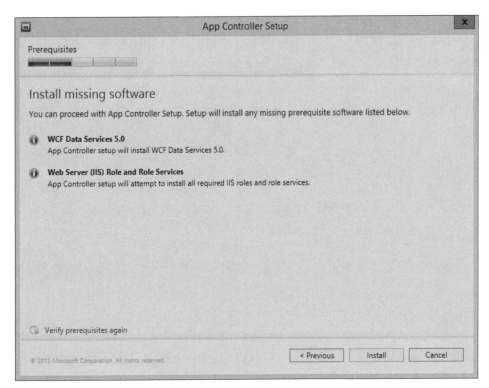

Figure 8.16
App Controller Setup display names of missing software.
Source: Windows Server 2012 R2/System Center App Controller 2012 R2.

1. Review the names and click Install.

2. Wait for the installation of roles and role services to complete.

Select Installation Path

On the next page, the default installation path is shown. The default location meets your needs.

1. Review installation path.

2. Click Next.

Configure the Services

On the next page, you enter the administrative account that will be used for configuration. The VMMAdmin account works just fine (see Figure 8.17).

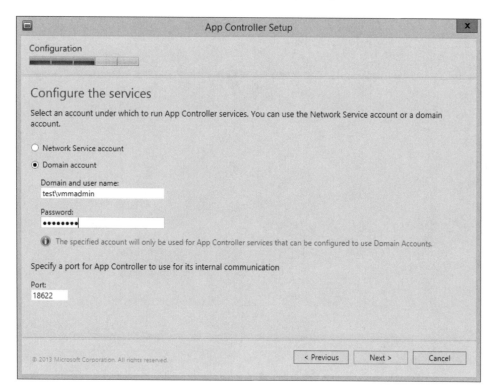

Figure 8.17
App Controller Setup specify Domain account for configuration.
Source: Windows Server 2012 R2/System Center App Controller 2012 R2.

1. Enter test\vmmadmin for the Domain account and Pa$$w0rd for the password.

2. Click Next.

Configure the Website

Figure 8.18 shows the website configuration. The IP address for the VMM virtual machine will work. Also, you must request a self-signed certificate, which is needed to secure the website.

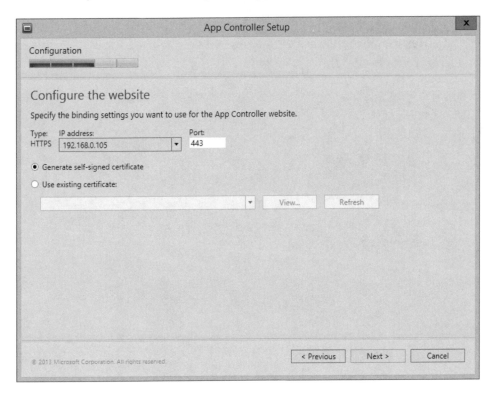

Figure 8.18
App Controller Setup Configure the website.

Source: Windows Server 2012 R2/System Center App Controller 2012 R2.

1. Click the IP address chevron and select 192.168.0.105.

2. Click Generate self-signed certificate.

3. Click Next.

Configure the SQL Server Database

On the next page, you configure the settings to connect to the existing SQL server and install the AppController database. The settings for the SQL server are shown in Figure 8.19.

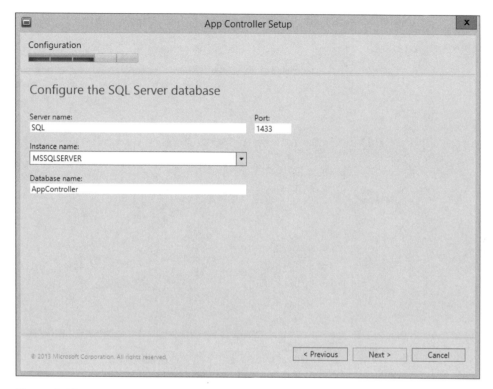

Figure 8.19
App Controller Setup Configure the SQL Server database.
Source: Windows Server 2012 R2/System Center App Controller 2012 R2.

1. Enter SQL for the Server name and 1433 for the Port.

2. Enter MSSQLSERVER for the Instance name.

3. Wait for the connection to the SQL server.

4. Click Next.

5. Wait for the configuration of the SQL server to complete.

Help Improve App Controller

The next page shows the Help Improve App Controller for System Center 2012 R2 page. Also, you can choose to receive updates for App Controller.

1. As your conscience dictates, choose No or Yes to the CEIP request.

2. Click Use Microsoft Update.

3. Click Next.

Confirm Settings

On the next page (see Figure 8.20), you can review the settings. If you like these settings, you are ready to install. Otherwise, return to the previous page and make the corrections.

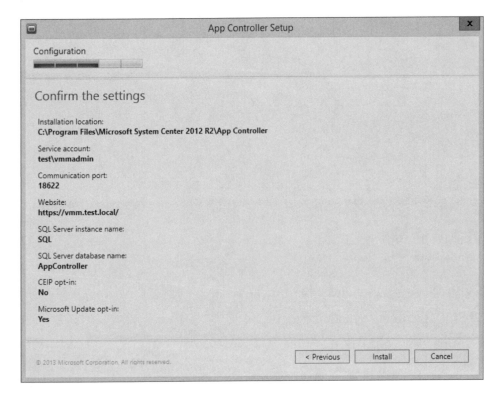

Figure 8.20
App Controller Setup Confirm the settings.
Source: Windows Server 2012 R2/System Center App Controller 2012 R2.

1. Review the settings. Click Previous to make changes.

2. Click Install.

Installing Components

Figure 8.21 shows the progress of the installation.

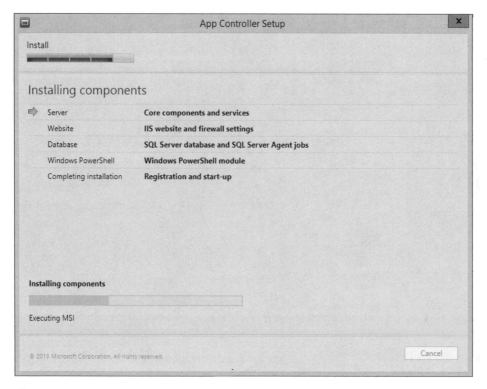

Figure 8.21
App Controller Setup Installing components.
Source: Windows Server 2012 R2/System Center App Controller 2012 R2.

Setup Completed Successfully

Figure 8.22 shows a successful installation. If Setup is unable to complete, you are provided with a list showing which items could not be installed, along with links to the related log files. Review these logs for more information about where the Setup issue occurred.

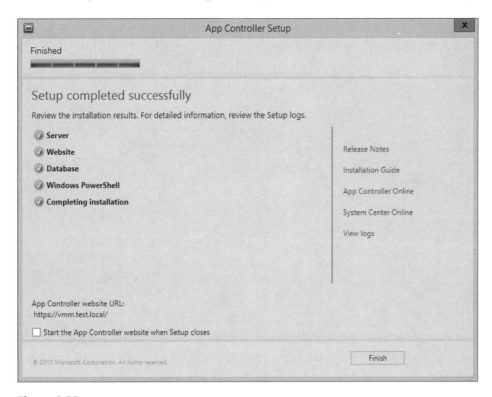

Figure 8.22
App Controller Setup completed successfully.

Source: Windows Server 2012 R2/System Center App Controller 2012 R2.

1. Review the Setup completed successfully page.

2. Click Finish.

3. Log off and restart the VMM virtual machine.

Deploying Virtual Machines

With the Private VM Template created by the administrator and the Self-Service Role created by the Tenant Administrator, you are ready for Sarah Self to deploy her four virtual machines.

Configuring App Controller Website

You will need to complete a few tasks the first time you access the App Controller website. You will see a certificate error with the text Continue to this website (not recommended). On the second access, the certificates will be copied and available to the Internet Explorer.

After you complete these tasks, you assume the persona of Sarah Self to access this website from the Internet Explorer and work with her virtual machines.

You sign in to the App Controller by entering your credentials, as shown in Figure 8.23.

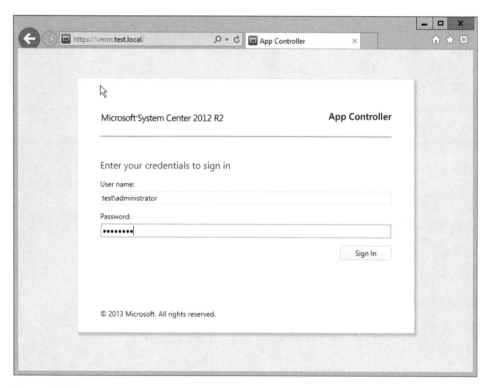

Figure 8.23
Sign in to the App Controller website.
Source: Windows Server 2012 R2/System Center App Controller 2012 R2.

To use the App Controller for the first time, you need to complete these steps:

1. Return to the CLIENT virtual machine.

2. To log out PCloud, press the Windows Key, click Peter Cloud, and click Sign out.

3. Log on with user test\administrator and a password of Pa$$w0rd.

4. To start Internet Explorer, press the Windows Key and click Internet Explorer.

5. When the Set up Internet Explorer 11 page appears, click Use recommended security and compatibility settings, and then click OK.

6. To access the App Controller website, enter https://vmm.test.local/ for the address and press Enter.

Website Work-around

If you are unable to connect to the App Controller website, use https://192.168.0.105/ in place of https://vmm.test.local/.

7. To access the website and avoid the certificate conflict, click Continue to this website (not recommended).

8. To install Silverlight, click Install now. Click Run. Click Install now.

9. Wait for Silverlight to be installed. Click Next and then click Close.

10. Press F5 to refresh the Web page.

11. Enter test\administrator for the user name and Pa$$w0rd for the password.

12. Click Sign In.

Add a New VMM connection

After you complete the connection information and connect the first time, you will be taken directly to the VMM.test.local website (see Figure 8.24).

Figure 8.24
Add a new VMM Connection.
Source: Windows Server 2012 R2/System Center App Controller 2012 R2.

1. Click Connect to a Virtual Machine Manager server and clouds under Common Tasks.

2. Enter PRIVATE for the Connection name.

3. Enter vmm.test.local for the Server name.

4. Retain the check in Automatically import SSL certificates.

5. Click OK.

6. Click Clouds node, click Connect, and then select VMM server.

7. Wait for the connection to be made.

8. To log out as Administrator, click Sign out in the App Controller menu.

Viewing the App Controller Web Pages

Since the website pages differ from the windows in the VMM console, you can take a look at these pages as the Self-Service user Sarah Self.

Review App Controller Overview Page

After sign-in, the App Controller Web page is displayed. Figure 8.25 shows the Overview node.

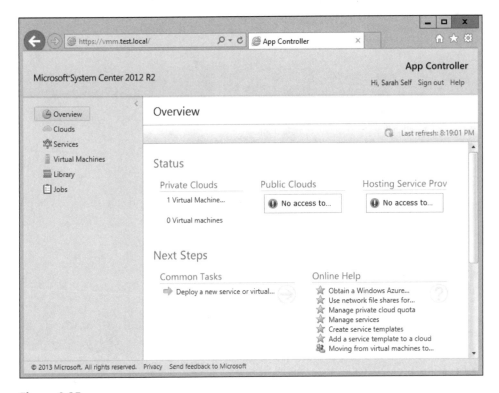

Figure 8.25
App Controller Overview page.
Source: Windows Server 2012 R2/System Center App Controller 2012 R2.

1. Log on to App Controller with user test\Self and a password of Pa$$w0rd.

2. Review the Overview.

Review App Controller Clouds Page

Figure 8.26 shows the Clouds node. Sarah has a connection to the PRIVATE cloud.

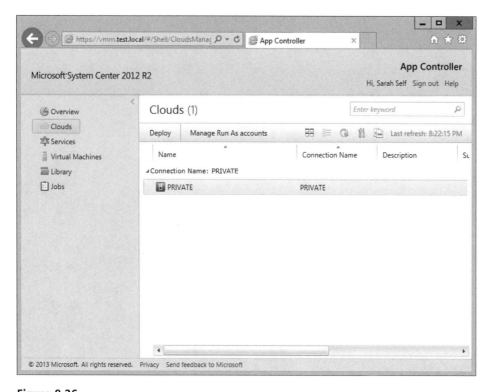

Figure 8.26
App Controller Clouds page.
Source: Windows Server 2012 R2/System Center App Controller 2012 R2.

1. Click the Clouds node.

2. Review the Clouds node.

Review App Controller Virtual Machines Page

On the Virtual Machines node, you can see where the running virtual machines are listed. Also, you can start and connect to virtual machines here. Figure 8.27 shows the Virtual Machines node.

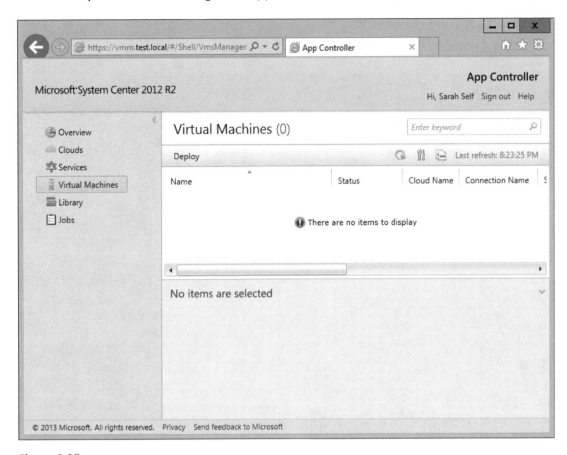

Figure 8.27
App Controller Virtual Machines page.
Source: Windows Server 2012 R2/System Center App Controller 2012 R2.

1. Click the Virtual Machines node.

2. Review the Virtual Machines node.

Review App Controller Library Page

Figure 8.28 shows the Library node. From this node, you can see the Private VM Template in the Templates node, which Sarah will use to deploy her virtual machines.

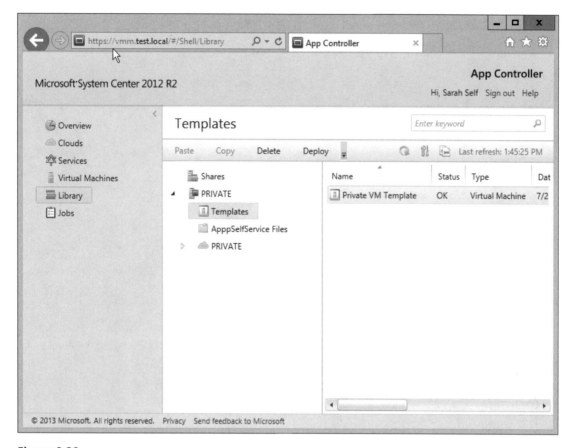

Figure 8.28
App Controller Templates page showing Private VM Template.
Source: Windows Server 2012 R2/System Center App Controller 2012 R2.

1. Click the Library node.

2. Review the Library node.

3. Expand PRIVATE and click Templates.

Review App Controller Jobs Page

When you create virtual machines, you can see the status of the running PowerShell script on the Jobs node. Figure 8.29 shows the Jobs node.

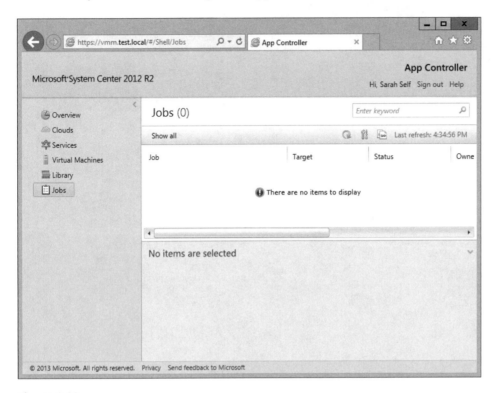

Figure 8.29
App Controller Jobs page.
Source: Windows Server 2012 R2/System Center App Controller 2012 R2.

1. Click the Jobs node.
2. Review the Jobs node.

Deploying a Virtual Machine

As an Application Administrator Self-Service User, Sarah Self can deploy virtual machines.

Start Deployment

From the Virtual Machines node, Sarah starts the virtual machine deployment. Figure 8.30 shows the Virtual Machines page.

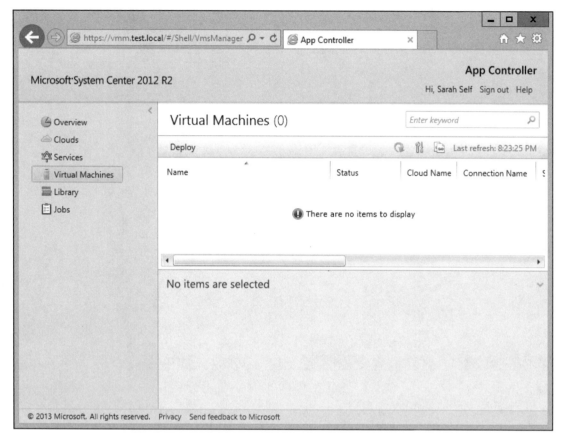

Figure 8.30
App Controller New Deployment page.
Source: Windows Server 2012 R2/System Center App Controller 2012 R2.

1. Click the Virtual Machines node.

2. Click the Deploy icon.

Select the Private Cloud

Figure 8.31 shows the Configure a cloud option for this New Deployment page. When you see a red star, this indicates you have a task to complete.

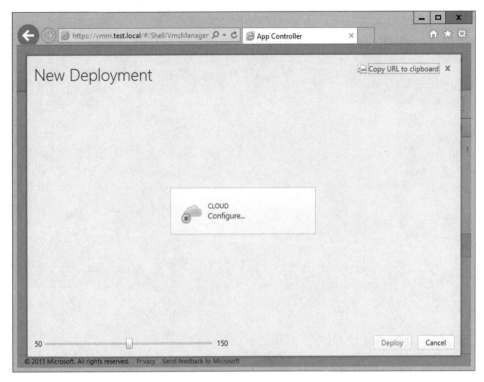

Figure 8.31
Configure a cloud for this deployment.

Source: Windows Server 2012 R2/System Center App Controller 2012 R2.

1. Click the Configure link.

2. Wait for the pop-up to appear.

Review Resources

After you select the Configure link, a pop-up appears. Figure 8.32 shows this pop-up where the remaining quotas are shown.

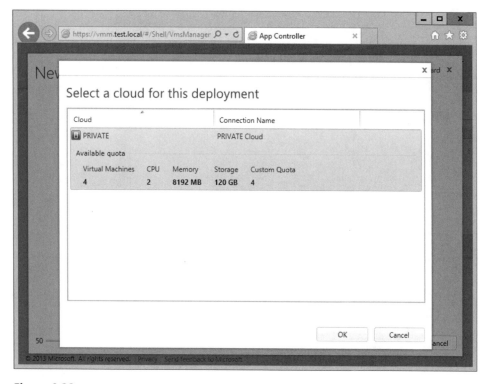

Figure 8.32
Cloud selected for this deployment.

Source: Windows Server 2012 R2/System Center App Controller 2012 R2.

1. Review the available resources.
2. Click OK.

Select a Template

The next step is to select the template to deploy the virtual machine, as shown in Figure 8.33.

Figure 8.33
Select a template for this deployment.

Source: Windows Server 2012 R2/System Center App Controller 2012 R2.

1. Click the Select a template link.

2. Wait for the pop-up to appear.

Choose a Template

Figure 8.34 shows the page where a VM template was selected. After a selection is made, the remaining quota resources are shown.

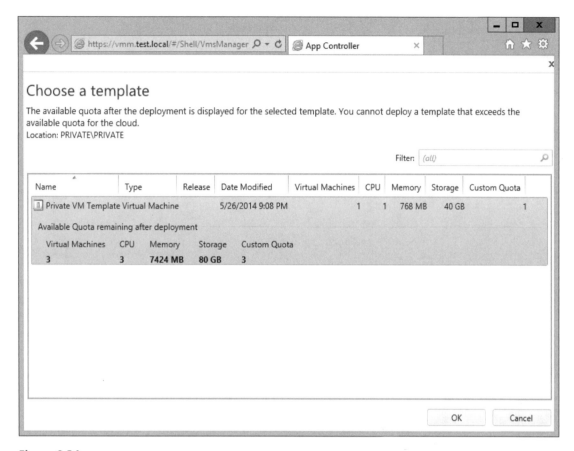

Figure 8.34
Template selected.
Source: Windows Server 2012 R2/System Center App Controller 2012 R2.

1. Click Private VM Template.

2. Review the remaining resources and then click OK.

Configure the Virtual Machine

On the next page, you can see that the VIRTUAL MACHINE requires further configuration (see Figure 8.35).

Figure 8.35
Configure Virtual Machine.

Source: Windows Server 2012 R2/System Center App Controller 2012 R2.

1. Review the deployment diagram.

2. Click the Configure for VIRTUAL MACHINE option.

Configure the Virtual Machine Pop-up

Figure 8.36 shows a completed virtual machine pop-up where you can review and configure settings for the deployment of the virtual machine.

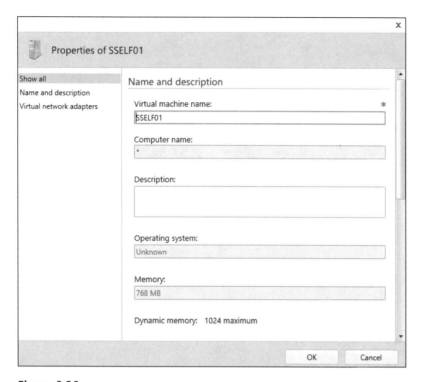

Figure 8.36
Virtual machine named.
Source: Windows Server 2012 R2/System Center App Controller 2012 R2.

1. Enter SSELF01 for the Virtual machine name.

2. Review the remaining entries and then click OK.

3. Click Deploy.

4. Wait for the deployment to complete.

Virtual Machine Creation

A PowerShell script runs and places the virtual machine in the PRIVATE cloud. A placement will be made to the COMPUTE host computer with the most available resources. Figure 8.37 shows a status of Under creation.

Wait for the deployment to complete.

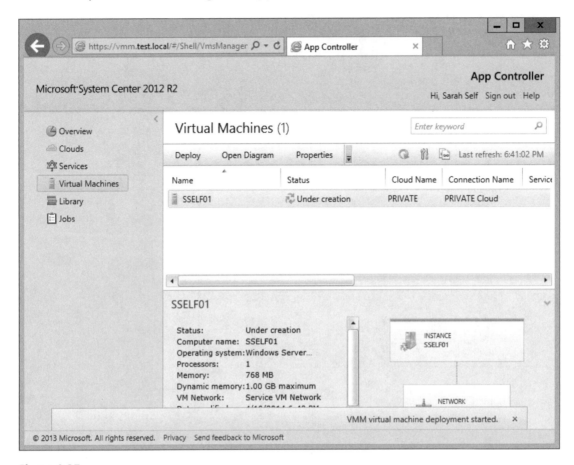

Figure 8.37
Virtual machine SSELF01 under creation.

Source: Windows Server 2012 R2/System Center App Controller 2012 R2.

Check Progress of Deployment

You can check the progress of the deployment in the Jobs node, as shown in Figure 8.38. Watch the Job status percentage.

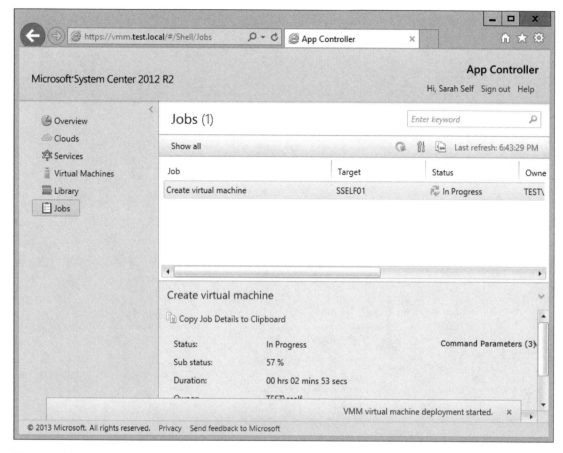

Figure 8.38
Job status for virtual machine deployment.
Source: Windows Server 2012 R2/System Center App Controller 2012 R2.

Start the Virtual Machine

Return to the Virtual Machines node where you manage the deployed virtual machine. Figure 8.39 shows the virtual machine ready to be started.

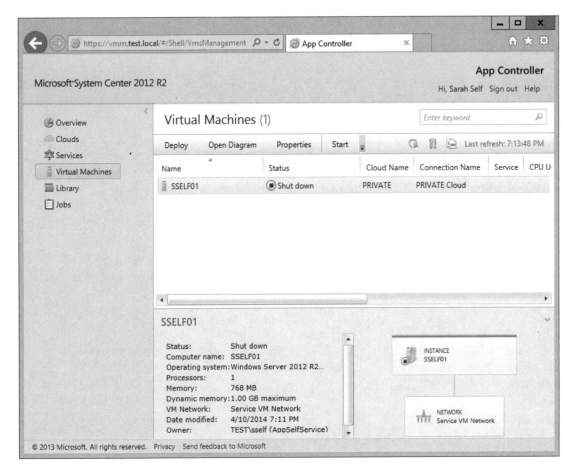

Figure 8.39
Virtual machine SSELF01 deployed.
Source: Windows Server 2012 R2/System Center App Controller 2012 R2.

1. Click the Virtual Machines node.

2. To start the virtual machine, click SSELF01 and then click the Start button.

3. Wait for the virtual machine to start.

4. Click the chevron next to Properties and then click Console. Click the Console tab.

5. If you see the message: This website wants to install System Center 2012 R2 Virtual Machine Manager, click Install. Enter test\administrator and a password of Pa$$w0rd. Click Yes. Click Install.

6. If the message that Webpage wants to run the following add-on appears, click Allow.

7. If necessary, log on with user test\administrator and a password of Pa$$w0rd.

8. To log on to the virtual machine, click Send Ctrl+Alt+Del. Enter Administrator and a password of Pa$$w0rd.

9. Click Local Server and review the Settings for the virtual machine.

Deploy Additional Virtual Machines

You have deployed the first virtual machine for Sarah Self. To deploy additional virtual machines, complete these steps for SSELF02, SSELF03, and SSELF04:

1. Click the App Controller tab.

2. Click the Virtual Machines node and click Deploy.

3. Click the Configure link.

4. Review the available resources and click OK.

5. Click the Select a template link.

6. Click Private VM Template.

7. Review the remaining resources and then click OK.

8. Review the deployment diagram.

9. Click the Configure link.

10. Enter SSELF02 for the Virtual machine name.

11. Review the remaining entries and then click OK.

12. Click Deploy.

13. Click the Jobs node.

14. Wait for the deployment to complete.

15. To start the virtual machine, click the Virtual machines node, click SSELF02, and then click the Start button.

16. Wait for the virtual machine to start.

17. Click the chevron next to Properties and then click Console.

18. Click the Console tab.

19. To log on to the virtual machine, click Send Ctrl+Alt+Del.

20. Enter Administrator and a password of Pa$$w0rd.

21. Click Local Server and review the Settings for the virtual machine.

22. Repeat steps 1 through 21 for SSELF03 and SSELF04.

SUMMARY

- You learned the purpose and features of the App Controller.

- You created a virtual machine template, which permits the deployment of a virtual machine.

- You created an Application Administrator Self-Service User, which deploys and manages virtual machines.

- You installed the App Controller, which provides Web pages to deploy and manage virtual machines.

- From the Application Administrator Self-Service, you deployed and managed four virtual machines.

CASE PROJECTS

Case 8-1: Microsoft Private Cloud Offering

Microsoft has a public cloud offering called Azure (meaning blue color of the clear sky). Do a Web search for Microsoft Azure.

Case 8-2: Try Microsoft Azure for Free

Microsoft is eager for you to try Microsoft Azure. To get started, search for Microsoft Azure try for free. Also, the App Controller has a link to Azure.

Case 8-3: Compare Microsoft Azure to Others

There are other public cloud providers available. To see comparisons, search for Azure vs. Amazon vs. RackSpace.

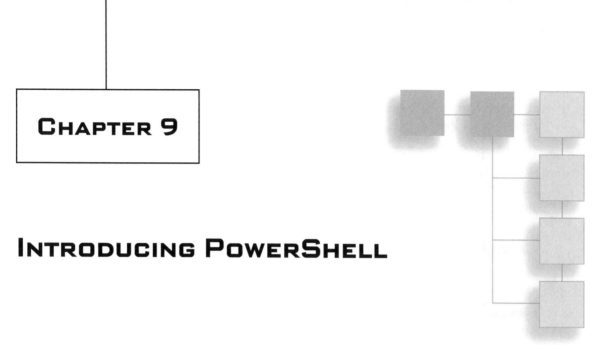

CHAPTER 9

INTRODUCING POWERSHELL

After reading this chapter and completing the exercises, you will be able to do the following:

- Describe the PowerShell environment.
- State reasons to learn PowerShell.
- Work with PowerShell cmdlets.
- Use cmdlets with Virtual Machine Manager.

This is the first of two chapters on PowerShell. PowerShell is a new Windows command-line shell designed especially for server administrators. You have been using PowerShell scripts, starting with Chapter 2. VMM creates and executes PowerShell scripts for administrative tasks. In this chapter, you will increase your ability to simplify tasks using PowerShell 4.0.

DESCRIBING THE POWERSHELL ENVIRONMENT

With your computers, you have worked from the command shell. For example, you have used the DIR command to get a listing of the folders and files in the current directory. When working from the command prompt, you interact with the Windows Server 2012 R2 command shell.

The command shell is a separate software program that provides direct communication between you and the operating system. When you enter a command, the command interpreter executes it, requests that the operating system perform the task for you, and displays text output on the screen. The command shell of the Windows server operating system uses the command interpreter CMD.EXE, which translates user input into a form that the operating system understands.

PowerShell is a new Windows command-line shell designed especially for server administrators. From the Windows PowerShell 4.0 interactive prompt, you can enter commands or invoke scripts. Scripts provide the ability to repeat commands in a scripting environment. You will learn to use scripts in Chapter 10, "Working with PowerShell Scripts." Unlike the command prompt, which accepts and returns text, PowerShell 4.0 is built on top of the .NET Framework and accepts and returns .NET Framework objects. The .NET Framework (pronounced dot net) is a software environment that runs primarily in Windows. It includes a large library and supports several programming languages, including PowerShell. This fundamental change in the environment brings entirely new tools into the management of Windows server roles.

The .NET Framework uses objects. As an example of an object, consider a bicycle. All real-world objects share two characteristics: state and behavior. A bicycle's state includes current gear ratio, current pedal cadence, current speed, and current direction. Bicycles also have behaviors, such as changing gear ratio, changing pedal cadence, applying brakes, and rotating handle bars. The state of an object is its data, and the behavior of an object is its methods. When you use an object, you pass along the data and the methods that can be used to transform the data.

Reasons to Learn PowerShell

You need to learn PowerShell for several reasons:

1. **It's here to stay.** For example, PowerShell version 4 is prominently displayed on the taskbar in Windows Server 2012 R2.

2. **Most Microsoft products will eventually use it.** You have used PowerShell since Chapter 2, "The Microsoft Private Cloud," starting with Virtual Machine Manager.

3. **Virtually all current Microsoft server products can be managed through PowerShell.** If you become proficient in PowerShell, you can manage most of Microsoft's newer products.

4. **It can make your job easier.** You can automate routine tasks. With a PowerShell script, you can complete these tasks with less effort.

5. **Many GUIs are PowerShell front ends.** Microsoft has been designing GUIs for various products that are actually front-end interfaces to PowerShell. One example is the Virtual Machine Manager console, in which the GUI actually generates a PowerShell script to complete your requested task.

6. **Microsoft certification exams contain PowerShell questions.** Microsoft has been adding questions about PowerShell to its certification exams. While you do not necessarily have to know the full command syntax, you do need to know which command you should use in a given situation.

7. **Microsoft considers it important.** The single most important skill you will need as a Windows administrator in the coming years is proficiency with Windows PowerShell.

8. **If you do not learn it, someone else will.** Given the intense competition for IT jobs, you need every edge you can get. Your chances for advancement might improve by knowing PowerShell.

WORKING WITH POWERSHELL CMDLETS

PowerShell introduces the concept of a cmdlet (pronounced command-let) or small command. These single-function command-line tools are built into PowerShell. You can use each cmdlet separately, but their power is realized when you chain these simple tools in sequence to perform complex tasks. PowerShell 4.0 includes more than 400 basic cmdlets. The PowerShell 4.0 command prompt is shown in Figure 9.1. Some cmdlets need to be run at an elevated command level. To do this, you run the PowerShell command prompt as an administrator.

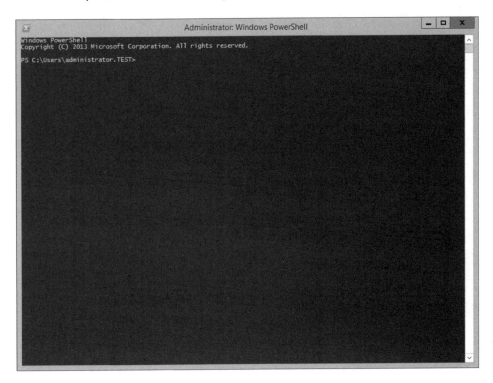

Figure 9.1
PowerShell command prompt.

Source: Windows Server 2012 R2/Windows PowerShell 4.0.

1. Return to VMM virtual machine.

2. Right-click the PowerShell 4.0 (blue icon with sigma) on the taskbar.

3. To run an elevated shell, click Run as Administrator.

Changing the Scheme Used in the PowerShell Console

You may find the white-on-blue color scheme or font sizes not to your liking. To make changes to these elements, right-click on the PowerShell window bar and select Properties. You may want to pick other colors, such as white for the background and black for the text. To pick a larger font, click the Font tab.

DIR Command in PowerShell

Many of your favorite commands will work in PowerShell. Consider the DIR command that you have used with the regular command prompt. Figure 9.2 shows the results of using the DIR command in PowerShell.

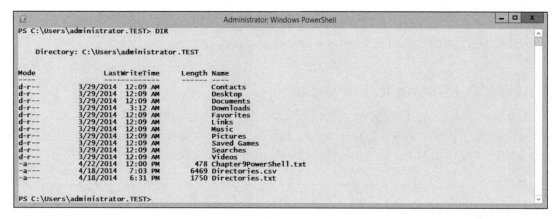

Figure 9.2
DIR command in PowerShell.
Source: Windows Server 2012 R2/Windows PowerShell 4.0.

1. Type DIR and then press Enter.
2. After reviewing the results, type CLS and then press Enter.

Get-Alias DIR Command in PowerShell

It is interesting to see how PowerShell 4.0 interprets this command. If you enter Get-Alias DIR, you see that PowerShell 4.0 uses Get-ChildItem to produce the output for the DIR command (see Figure 9.3).

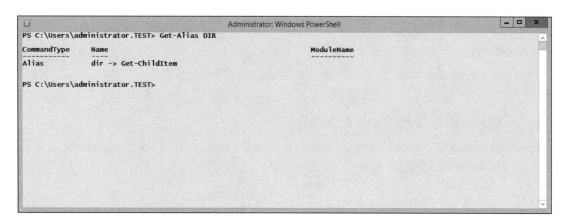

Figure 9.3
Get-Alias DIR command in PowerShell.
Source: Windows Server 2012 R2/Windows PowerShell 4.0.

1. Type Get-Alias DIR and then press Enter.

2. After reviewing the results, type CLS and then press Enter.

Get-Alias Command in PowerShell

To see the alias for other familiar commands, use Get-Alias COPY or Get-Alias CLS. The Get-Alias command is a quick way to learn equivalent PowerShell 4.0 commands for commands that you learned when working with other shells (see Figure 9.4).

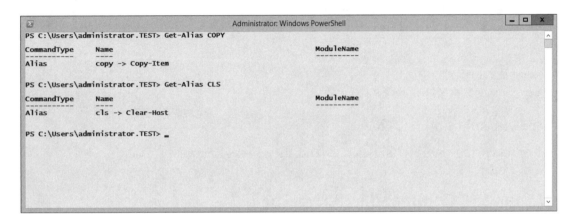

Figure 9.4
Get-Alias command in PowerShell.
Source: Windows Server 2012 R2/Windows PowerShell 4.0.

1. Type Get-Alias COPY and then press Enter.

2. Type Get-Alias CLS and then press Enter.

3. After reviewing the results, type CLS and then press Enter.

Linux ls Command in PowerShell

You will find aliases for many of your favorite Linux commands as well. Consider the ls command, as shown in Figure 9.5.

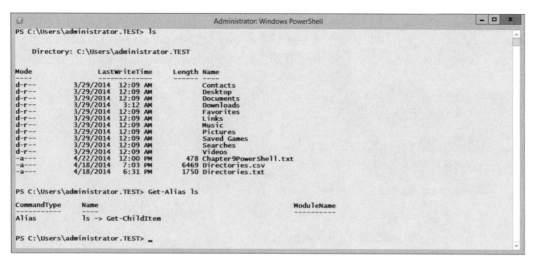

Figure 9.5
Linux `ls` command in PowerShell.
Source: Windows Server 2012 R2/Windows PowerShell 4.0.

1. Type `ls` and then press Enter.

2. Type `Get-Alias ls` and then press Enter.

3. After reviewing the results, type `CLS` and then press Enter.

PowerShell Verbs and Nouns

As an example of a basic cmdlet, consider `Get-Date`, as shown in Figure 9.6. Like all cmdlets, `Get-Date` is constructed from a verb and a noun and may be followed by qualifying information that is used to customize the actions of the cmdlet.

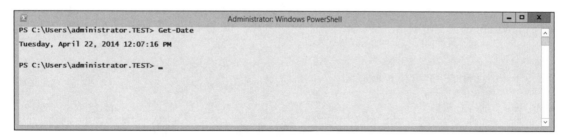

Figure 9.6
`Get-Date` cmdlet.
Source: Windows Server 2012 R2/Windows PowerShell 4.0.

1. Type `Get-Date` and then press Enter.

2. After reviewing the results, type `CLS` and then press Enter.

PowerShell Verbs

The verb and noun are separated by a hyphen. As in any language, a verb conveys action. Table 9.1 describes some verbs that you might encounter when working with PowerShell.

Table 9.1 Standard PowerShell 4.0 Verbs

Verb	Description
Get	Retrieves a resource.
Set	Creates or replaces data for a resource.
Copy	Copies a resource to another container; also renames a resource.
Out	Sends data out of the environment.
New	Creates an empty resource that is not associated with any content.
Add	Adds a resource to a container; paired with Remove.
Remove	Deletes a resource from a container; paired with Add.
Clear	Sets the contents to the null value.
Import	Creates a resource from a file.
Select	Locates a resource in a container.
Show	Makes a resource visible to the user.
Test	Verifies the operation of a resource.

© 2014 Cengage Learning®.

PowerShell Verb/Noun Pairs

Cmdlets are named as verb/noun pairs. Table 9.2 lists some verb/noun pairs you might encounter when working with PowerShell.

Table 9.2 PowerShell 4.0 Verb/Noun Pairs

Noun	Cmdlet	Description
Alias	Get-Alias	Returns alias names for cmdlets.
ChildItem	Get-ChildItem	Gets child items, which are contents of a folder or registry key.
Command	Get-Command	Retrieves basic information about a command.

Computer	Stop-Computer	Stops (shuts down) a computer.
Content	Set-Content	Puts content in the item.
Counter	Import-Counter	Imports performance counter log files.
Date	Set-Date	Sets the system date on the host system.
EventLog	Get-EventLog	Gets event log data.
History	Clear-History	Deletes entries from the session history.
Item	New-Item	Creates a new item in a namespace.
ItemProperty	Clear-ItemProperty	Removes the property value from a property.
Location	Set-Location	Sets the current working directory.
Module	Import-Module	Adds a module to the session.
Object	New-Object	Creates a new .NET object.
Path	Test-Path	Returns true if the path exists; otherwise, returns false.
Process	Stop-Process	Stops a running process.
Service	Start-Service	Starts a stopped service.

© 2014 Cengage Learning®.

Updating the Get-Help

To install the latest Get-Help files, you run the Update-Help cmdlet, which is shown in Figure 9.7. The Update-Help cmdlet downloads the newest help files for Windows PowerShell modules and installs them on your computer.

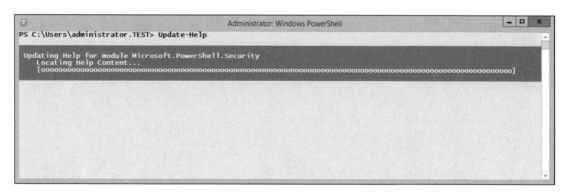

Figure 9.7
Update-Help.
Source: Windows Server 2012 R2/Windows PowerShell 4.0.

1. Type Update-Help and then press Enter.

2. Wait for the Get-Help files to be downloaded and installed.

3. After reviewing the results, type EXIT and then press Enter.

4. Right-click PowerShell 4.0 and click Run as Administrator.

Using Get-Help with a cmdlet

To be successful with PowerShell, you need to learn to work with the Get-Help command, which provides information about a cmdlet. For example, to see information about the Get-Date cmdlet, enter Get-Help Get-Date. The results are shown in Figure 9.8.

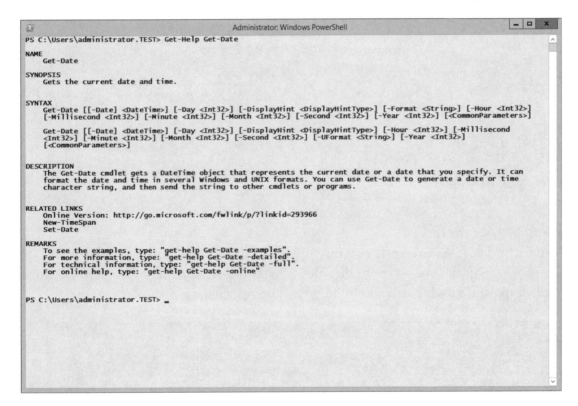

Figure 9.8
Get-Help Get-Date cmdlet.
Source: Windows Server 2012 R2/Windows PowerShell 4.0.

1. Type Get-Help Get-Date and then press Enter.

2. After reviewing the results, scroll to the prompt, type CLS and then press Enter.

Get-Date with -example switch

If you learn better by seeing examples, you can add the -example switch and run the cmdlet shown in Figure 9.9. A switch controls the action of the cmdlet. Using the -example switch provides real examples and helps reduce the learning curve for PowerShell.

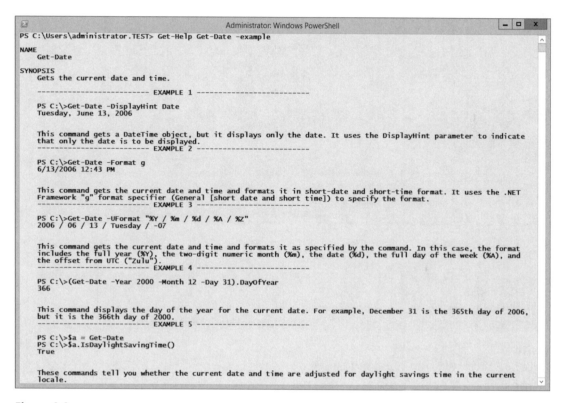

Figure 9.9
Get-Help Get-Date with –example switch.
Source: Windows Server 2012 R2/Windows PowerShell 4.0.

1. Type Get-Help Get-Date –example and then press Enter.

2. Scroll to see all of the results.

3. After reviewing the results, scroll to the prompt, type CLS and then press Enter.

Get-Date with -detailed switch

If you need more information, you can use the -detailed switch, as shown in Figure 9.10.

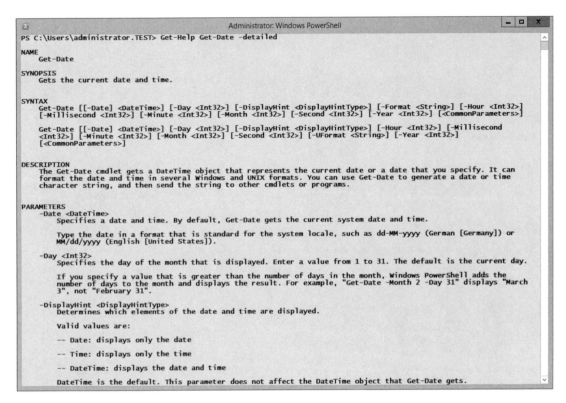

Figure 9.10
Get-Help Get-Date with —detailed switch.
Source: Windows Server 2012 R2/Windows PowerShell 4.0.

1. Type Get-Help Get-Date —detailed and then press Enter.

2. Scroll to see all of the results.

3. After reviewing the results, scroll to the prompt, type CLS and then press Enter.

Get-Date with -full switch

When you are not sure about the results of a command, the -full switch provides technical information that might help you correct the problem. Figure 9.11 shows the results of using the -full switch.

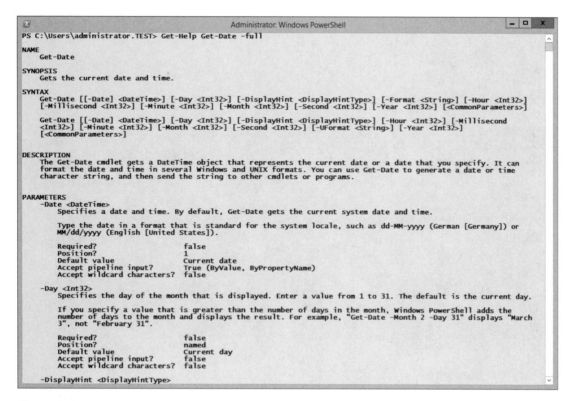

Figure 9.11

Get-Help Get-Date with —full switch.

Source: Windows Server 2012 R2/Windows PowerShell 4.0.

1. Type Get-Help Get-Date —full and then press Enter.

2. Scroll to see all of the results.

3. After reviewing the results, scroll to the prompt, type CLS and then press Enter.

You can use the -example, -detailed, and -full switches with most cmdlets. This provides a consistent approach when you learn to use the PowerShell 4.0 cmdlets.

Case Sensitivity

PowerShell is not case sensitive. In the cmdlets used so far, the first letter of each word was capitalized to match the PowerShell 4.0 documentation. However, any of the following cases will work:

Get-Date

get-date

GET-DATE

See Figure 9.12 for these examples.

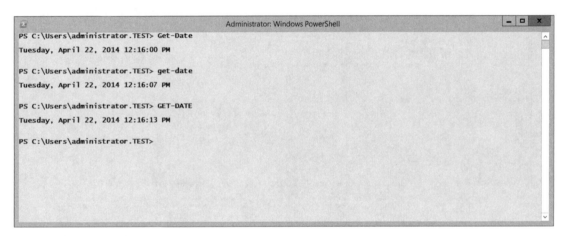

Figure 9.12
Case Sensitivity with Get-Date.
Source: Windows Server 2012 R2/Windows PowerShell 4.0.

1. Type Get-Date and then press Enter.

2. Type get-date and then press Enter.

3. Type GET-DATE and then press Enter.

4. After reviewing the results, type CLS and then press Enter.

Although PowerShell 4.0 is not case sensitive, it requires proper syntax and spelling. When you enter a cmdlet in the wrong syntax or misspell a word, a red message appears underlining the item in error to indicate that something is wrong.

Tab Autocomplete

A tool that you can use to enter long commands correctly is tab autocomplete. To use this tool to complete a noun, type the first few characters and then press the Tab key. Figure 9.13 shows tab autocomplete results. You must enter the minimum number of characters to complete the noun before you press Tab.

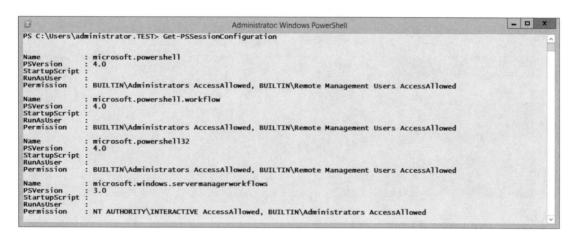

Figure 9.13
Using tab autocomplete.
Source: Windows Server 2012 R2/Windows PowerShell 4.0.

1. To get Get-PSSession, type Get-PSSe and press Tab.

2. To get Get-PSSessionConfiguration, type C and press Tab.

3. Press Enter.

4. After reviewing the results, type CLS and then press Enter.

Up Arrow Key

Another handy tool that saves typing is the Up arrow key. You have used this tool in the regular command prompt to cycle back through your history of commands and locate a previously used command. To reuse the command after you have located and selected it, press Enter. Of course, you can also use the Left arrow key or Backspace key to edit the command.

Using Parameters

Parameters allow you to modify the information that a cmdlet returns. When you run a cmdlet, the results contain properties and values that correspond to the nouns in your cmdlets. Parameters allow you finer control over the properties that PowerShell 4.0 returns in the resulting table. Parameters are unique to the nouns in your cmdlet. For example, Figure 9.14 shows the -name parameter used with DIR to show the alias for the DIR command.

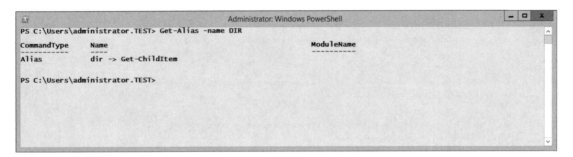

Figure 9.14

Get-Alias with —name parameter.

Source: Windows Server 2012 R2/Windows PowerShell 4.0.

1. Type Get-Alias —name DIR and then press Enter.

2. After reviewing the results, type CLS and then press Enter.

The -name parameter is a keyword parameter that you explicitly specify in the cmdlet: Get-Alias -name DIR. You do not need to use the keyword. Get-Alias DIR returns the same results. When there is more than one keyword, you enter the parameters in the order of the keywords for the cmdlet. These are known as *positional parameters*.

You need to remember two things when using positional parameters. First, you need to know the correct position of the parameter when you enter the cmdlet syntax. Second, not all parameters are positional. Some are named parameters, and you must use the keyword. Figure 9.15 shows an example of each type.

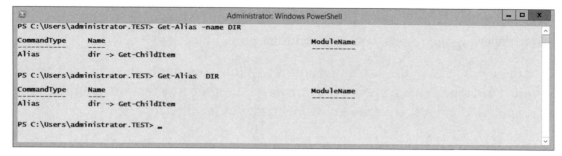

Figure 9.15
Get-Alias with –name parameter.
Source: Windows Server 2012 R2/Windows PowerShell 4.0.

1. Type Get-Alias –name DIR and then press Enter.

2. Press Up arrow.

3. Edit Get-Alias –name DIR to Get-Alias DIR and then press Enter.

4. After reviewing the results, type CLS and then press Enter.

Working with Properties

Properties have two parts in PowerShell: property names and property values. Property names are column headings, and property values are the data shown below the headings. For example, in Figure 9.16, the Get-ChildItem property names are Mode, LastWriteTime, Length, and Name. The property values are shown in the rows below the heading names. Since these properties are for folders, the length property values are omitted.

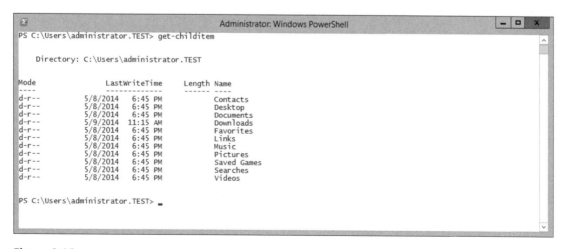

Figure 9.16
Get-ChildItem property names.
Source: Windows Server 2012 R2/Windows PowerShell 4.0.

1. Type Get-ChildItem and then press Enter.

2. After reviewing the results, type CLS and then press Enter.

Think of these property values as being read-only. While you cannot directly use properties in your PowerShell commands, you can control the properties shown as output. For example, enter Get-ChildItem -name to list the names of the directory items.

Working with the Pipe Operator

You might have used the More command in a regular command prompt to page through a large file. In a command such as DIR | More, you use the pipe operator (|) to pass the output to the More command.

Piping cmdlets together is called *pipelining*, in which you take the output of one cmdlet and pass it to the next cmdlet. The PowerShell equivalent of DIR | More is Get-ChildItem | More. This is shown in Figure 9.17.

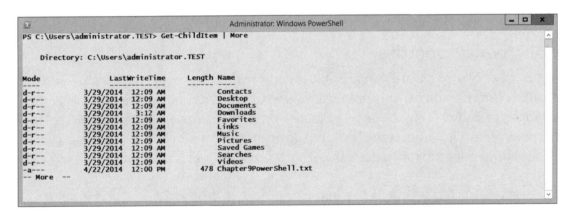

Figure 9.17
Pipelining Get-ChildItem to More.
Source: Windows Server 2012 R2/Windows PowerShell 4.0.

1. Type Get-ChildItem | More and then press Enter.

2. When the -- More-- text appears, press the spacebar.

3. After reviewing the results, scroll to the prompt, type CLS, and then press Enter.

Scrolling Shortcuts

If you are tired of scrolling to read the Get-Help *cmdlet* text, consider using the Help *cmdlet*, which is equivalent to the Get-Help *cmdlet* | More.

Also to terminate the list prematurely and advance to the prompt, use *Ctrl + c*.

Using the Get-Command cmdlet

The Get-Command cmdlet lists all of the cmdlets that are available in the current session. Where the Get-Help or Help cmdlets provide information from the help files, the Get-Command cmdlet gets its information directly from the code for the cmdlet.

Locating cmdlets with Get-Command

There are numerous cmdlets supplied with the default installation of PowerShell 4.0. To see all of the cmdlets, you use Get-Command -type Cmdlet, as shown in Figure 9.18. The ModuleName indicates the PowerShell module where the cmdlet is located. Modules are used to group cmdlets into a common module. Modules can be used to extend the functionality of PowerShell. For example, there is a common module for System Center of which VMM is a component, Modules are similar to the libraries that an application developer might use with a particular programming language.

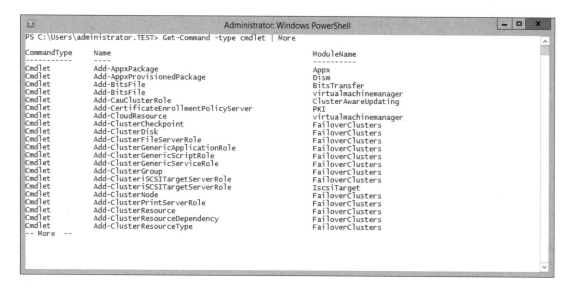

Figure 9.18
Get-Command cmdlet lists available cmdlets.
Source: Windows Server 2012 R2/Windows PowerShell 4.0.

1. Type Get-Command –type cmdlet | More and then press Enter.

2. After reviewing the results, press the spacebar and scroll to the prompt, type CLS, and then press Enter.

Locating cmdlets with Common Nouns

One technique is to request cmdlets with common nouns. For example, when moving from directory to directory, you use the Set-Location cmdlet, which corresponds to the CD command. A quick way to locate similar commands is to use the –noun parameter. For example, consider this cmdlet: Get-Command –noun Location. The results are shown in Figure 9.19. Since you suspect that Get-Location is the cmdlet that you are looking for, you issue a Help Get -Location cmdlet.

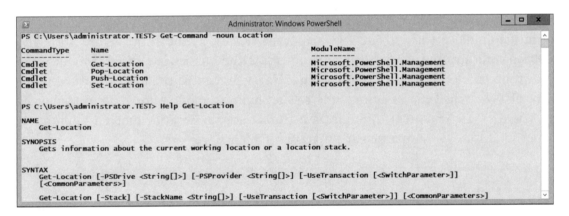

Figure 9.19
Cmdlets with common nouns.

Source: Windows Server 2012 R2/Windows PowerShell 4.0.

1. Type Get-Command –noun Location and then press Enter.

2. Type Help Get-Location and then press Enter.

3. After reviewing the results, press the spacebar and scroll to the prompt, type CLS, and then press Enter.

Locating cmdlets with a Common ModuleName

Another way to narrow down the list of cmdlets is to refer to the module that contains the cmdlet. Figure 9.20 shows a listing of the cmdlets in the Microsoft.PowerShell.Management module. By adding -verb Get (not shown), you narrow the list to those cmdlets that return information.

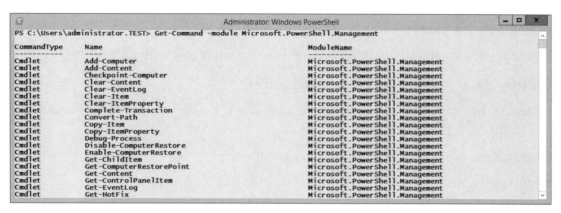

Figure 9.20
Cmdlets with a common ModuleName.

Source: Windows Server 2012 R2/Windows PowerShell 4.0.

1. To get all of the cmdlets, type the following command and then press Tab:

   Get-Command —module Mi

2. Press Enter.

3. After reviewing the results, press the spacebar and scroll to the prompt, type CLS, and then press Enter.

4. Press the Up arrow twice.

5. To get all of the Get cmdlets, edit the command, as shown, and then press Enter:

   Get-Command —module Microsoft.PowerShell.Management —verb Get

Don't Split Commands

In this book, you will see the longer commands split into two or more lines, which is done to accommodate the format of the book. In the PowerShell console, command lines are 120 characters long. Commands longer than 120 characters wrap onto the next line. When commands wrap, PowerShell considers these lines to be continuous. The point is just for you to type and let PowerShell take care of this wrapping onto the next line.

6. After reviewing the results, press the spacebar and scroll to the prompt, type CLS, and then press Enter.

Working with PowerShell Output

The previous section explained how to locate cmdlets that serve a particular purpose. Yet, the results can be a bit unwieldy. In this section, you will learn about cmdlets that control output and how the pipe operator is used with them.

The pipe operator is typically used with the following types of commands:

- **Sorting:** Arranging a table in a particular order.

- **Filtering:** Selecting items to remain in a table after filtering out unwanted items using the Where-Object cmdlet.

- **Formatting:** Making the output look more pleasing.

- **Redirecting:** Sending output to a file.

Sorting a Table of Cmdlets

The only cmdlet you need to learn in order to sort tables is Sort-Object. You also need to know the parameters of an object to sort the table. For example, if you want to sort a table of cmdlets, run the cmdlets as shown in Figure 9.21.

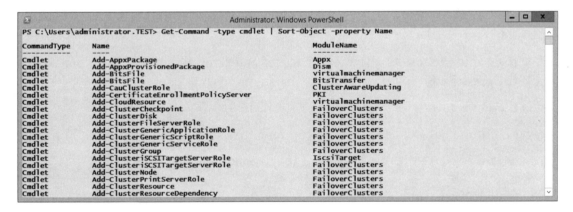

Figure 9.21
Sorting a table of cmdlets.
Source: Windows Server 2012 R2/Windows PowerShell 4.0.

1. To sort the list by Name, type the following command and press Enter:

```
Get-Command –type cmdlet| Sort-Object -property Name
```

2. After reviewing the results, scroll to the prompt, type CLS, and then press Enter. If you want to page through the sorted output, add | more to the end of the previous command.

Sorting a Table of Cmdlets by Two Properties

Where there are multiple properties, you might sort by two or more properties. For a sort by the Name within ModuleName, you use the cmdlets shown in Figure 9.22.

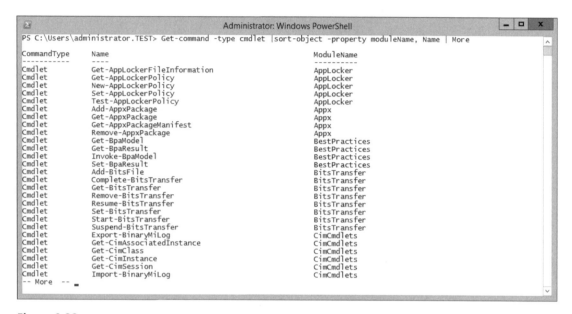

Figure 9.22
Sorting a table of cmdlets by two properties.
Source: Windows Server 2012 R2/Windows PowerShell 4.0.

1. To sort the list by ModuleName and Name, type the following command and press Enter:

   Get-Command –type cmdlet| Sort-Object -property ModuleName, Name | More

2. When the -- More -- text appears, press the spacebar.

3. After reviewing the results, scroll to the prompt, type CLS, and then press Enter.

Filtering a Table of Cmdlets

In some situations, you might need to see only a part of the complete table. If so, you can use PowerShell's filtering capabilities with the Where-Object cmdlet. You need to know the comparison operators defined in Table 9.3.

Table 9.3 Comparison Operators Used with `Where-Object`

Operator	Definition
`-eq`	Equals, which is used for finding identical values
`-ne`	Not equals, which includes values that are not identical
`-gt`	Greater than
`-ge`	Greater than or equal to
`-lt`	Less than
`-le`	Less than or equal to
`-like`	Matching operator that uses the * wildcard operator
`-match`	Allows you to find the values of a string that do match
`-contains`	Allows you to see whether an identical value exists in a list of values
`-notlike`	Allows you to identify the value that does not match
`-notmatch`	Allows you to find the values of a string that do not match
`-notcontains`	Allows you to find the values in a list that do not match

© 2014 Cengage Learning®.

Select and Sort Objects

In an earlier example, you used the

```
Get-Command –type cmdlet| Sort-Object -property ModuleName, Name
```

cmdlet to obtain a sorted list of available cmdlets. If you want to only include cmdlets that start with Get in their name, you add a `Where-Object`, shown in bold, to this command.

```
Get-Command –type cmdlet| Where-Object Name –Like "Get-*" | Sort-Object -property
ModuleName, Name | More
```

This is shown in Figure 9.23.

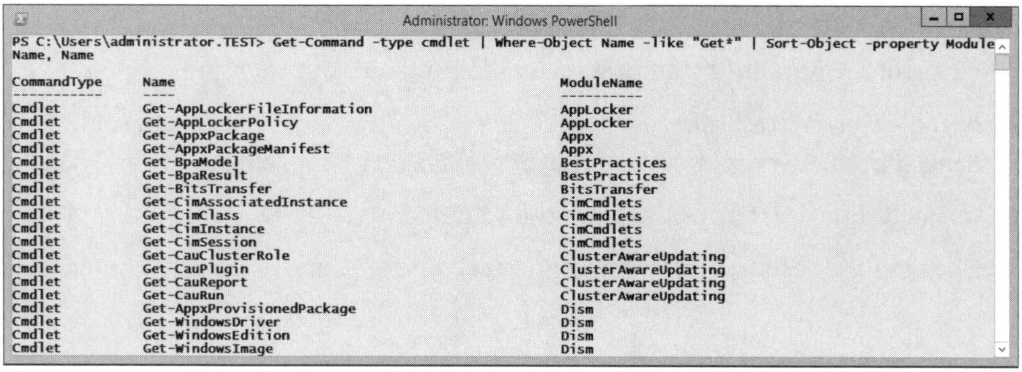

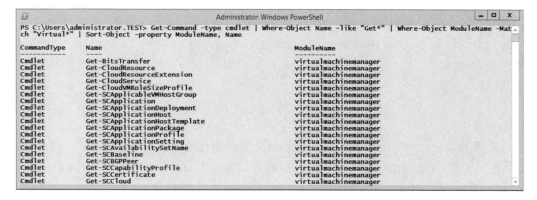

Figure 9.23
Select and sort a table of cmdlets.
Source: Windows Server 2012 R2/Windows PowerShell 4.0.

1. Press the Up arrow twice.

2. Edit the existing command by adding the cmdlet in bold and then press Enter.

   Get-Command –type cmdlet| **Where-Object Name –like "Get-*"** | Sort-Object -property ModuleName, Name | More

3. When the - - More - - text appears, press the spacebar.

4. After reviewing the results, scroll to the prompt, type CLS, and then press Enter.

Figure 9.24 shows the effects of filtering on two objects: Names that start with "Get-*" and ModuleNames that match "Virtual*". This produces a list of the Get cmdlets that you can use with Virtual Machine Manager. This list will be useful later in this chapter.

Figure 9.24
Select by two objects and sort a table of cmdlets.
Source: Windows Server 2012 R2/Windows PowerShell 4.0.

1. Press the Up arrow twice.

2. Edit the existing command by adding the cmdlet in bold and then press Enter.

   Get-Command —type cmdlet| Where-Object Name —Like "Get-*" | **Where-Object ModuleName —Match "Virtual*"** | Sort-Object -property ModuleName, Name | More

3. When the -- More -- text appears, press the spacebar.

4. After reviewing the results, scroll to the prompt, type CLS, and then press Enter.

Alternative Entries for Where-Object

There are a number of legal ways to complete the Where-Object cmdlet. All of the following produce the same results:

Get-Command —type cmdlet|Where-Object —Property Name —Like "Get-*"

Get-Command —type cmdlet| Where —Property Name —Like "Get-*"

Get-Command —type cmdlet| Where Name —Like "Get-*"

Get-Command —type cmdlet| Where-Object {$_ .Name —Like "Get-*"}

The last entry is the format for versions of PowerShell prior to PowerShell 3.0.

Formatting a Table of Cmdlets

You have seen examples of the Format-Table cmdlet in the previous exercises, which is one of the formatting options available in PowerShell. Two other options are available as well: Format-Wide and Format-List.

Unless you specify the properties, the cmdlet displays the properties in the order that they appear in the object. With the —Property parameter, you can change the order in which properties are displayed. The exception is the one that Format-Wide takes, which only shows a single property.

Using Format-Wide

The Format-Wide cmdlet, by default, displays only the default property of an object, as shown in Figure 9.25. The information associated with each object is displayed in a single column.

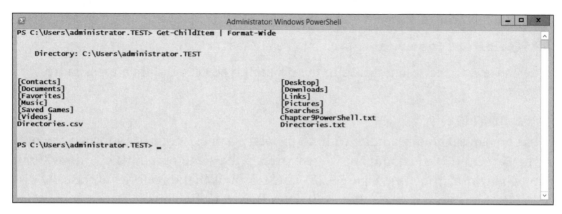

Figure 9.25
Data with `Format-Wide`.
Source: Windows Server 2012 R2/Windows PowerShell 4.0.

1. Type Get-ChildItem | Format-Wide and then press Enter.

2. After reviewing the results, scroll to the prompt, type CLS, and then press Enter.

Using Format-List

The Format-List cmdlet displays an object in the form of a listing, with each property labeled and displayed on a separate line. With the –Property parameter, you can control which property values are displayed and in which order (see Figure 9.26).

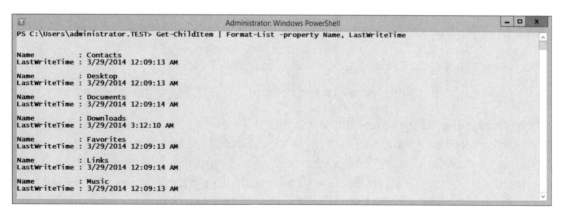

Figure 9.26
Data with `Format-List`.
Source: Windows Server 2012 R2/Windows PowerShell 4.0.

1. Type the following command and press Enter:

   `Get-ChildItem | Format-List –property Name, LastWriteTime`

2. After reviewing the results, scroll to the prompt, type CLS, and then press Enter.

Using Format-Table

If you use the `Format-Table` cmdlet with no property names specified to format the output of the `Get-ChildItem` command, you get exactly the same output as you do without performing any formatting (see Figure 9.27). The reason is that directories are usually displayed in a tabular format, as are most Windows PowerShell objects.

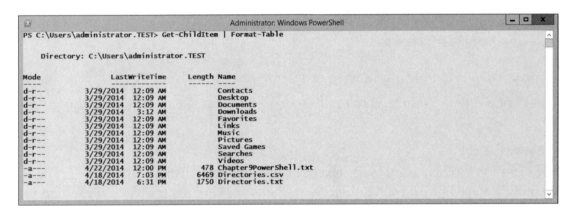

Figure 9.27
Data with `Format-Table`.
Source: Windows Server 2012 R2/Windows PowerShell 4.0.

1. Type `Get-ChildItem | Format-Table` and then press Enter.

2. After reviewing the results, scroll to the prompt, type CLS, and then press Enter.

You might choose the tabular view for displaying a lot of comparable data, but it may be difficult to interpret the data if the display is too narrow. The tabular view can be made more readable by adding –Autosize at the end of the command. However, data values may be truncated at the end of the line. To remedy this problem, use the –Property parameter to control which values are displayed and their sequence.

For very long output lines, you might consider the –Wrap parameter. You would use this instead of –Autosize.

Working with File Output

The results of almost any PowerShell cmdlet can be sent or redirected to a file. You can redirect output in several different types of files, including CSV for spreadsheets, HTML, or text files. Table 9.4 shows the types of output you can use with PowerShell.

Table 9.4 File Output Options

Out cmdlets	Description
Out-File	Creates a text file.
Out-GridView	Creates a grid in a separate window that you can sort and filter.
Out-Host	Displays the results in the PowerShell session (default option).
Out-Null	Deletes the output.
Out-Printer	Sends output to a connected printer.
Out-String	Outputs the results in an array of strings, which is useful for setting up variables for scripting operations.
Export-CSV	Outputs a file in CSV format (spreadsheet format).

© 2014 Cengage Learning®.

Using Out-File

You can send output to a file instead of the console (Out-Host) by using Out-File. For an example, see Figure 9.28. By default, Out-File produces a file in the Unicode (16-bit characters) format. You can change the behavior by using –Encoding ASCII.

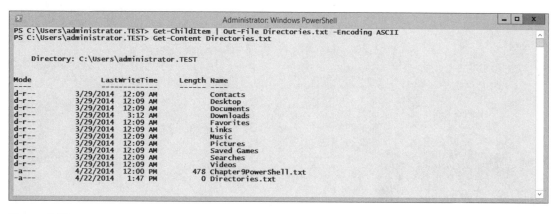

Figure 9.28
Using Out-File.
Source: Windows Server 2012 R2/Windows PowerShell 4.0.

1. Type the following command and press Enter:

   `Get-ChildItem | Out-File Directories.txt —Encoding ASCII`

2. To see the text within the Directories.txt file, type `Get-content Directories.txt` and then press Enter.

3. After reviewing the results, scroll to the prompt, type `CLS`, and then press Enter.

Using Out-GridView

The `Out-GridView` cmdlet sends the output to a new window where you can interact with the table (see Figure 9.29). You can use the following features of the table to examine your data:

- **Manage Columns.** To hide, show, or reorder a column, right-click a column header and then click Select Columns.

- **Sort.** To sort the data, click a column header.

- **Quick Filter.** Use the Filter box at the top of the window to search the text in the table.

- **Criteria Filter.** Use the Add criteria drop-down menu to create rules to filter the data. This is very useful for very large data sets, such as event logs.

- **Copy and paste.** To copy rows of data, press Ctrl+c (copy). You can paste the data into your text or spreadsheet program.

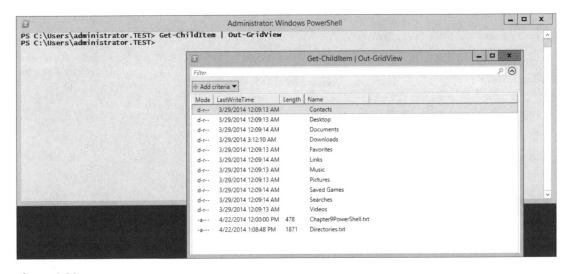

Figure 9.29
Using Out-GridView.

Source: Windows Server 2012 R2/Windows PowerShell 4.0.

1. Type `Get-ChildItem | Out-GridView` and then press Enter.

2. To sort the Directories in ascending order, click Name.

3. To sort the Directories in descending order, click Name.

4. To remove the length column, right-click Name, click Select Columns, click Length and click <<.

5. To rearrange the columns, click Name, click Move up twice, and then click OK.

6. Close the Get-ChildItem | Out-GridView window.

7. After reviewing the results, scroll to the prompt, type `CLS`, and then press Enter.

Using Export-CSV

You use the `Export-CSV` cmdlet to create a CSV file. Each object is represented as a row of the CSV. The row consists of a comma-separated list of the values of object properties, including properties you may not have previously seen. You can use this cmdlet to create spreadsheets and share data with programs that take CSV files as input, as shown in Figure 9.30.

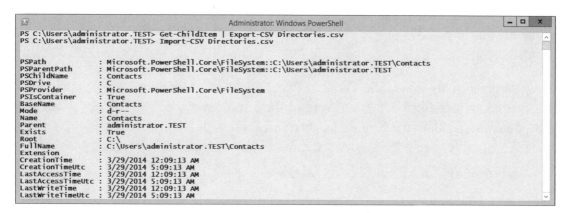

```
PS C:\Users\administrator.TEST> Get-ChildItem | Export-CSV Directories.csv
PS C:\Users\administrator.TEST> Import-CSV Directories.csv


PSPath              : Microsoft.PowerShell.Core\FileSystem::C:\Users\administrator.TEST\Contacts
PSParentPath        : Microsoft.PowerShell.Core\FileSystem::C:\Users\administrator.TEST
PSChildName         : Contacts
PSDrive             : C
PSProvider          : Microsoft.PowerShell.Core\FileSystem
PSIsContainer       : True
BaseName            : Contacts
Mode                : d-r--
Name                : Contacts
Parent              : administrator.TEST
Exists              : True
Root                : C:\
FullName            : C:\Users\administrator.TEST\Contacts
Extension           :
CreationTime        : 3/29/2014 12:09:13 AM
CreationTimeUtc     : 3/29/2014 5:09:13 AM
LastAccessTime      : 3/29/2014 12:09:13 AM
LastAccessTimeUtc   : 3/29/2014 5:09:13 AM
LastWriteTime       : 3/29/2014 12:09:13 AM
LastWriteTimeUtc    : 3/29/2014 5:09:13 AM
```

Figure 9.30
Using Export-CSV.
Source: Windows Server 2012 R2/Windows PowerShell 4.0.

1. Type the following command and then press Enter:

    `Get-ChildItem | Export-CSV Directories.csv`

2. To view the results, type `Import-CSV Directories.csv` and then press Enter.

3. After reviewing the results, scroll to the prompt, type `CLS`, and then press Enter.

Using Variables in PowerShell

If you have worked with a scripting language, such as Perl or Python, you're accustomed to variables being nothing more than a place to store data. PowerShell has variables, too, but they're much more powerful than the variables in older scripting languages.

One reason is that PowerShell variables are actually mapped to the underlying classes in the Microsoft .NET Framework. And in the Framework, variables are objects, meaning they can store data and also manipulate it in many ways. In fact, the robust capabilities of variables in Windows PowerShell are the reason why the Windows PowerShell scripting language doesn't require any data manipulation functions.

You can create variables as needed, on the fly, by assigning a value. Here's an example of the ubiquitous "Hello World."

```
$msg = "Hello World"
```

In PowerShell, variable names always start with a dollar sign ($) and can contain a mix of letters, numbers, or symbols. This example created a new variable named `$msg` and assigned it the initial value of `"Hello World."` Because in this case the value is a string of characters, PowerShell will use the string data type to store the value.

Now, what if you created a variable and assigned a digit? In this example, PowerShell would use an int32 type, 32-bit integer, to store the value for start.

```
$start=5
```

Allowing PowerShell to assign the variable types might not work for you. Suppose that you are reading values from a file and one of the variables appears as all digits but will never be used in calculations. You can override PowerShell by declaring the type when declaring the variable. Table 9.5 shows the more common variable types.

Here's an example of a string variable consisting of the digits 555.

```
[String]$tart = 555
```

Table 9.5 Common Types for Variables

Shortcut	Data Type
[datetime]	Date or time
[string]	String of characters
[char]	Single character

[double]	Double-precision floating number
[single]	Single-precision floating number
[int]	32-bit integer
[wmi]	Windows Management Instrumentation (WMI) instance or collection
[adsi]	Active Directory Services object
[Boolean]	True or False value

© 2014 Cengage Learning®.

USING CMDLETS WITH VIRTUAL MACHINE MANAGER

The PowerShell 4.0 library for Virtual Machine Manager is extensive. In fact, there are 615 cmdlets. You can do just about everything that you do with the GUI, and many things you might do are easier in PowerShell. In this section, you will try out a few of the simpler Get cmdlets. In Chapter 10, "Working with PowerShell Scripts," you will expand your knowledge of PowerShell by building scripts of PowerShell cmdlets.

Using Get-SCCloud

The Get-SCCloud cmdlet gets a private cloud object from the Virtual Machine Manager (VMM). For further use, you can store the object in a variable. Figure 9.31 shows this cmdlet. To see the name of the cloud, you append .Name to the variable $Cloud.

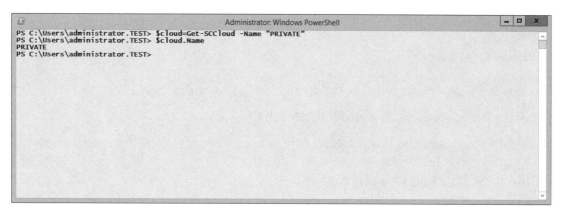

Figure 9.31
Using Get-SCCloud.
Source: Windows Server 2012 R2/Windows PowerShell 4.0.

1. To start a new session, close the PowerShell window and then click the PowerShell icon on the taskbar.

2. To get the cloud object, type the following command and press Enter:

   `$cloud =Get-SCCloud —Name "PRIVATE"`

3. To see the name of the cloud object, type `$cloud.Name` and press Enter.

Using Get-SCVMHost

You use this command to get the virtual machine host objects from the Virtual Machine Manager database. To save the host objects for further use, you store these objects in the variable `$hosts`. To see a single property, such as `ComputerName`, you concatenate the property to the variable. Figure 9.32 shows these commands.

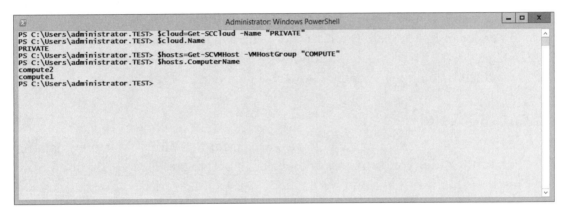

Figure 9.32
Using Get-SCVMHost.
Source: Windows Server 2012 R2/Windows PowerShell 4.0.

1. To get the hosts object, type the following command and press Enter:

   `$hosts =Get-SCVMHost —VMHostGroup "COMPUTE"`

2. To see the names of the host objects, type `$hosts.ComputerName` and press Enter.

Using Get-SCVirtualMachine

The Get-SCVirtualMachine cmdlet gets one or more virtual machine objects from the System Center Virtual Machine Manager (VMM) database. A virtual machine can be deployed on a virtual machine host or can be stored in the VMM library. Since you are using the cloud property, you see the virtual machines deployed to the cloud. Figure 9.33 shows the commands to store the virtual machine objects in `$vms` and display the computer names.

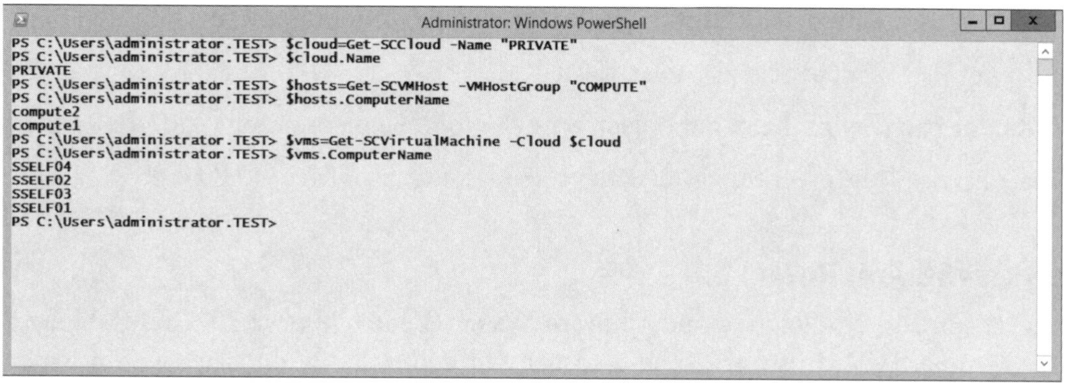

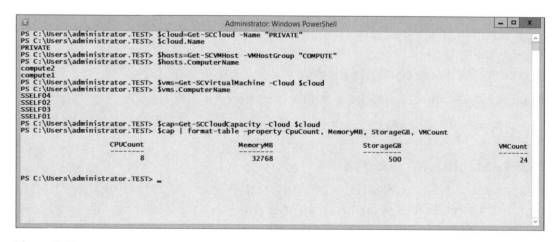

Figure 9.33
Using Get-SCVirtualMachine.
Source: Windows Server 2012 R2/Windows PowerShell 4.0.

1. To get the virtual machine objects, type the following command and press Enter:

   $vms =Get-SCVirtualMachine —Cloud $cloud

2. To see the names of the virtual machine objects, type $vms.ComputerName and press Enter.

Using Get-SCCloudCapacity

The Get-SCCloudCapacity cmdlet gets the cloud capacity for a private cloud in System Center Virtual Machine Manager (VMM). Cloud capacity includes settings for the number of virtual machines, number of virtual CPUs, custom quota points, storage, and memory assigned to a private cloud. Figure 9.34 shows the cloud capacity.

Figure 9.34
Using Get-SCCloudCapacity.
Source: Windows Server 2012 R2/Windows PowerShell 4.0.

1. To get the cloud capacity object, type the following command and press Enter:

   `$cap =Get-SCCloudCapacity –Cloud $cloud`

2. To see the capacity of the cloud object, type the following command and press Enter:

   `$cap | Format-Table –property CPUCount, MemoryMB, StorageGB, VMCount`

Using `Get-SCUserRole`

The `Get-SCUserRole` cmdlet gets one or more System Center Virtual Machine Manager (VMM) user roles. VMM uses role-based security to define the boundaries within which members of a given user role can operate and the set of allowed operations members that a user role can perform. Figure 9.35 shows the user role object stored in `$userrole`.

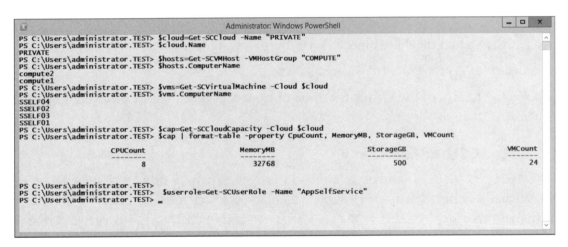

Figure 9.35
Using `Get-SCUserRole`.
Source: Windows Server 2012 R2/Windows PowerShell 4.0.

1. To get the user role object, type the following command and press Enter:

   `$userrole =Get-SCUserRole –Name "AppSelfService"`

2. To see the name of the user role object, type `$Userrole.Name` and press Enter.

Using `Get-SCUserRoleQuota`

The `Get-SCUserRoleQuota` cmdlet gets a System Center Virtual Machine Manager (VMM) user role quota object. Figure 9.36 shows the user role stored in `$selfcap`. The `$selfcap` object is piped to a `Format-Table` to display the selected properties.

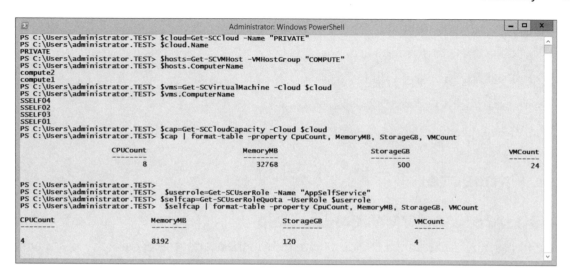

Figure 9.36
Using Get-SCUserRole.
Source: Windows Server 2012 R2/Windows PowerShell 4.0.

1. To get the user role capacity object, type the following command and press Enter:

   ```
   $selfcap =Get-SCUserRoleQuota –UserRole $userrole
   ```

2. To see the capacity of the user role object, type the following command and press Enter:

   ```
   $selfcap | Format-Table –property CPUCount, MemoryMB, StorageGB, VMCount
   ```

Congratulations! You have written your first script. Now go to Chapter 10 and learn more about the "power" in PowerShell.

SUMMARY

PowerShell is a Windows command-line shell designed especially for server administrators. You can use the features and components of PowerShell to perform the following tasks:

- Use familiar CLI Windows commands like DIR or Linux commands like ls.
- Create aliases for PowerShell cmdlets.
- Gain knowledge of PowerShell cmdlets with Get-Help.
- Use Tab autocomplete to speed typing of cmdlets.

- Pipe objects from cmdlet to cmdlet.

- Filter object lists to select objects.

- Sort objects by property values.

- Format output to improve readability.

- Use VMM-specific cmdlets to get information about the private cloud.

Case Projects

Case 9-1: Access the VMM Cmdlet Help

Microsoft has an article that provides help information about the cmdlets to support PowerShell in a VMM environment. Do a Web search for Cmdlet Reference for System Center 2012 - Virtual Machine Manager.

Case 9-2: Locate Information about Using the VMM Cmdlets

Ed Wilson is a well-known scripting expert. He is a Microsoft Certified Trainer who has delivered a popular Windows PowerShell workshop to Microsoft Premier Customers worldwide. Search the Web for Ed Wilson Scripting Guy.

Case 9-3: Locate Information about Others Using PowerShell

Another site to consider is PowerShell.org, which is owned and operated by PowerShell.org, Inc., a Nevada not-for-profit corporation. Search for PowerShell.org. What does this organization provide that will help you use PowerShell?

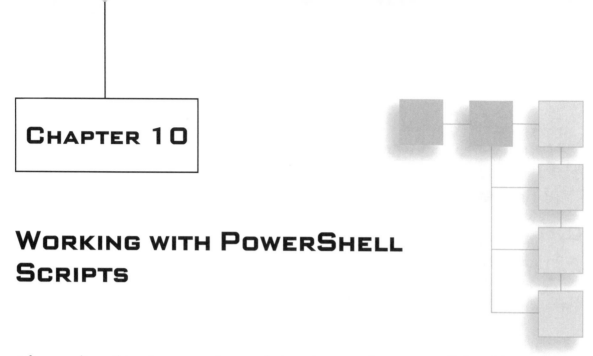

CHAPTER 10

WORKING WITH POWERSHELL SCRIPTS

After reading this chapter and completing the exercises, you will be able to do the following:

- Use the Windows PowerShell Integrated Scripting Environment (ISE).
- Write scripts to manage virtual machines.
- Write scripts to create user accounts.
- Write scripts to deploy virtual machines.

This is the second of two chapters on PowerShell. In Chapter 9, "Introducing PowerShell," you learned about the basics of PowerShell. In this chapter, you will construct scripts to simplify tasks using PowerShell 4.0. While you complete most activities to manage virtual machines, create user accounts, or deploy virtual machines with the GUI tools, you gain efficiency by creating PowerShell scripts for repetitive tasks.

USING THE WINDOWS POWERSHELL INTEGRATED SCRIPTING ENVIRONMENT (ISE)

To make PowerShell easier to use, Microsoft provides the Integrated Scripting Environment (ISE), which provides a rich scripting experience. The ISE enables you to write, run, and test scripts in a graphical and intuitive environment. Key features in ISE include:

- **Brace Matching:** Locates the closing brace, if you have an opening brace selected.
- **Intellisense:** Displays clickable menus of potentially matching cmdlets, parameters, parameter values, files, or folders as you type.

- **Snippets:** Displays short sections of PowerShell code that you can insert into the scripts.

- **Show-Command:** Composes or runs a cmdlet by filling in a graphical form.

- **Drag-and-drop text editing:** Selects any block of text and drags that text to another location in the editor.

- **Parse error display:** Indicates errors with red underlines. When you hover over an indicated error, tooltip text displays the problem that was found in the code.

- **Context-sensitive Help:** Opens context-sensitive Help about the highlighted cmdlet if you press F1 when your cursor is in a cmdlet, or if you have part of a cmdlet highlighted.

- **AutoSave:** Automatically saves your open scripts every two minutes.

Identify ISE Panes

The ISE has three panes, as shown in Figure 10.1: Script, Console, and Command Add-on.

Starting at the bottom left, the Console pane is similar to the PowerShell command prompt that you have already used. Also, the output of scripts appears in the Console pane as you run them in the ISE. Next to Console pane is the Command Add-on pane where you can search for cmdlets. You can also restrict your search to a particular module, such as the virtualmachinemanager cmdlets.

At the top, the Script pane makes it very convenient to have an editor in the PowerShell ISE. Because the ISE is a GUI tool, you can use the familiar cut, copy, and paste features.

The ISE's true power is that it helps you enter and update PowerShell commands easily. Although you can edit commands and scripts in Notepad and then run them in Power-Shell command windows, it is much easier to do everything in one place. An added bonus is that you can work with up to eight sessions at the same time, which is particularly useful when you want to borrow some commands from a previous script.

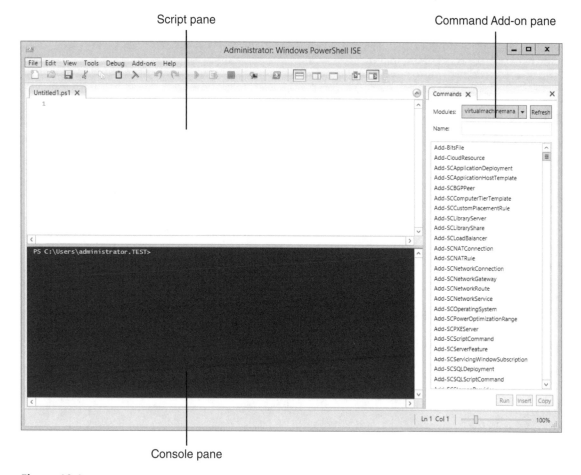

Figure 10.1
ISE with three panes identified.
Source: Windows Server 2012 R2/Windows PowerShell 4.0 ISE.

1. Go to the VMM virtual machine.

2. Press the Windows key, type Power, right-click the Windows PowerShell ISE icon, and then click Pin to taskbar. Click the Desktop.

3. To open the ISE, click the ISE icon on the taskbar.

4. To add the Script pane, click View and then click Show Script Pane.

5. To change the Command Add-on to Virtual Machine Manager scripts, click the Modules chevron, scroll, and select virtualmachinemanager.

Changing the Font Used in the ISE Console

You may find font sizes not to your liking. To make these changes, click Tools and select Options. To pick a larger font, click the Font size chevron.

Overview of ISE Toolbar

Figure 10.2 indicates the multitude of buttons on the toolbar. If you have used a recent Microsoft Office product, you are familiar with the first nine buttons. To clear the output pane, click the Clear Output Pane button, which looks like a blue squeegee.

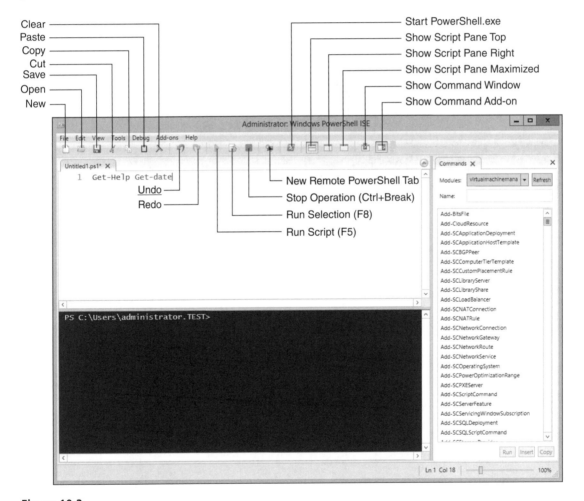

Figure 10.2
ISE toolbar buttons identified.

Source: Windows Server 2012 R2/Windows PowerShell 4.0 ISE.

The next five buttons control the execution of scripts. You can launch a script directly from the PowerShell ISE by pressing F5. If you have several versions of the cmdlets in the editor, just select a particular line and press F8. You can also run part of a set of cmdlets in the editor by highlighting the portion and then pressing F8.

To run a PowerShell script on a remote computer, select the New Remote PowerShell Tab button. After entering a computername, username, and password, the script runs on the remote computer. To run PowerShell cmdlets in a new session on the same computer, you select the Start PowerShell.exe button.

Of the remaining five buttons, the next three control the display and placement of the three panes in the ISE. If you need more information about the properties of a cmdlet, highlight the cmdlet and select Show Command Window. A pop-up appears that shows the properties of the cmdlet. By highlighting a cmdlet and pressing the F1 key, you can see a Help pop-up. The Show Command Add-on button toggles the Command Add-on pane.

Changing the Theme Used in the ISE Console

You may want to change the colors for the script and command panels. To make these changes, click Tools and select Options. To pick a Theme, click Manage Themes. Select the theme of your choice and click OK. Click Apply to see your choice.

Working with Intellisense

Microsoft touts Intellisense as an automatic-completion assistance feature. It displays clickable menus of potentially matching cmdlets, parameters, and parameter values as you type.

With the addition of Intellisense, it is easier to discover cmdlets and syntax when you use ISE to create scripts. Of course, you can ignore the Intellisense suggestions, as you must double-click the suggestion to include it in your script.

Using PowerShell Profiles

The ISE profile is simply a script or text file that runs each time ISE starts. You can use the profile to set up your ISE environment. These items enable you to use ISE more easily:

`Set-ExecutionPolicy unrestricted —force`—Without this cmdlet, the profile will not load.

`$cloud =Get-SCCloud —Name "PRIVATE"`—This cmdlet provides the cloud object for PRIVATE.

`$hosts =Get-SCVMHost –VMHostGroup "COMPUTE"`—This cmdlet provides the host objects for the host computers in COMPUTE.

`$psISE.Options.FontSize = 14`—This cmdlet changes the font size to 14 points.

Establish $profile File

Since you use the ISE to run Windows PowerShell, you can create an ISE-specific profile for users to run scripts on your hosts. Figure 10.3 shows the creation of the `$profile` file.

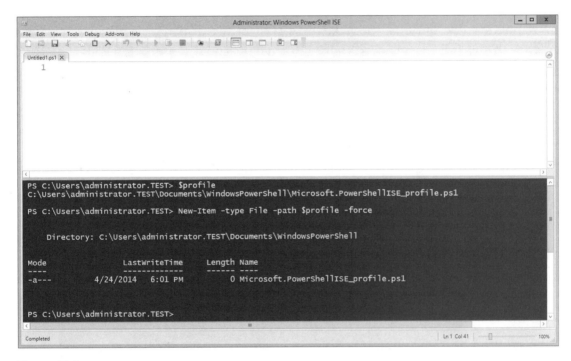

Figure 10.3
`$profile` file created.
Source: Windows Server 2012 R2/Windows PowerShell 4.0 ISE.

1. To toggle the Command Add-on pane off, click the Show Command Add-on button.

2. In the command pane, type this variable and press Enter.

   `$profile`

3. In the command pane, type this cmdlet and press Enter.

   `New-Item –Type file –path $profile –Force`

4. Click the Clear Console Pane button (blue squeegee).

Changing the Pane Sizes

From time to time, you might want to change the sizes of the Script and Console panes. Grasp the top of the Console pane and drag up or down.

Create $profile Script

You can create a script with ISE and save it in a path indicated by the $profile path (see Figure 10.4). This will be your first exposure to ISE Intellisense. When the ISE is restarted, your cmdlets are applied.

Figure 10.4
$profile script created.

Source: Windows Server 2012 R2/Windows PowerShell 4.0 ISE.

1. To open and edit the profile, click File, click Open, and navigate to the Microsoft.PowerShellISE_profile. Click Open.

2. To use Intellisense to complete the cmdlet, type Set-E. Double-click Set-ExecutionPolicy.

3. Type unrestricted –force and press Enter.

4. Type this cmdlet and press Enter.

   $cloud =Get-SCCloud –Name "PRIVATE"

5. Type $hosts =Get-SCVMHost –VM. Double-click VMHostGroup. Type "COMPUTE" and press Enter.

Intellisense Not Working

If Intellisense is not assisting with the creation of VMM cmdlets, you need to load the Virtual Machine Manager module. To do this, click the View menu and click Show Command Add-on. Then click the Modules chevron, scroll, and select virtualmachinemanager.

6. Type this cmdlet and press Enter.

   $psISE.Options.FontSize = 14

7. Review entries and make corrections as need. These entries are in the Using PowerShell Profiles section.

8. When editing is completed, click File and select Save.

9. Close the ISE window.

10. To open the ISE, click the ISE icon on the taskbar.

11. Wait for the $profile script to complete.

12. To verify the $cloud variable, type $cloud.Name in the Command pane and press Enter.

13. To verify the $hosts variable, type $hosts.ComputerName in the Command pane and press Enter.

WRITING SCRIPTS TO MANAGE VIRTUAL MACHINES

In this section, you will learn to write scripts to manage virtual machines. The module for the Virtual Machine Manager module contains 615 cmdlets. (Hereafter, the Virtual Machine Manager module is called *VMM module*.) With these cmdlets, you can create scripts to manage your virtual machines.

An easy way to build and test scripts is to use incremental development. You can implement and test the script incrementally, adding a little more each time until the script is finished. By using this technique, you minimize potential scripting errors. You maximize your success at scripting by breaking a complex script into small increments, which have a high probability of producing usable results. Should you not get the intended results, only a small change is required to correct the problem.

Gaining Information about Virtual Machines

The VMM module has a number of cmdlets that determine the status of virtual machines on a given host computer. To save time when working with these cmdlets, you created a variable named $cloud in the ISE profile, which holds the object with the name for the cloud. $hosts contains the two names of the host computers. To see the names of the host computers and the virtual machines, you construct a PowerShell script. Figure 10.5 shows the first cmdlet for this script.

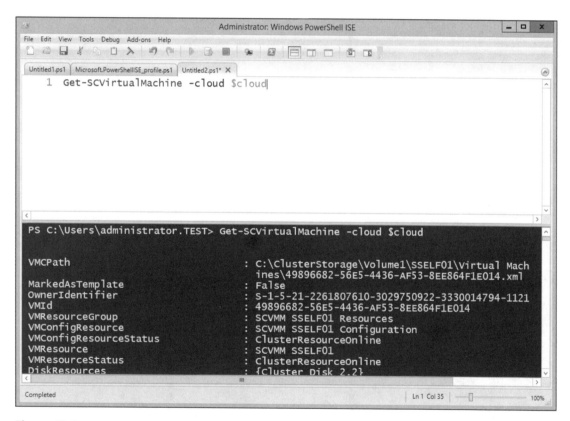

Figure 10.5
Script to see virtual machines properties.
Source: Windows Server 2012 R2/Windows PowerShell 4.0 ISE.

1. To start a new script, click the New button.

2. Type Get-SCV, scroll, and double-click Get-SCVirtualMachine.

3. Type –Cloud $cloud and press Enter.

4. Click the Clear Console Pane button.

5. Click the Run Script button or the F5 key.

6. Correct any errors and rerun the script.

7. Scroll the output pane back to the start of the output.

Add Sort by Host and Virtual Machine to Script

There are numerous properties that are available. You can scroll the property lists and locate the properties for the host computer and virtual machine. Next, you add the Sort-Object cmdlet to your script. Since this is a basic tool for many future scripts, you save it.

You can place cmdlets on successive lines, by placing the pipe symbol | at the end of the line (see Figure 10.6).

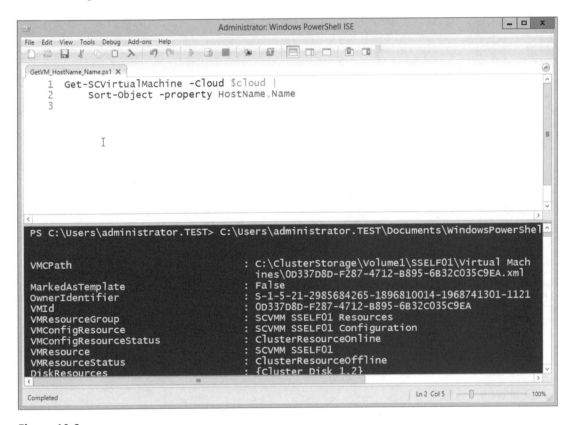

Figure 10.6
Script with properties sorted by the host and virtual machine.

Source: Windows Server 2012 R2/Windows PowerShell 4.0 ISE.

1. Type | at the end of line 1 and press Enter. Press Tab.

2. Type Sort- and double-click Sort-Object. Type –property.

3. Scroll the property list in the Command pane and locate the property for the host computer. (Value is compute1.test.local or compute2.test.local.)

4. Type the property you found in step 3. Type , (comma).

5. Scroll the property list in the Command pane and locate the property for the virtual machine. (Value is SSELF01, SSELF02, SSELF04, or SSELF04.)

6. Type the property you found in step 5.

7. Click the Clear Console Pane button.

8. To run the script, press F5.

9. Correct any errors and rerun the script.

10. To save the script, click File, click Save As, enter GetVM_SortHostName_Name, and then click Save.

Save Script Before Running

If you run a script after you save it, you will be asked to confirm a save prior to running the script.

Add Format-Table to Script

From the available properties, you can decide to format with only the HostName and Name. You want the virtual machine names (property Name) to appear grouped by the host computers (property HostName). To do this you append -GroupBy Hostname after the –Property Name.

Recall that you can copy (Ctrl+c) and paste (Ctrl+v), which provides speed and accuracy when building scripts. This addition is shown in Figure 10.7.

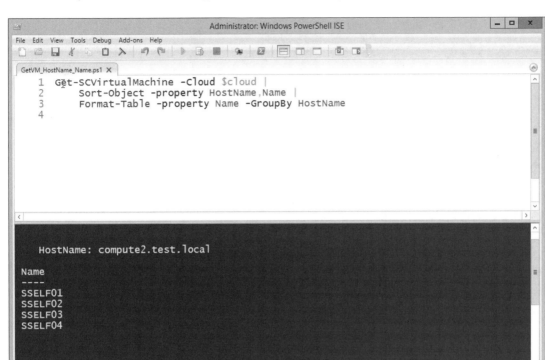

Figure 10.7
Script to see virtual machine properties sorted by host and virtual machine.
Source: Windows Server 2012 R2/Windows PowerShell 4.0 ISE.

1. Type | at the end of line 1 and press Enter. Press Tab.

2. Type Format- and double-click Format-Table.

3. With your mouse, select –property HostName, Name. Press Ctrl+c.

4. Move the mouse pointer after Format-Table. Press Ctrl+v.

5. Remove the HostName,.

6. To add the grouping, type –GroupBy HostName after Name.

7. Click the Clear Console Pane button.

8. To run the script, press F5.

9. Correct any errors and rerun the script.

10. Leave the script for further exercises.

Useful Properties about Virtual Machines

There are over 150 properties for the Get-SCVirtualMachine cmdlet. Table 10.1 lists ones that you might find to be the most useful. You will want to consider these as you build scripts to gain information for your virtual machines.

Table 10.1 Useful Properties for Virtual Machines

Property	Example
ComputerName	SSELF01
UserRole	AppSelfService
Owner	TEST\sself
Status	Running
PerfCPUUtilization	0
PerfMemory	512
PerfDiskBytesRead	0
PerfDiskBytesWrite	1023
PerfNetworkBytesRead	0
PerfNetworkBytesWrite	0
CreationSource	Private VM Template
CheckpointLocation	C:\ClusterStorage\Volume1\SSELF01
SelfServiceUserRole	AppSelfService
Location	C:\ClusterStorage\Volume1\SSELF01
CreationTime	4/13/2014 52216 PM
OperatingSystem	Windows Server 2012 R2 Standard
TotalSize	8528494592 (Bytes)
Name	SSELF01 (VHD)
AddedTime	4/13/2014 52216 PM
ModifiedTime	4/24/2014 35507 PM

Documenting Virtual Machines

It is a good practice to document your virtual machines. To do so, you continue with the script that you created previously and select the properties for the documentation (see Figure 10.8).

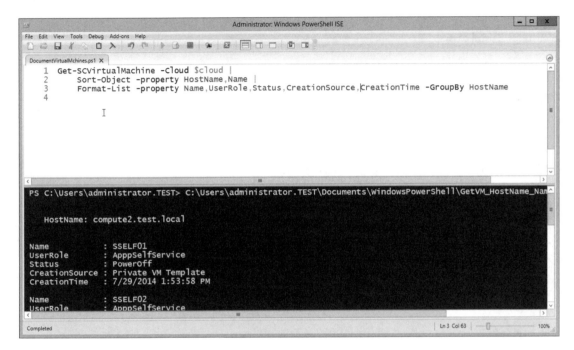

Figure 10.8
Script to see virtual machine properties sorted by host and virtual machine.
Source: Windows Server 2012 R2/Windows PowerShell 4.0 ISE.

1. Edit `Format-Table` to be `Format-List`.

2. To add additional properties, type `UserRole`, `Owner`, `Status`, `CreationSource`, `CreationTime` after `Name`.

3. Click the Clear Console Pane button.

4. If necessary, close the Get Command window.

5. To run the script, press F5.

6. Correct any errors and rerun the script.

7. To save the script, click File, click Save As, enter DocumentVirtualMachines, and then click Save.

Using Arrays in Scripts

Variables can be used to store arrays. Think of an array as an indexed list of values. Each element in the array is accessed by its index number. Figure 10.9 shows an array of colors, such as the cable colors used to identify the cables for the four networks used in the private cloud. The numbers 0, 1, 2, and 3 are the index numbers that are used to retrieve each element. For example, $Colors[2] would be the third element (PowerShell starts the indices with zero) with a value of Red.

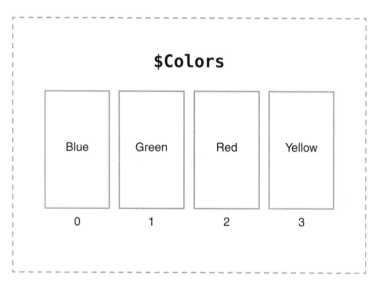

$Colors

Blue	Green	Red	Yellow
0	1	2	3

Figure 10.9
$Colors array has four elements.
© 2014 Cengage Learning®.

To load the $Colors array, you use this command:

```
$Colors = @("Blue","Green","Red","Yellow")
```

You use ForEach to process the elements of the array. Here is a block of PowerShell code that illustrates the use of ForEach to output the values for the $Colors array. The nice thing about ForEach is that it knows how many elements to process. In this case, $Colors[0], $Colors[1], $Colors[2], and $Colors[3] are selected.

```
ForEach ($Color in $Colors) {
$Color
}
```

Pay close attention to the syntax. You could have used any appropriate variable for $Color, such as $I. Notice that the braces { } while on separate lines are paired. Figure 10.10 shows this code.

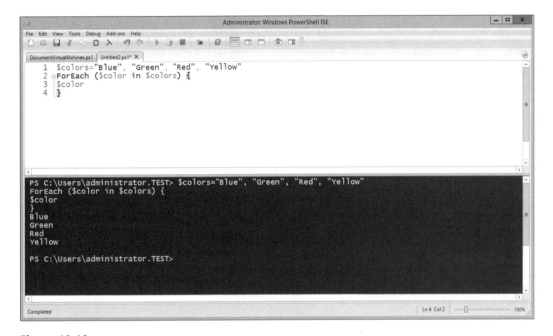

Figure 10.10
Sample script to output the colors.
Source: Windows Server 2012 R2/Windows PowerShell 4.0 ISE.

1. To open a new session, click File and then click New.

2. To load the $Colors array, enter the following command and press Enter.
   ```
   $Colors="Blue","Green","Red","Yellow"
   ```

3. To step through the array, enter the following command and press Enter.
   ```
   ForEach ( $Color in $Colors) {
   ```

4. To output each color, type $Color and press Enter.

5. To close the code block, type } and press Enter.

6. To run the script, press F5.

7. Correct any errors and rerun the script.

Now, you probably will never need to output these four colors. But this technique is useful when you need to process multiple virtual machines when working with a cmdlet that only accepts one virtual machine at a time. This is true for many of the Get- cmdlets in the next section.

Useful Get- cmdlets

There are over 170 Get- cmdlets in the VMM module. Table 10.2 shows the most useful cmdlets with their suggested usage. You use this table when locating a cmdlet to obtain information about your VMM environment.

Table 10.2   Useful Get- Cmdlets

cmdlet	Suggested Usage for a Private Cloud
Get-SCCloud	Returns cloud object.
Get-SCCloudCapacity	Returns the number of virtual CPUs, custom quota points, storage, and memory assigned.
Get-SCCloudUsage	Gets cloud usage data. (See Get-SCCloudCapacity.)
Get-SCGuestOSProfile	Gets a guest operating system profile object from the VMM library.
Get-SCHardwareProfile	Gets hardware profile objects from the VMM library.
Get-SCHostReserve	Gets the host reserve and placement settings for a host group.
Get-SCIPAddress	Gets allocated static and virtual IP addresses.
Get-SCLibraryShare	Gets VMM library shares.
Get-SCLogicalNetwork	Gets a logical network object.
Get-SCLogicalNetworkDefinition	Gets a logical network definition.
Get-SCLogicalSwitch	Gets a logical switch.
Get-SCPerformanceData	Gets performance data for host groups, clusters, hosts, and virtual machines.
Get-SCStorageDisk	Gets a storage disk object for the specified host from the VMM database.
Get-SCStorageLogicalUnit	Gets a storage logical unit object.
Get-SCUserRole	Gets a VMM user role.
Get-SCUserRoleMembership	Gets information about the user roles of which the current user or a specified user is a member.
Get-SCUserRolePermission	Gets a user role permission instance.
Get-SCVirtualNetwork	Gets virtual network objects configured on a VMM host.

(Continued)

Table 10.2   Useful **Get-** Cmdlets (*Continued*)

cmdlet	Suggested Usage for a Private Cloud
Get-SCVMHost	Gets virtual machine host objects from the Virtual Machine Manager database.
Get-SCVMHostGroup	Gets a host group object from the VMM database.
Get-SCVMNetworkAdapter	Gets physical network adapter objects on a VMM host.
Get-SCVMNetwork	Gets a VM network.
Get-SCVMSubnet	Gets a VM subnet.

Report Memory Usage for Virtual Machines

One of the performance measures that you need to track is memory usage. To do this you use the Get-SCPerformanceData cmdlet. However, this cmdlet can only retrieve memory usage for one virtual machine at a time. The ForEach command provides the methodology to remedy this problem. Figure 10.11 shows the completed script for this task. In the steps that follow, you will use Intellisense to aid in the construction of this script.

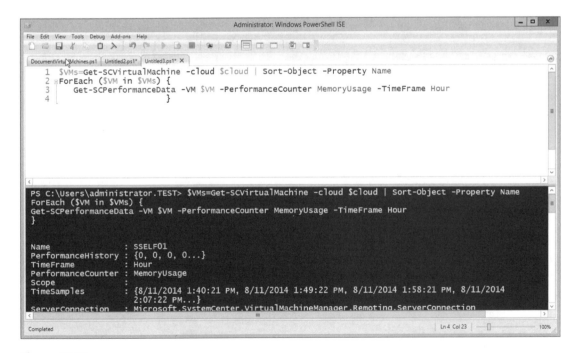

Figure 10.11
Report performance data for virtual machines.
Source: Windows Server 2012 R2/Windows PowerShell 4.0 ISE.

1. Click the Clear Console Pane button.

2. To start a new script, click File and then select New.

3. To get the sorted names of the virtual machine, enter the following command on one line and press Enter.

   ```
   $VMs=Get-SCVirtualMachines —cloud $cloud | Sort-Object —Property Name
   ```

4. To process one virtual machine at a time, enter the following command on one line and press Enter.
   ```
   ForEach ($VM in $VMs) {
   ```
5. To create the performance data cmdlet, type `Get-SCP` and double-click `Get-SCPerformanceData`.

6. To enter the virtual machine array, type `–`, double-click `–VM`, type `$`, and double-click `$VM`.

7. To enter a performance counter, type `-P` and then double-click `–PerformanceCounter` and press the spacebar. Double-click `MemoryUsage`.

8. To enter the time frame, type `–`, double-click `–TimeFrame`, press the spacebar, and double-click `Hour`.

9. To close the braces, press Enter and then type `}`.

10. To run the script, press F5.

11. Correct any errors and rerun the script.

12. To save the script, click File, click Save As, enter ReportMemoryUsage, and then click Save.

Use Tab to Offset the Embedded Cmdlets

It's a good practice to offset embedded cmdlets to show blocking and increase the readability of your scripts.

Using Get-Member to Design a Report

When designing a report, you might find it helpful to use `Get-Member` to determine the available properties. For example there are over 160 properties for `Get-SCVirtualMachine`. The old saying goes: If it's not here, you don't need it!

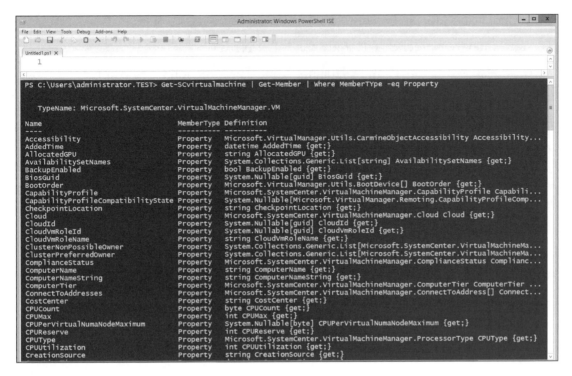

Figure 10.12
List properties for `Get-SCVirtualMachine` cmdlet.
Source: Windows Server 2012 R2/Windows PowerShell 4.0 ISE.

1. Click the Clear Console Pane button.

2. Type the following line in the Command Console and press Enter.

   `Get-SCVirtualMachine | Get-Member | Where MemberType —eq Property`

3. Scroll through the output in the Command Console and view the properties that you find interesting.

Modify Existing Report

When creating scripts, you can save time and effort by starting with an existing script file (see Figure 10.13). Of course, you copied five properties down for your new report.

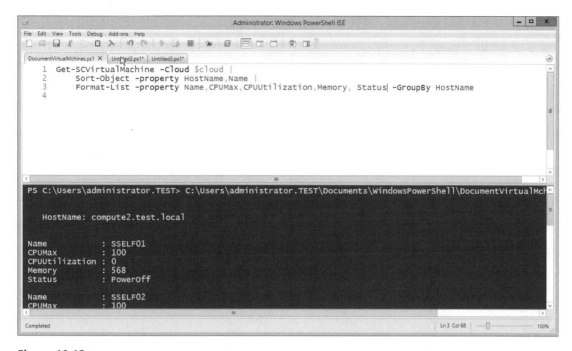

Figure 10.13
Using existing script.

Source: Windows Server 2012 R2/Windows PowerShell 4.0 ISE.

1. To open an existing script, click File, click Open, select DocumentVirtualMachines, and then click Open.

2. Click the Clear Console Pane button.

3. Edit the script to replace the `UserRole`, `Owner`, `Status`, `CreationSource`, and `CreationTime` with your five properties.

4. To run the script, press F5.

5. Correct any errors and rerun the script.

6. Keep the script for further exercises.

Replacing Items in a Script

Recall from using Microsoft Office that you can replace a word by doubling-clicking on the word and then typing the new word. This makes it easy to edit scripts where you are overtyping a property.

Working with Machine States

You will benefit from learning PowerShell to construct scripts to manage virtual machines. In this section, you will learn to construct such scripts.

Determining Virtual Machine Status

One of the properties available with Get-SCVirtualMachine is Status. With this property, you can determine whether a virtual machine is Running or Stopped.

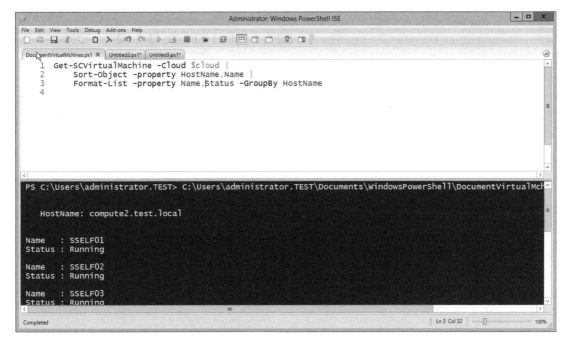

Figure 10.14
Determine the status of a virtual machine.

Source: Windows Server 2012 R2/Windows PowerShell 4.0 ISE.

1. Click the Clear Console Pane button.

2. Edit the script to replace your five properties with Status.

3. To run the script, press F5.

4. Correct any errors, and rerun the script.

5. Keep the script for further exercises.

If Construct

The If construct in PowerShell operates as the If in other scripting languages. The If is followed by a conditional statement in paired parentheses (...). This is followed by the open brace {. Then you place the cmdlet(s) and follow the cmdlet(s) with a close brace }.

```
If (condition)  {
"cmdlet(s) do something"
                }
```

You use If to control execution of cmdlets. As an example of an If condition consider this:

```
If ($Color –eq "Blue")
```

And when combined with a cmdlet, you have something this:

```
If ($Color –eq "Blue")    {
    Write-Host "Management"
                    }
```

Shut Down Running Virtual Machines

You cannot shut down a stopped machine. With If, you check to see if the virtual machine is running before stopping the virtual machine. The If is shown in the script being constructed in Figure 10.15.

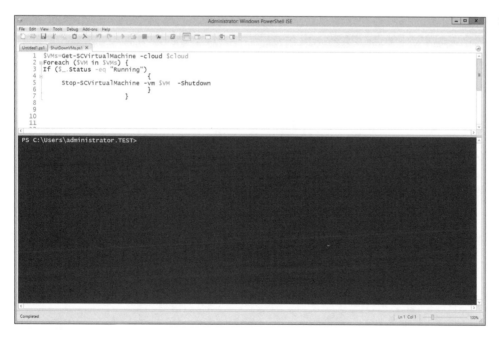

Figure 10.15
Shut down running virtual machines.

Source: Windows Server 2012 R2/Windows PowerShell 4.0 ISE.

1. To open an existing script, click File, click Open, select DocumentVirtualMachines, and then click Open.

2. To copy a line from a previous script, highlight the first line (without the |) with your mouse, click Edit, and then select Copy.

3. Click the Untitled.ps1 tab, click Edit, and select Paste.

4. Edit $VMs= at the beginning of line 1. Press End and then press Enter.

5. On the second line, type this command and press Enter.

   ```
   ForEach ($VM in $VMs) {
   ```

6. Type this command and press Enter.

   ```
   If ($VM.Status –eq "Running")  {
   ```

7. Type this command and press Enter.

   ```
   Stop-SCVirtualMachine –vm $VM –Shutdown
   ```

8. Type the two closing braces aligned with the opening braces.

9. To run the script, press F5.

10. Wait for the virtual machines to be shutdown. The Stop Operation button changes from red to gray.

11. Correct any errors and rerun the script.

12. To save the script, click File, click Save As, enter ShutDownVMs, and then click Save.

13. Return to the VMs and Services view and verify the status of the four virtual machines.

Start Stopped Virtual Machines

It will be an easy task to modify the previous script to start stopped virtual machines. Just replace Running with PowerOff and Stop with Start. Figure 10.16 shows the solution.

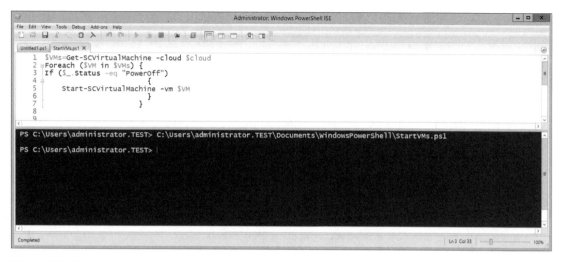

Figure 10.16
Start stopped virtual machines.
Source: Windows Server 2012 R2/Windows PowerShell 4.0 ISE.

1. Edit "Running" to "PowerOff" in line 3.

2. Edit Stop- to Start- in line 5. Remove the –Shutdown.

3. To run the script, press F5.

4. Wait for the virtual machines to be started. The Stop Operation button changes from red to gray.

5. Correct any errors and rerun the script.

6. To save the script, click File, click Save As, enter StartVMs, and then click Save.

7. Return to the virtual machine and verify the status of the four virtual machines.

WRITING SCRIPTS TO CREATE USER ACCOUNTS

The Active Directory module for Windows PowerShell consolidates a group of Active Directory Domain Services (AD DS) cmdlets. You use these 76 cmdlets to manage your AD DS. For example, you can use the Active Directory module to accomplish many of the common tasks that are associated with account management.

You accomplish these tasks by running PowerShell on the ADDS virtual machine.

Preparing the ISE on ADDS

To prepare the ISE on ADDS to create and run scripts, complete these steps:

1. Go to the ADDS virtual machine.

2. Click Local Server on Server Manager.

3. To open the ISE, click Tools and select Windows PowerShell ISE.

4. To add the Script pane, click View and then click Show Script Pane.

5. In the command pane, type this variable and press Enter.

   ```
   $profile
   ```

6. In the command pane, type this cmdlet and press Enter.

   ```
   New-Item –Type file –path $profile –Force
   ```

7. Click the Clear Console Pane button.

8. To open and edit the profile, click File, click Open, and navigate to Microsoft.PowerShellISE_profile. Click Open.

9. To use Intellisense to complete the Set-ExecutionPolicy cmdlet, type Set-E. Double-click Set-ExecutionPolicy.

10. Type unrestricted –force and press Enter.

11. To increase the font size, type this cmdlet and press Enter.

    ```
    $psISE.Options.FontSize = 14
    ```

12. To load the Active Directory Module, type Import-Module ActiveDirectory and press Enter.

13. Review the entries and make corrections as needed.

14. When editing is completed, click File and select Save.

15. Type Update-Help in the command pane and then press Enter.

16. Wait for the Get-Help files to be downloaded and installed.

17. Close the ISE window.

18. To open the ISE and activate the profile, click Tools and select Windows PowerShell ISE.

19. Wait for the Active Directory module to load.

Creating a New User Account

One repetitive task for which scripting is highly effective is the creation of numerous new users in Active Directory. You can use the `New-ADUser` cmdlet to create a new user account.

```
New-ADUser –Name "MSmart" -SamAccountName "MSmart"
–GivenName "Miles" –Surname "Smart"
–DisplayName "Miles Smart"
-Path "CN=Users,DC=Test,DC-Local"
-AccountPassword (ConvertTo-SecureString -AsPlainText "Pa$$w0rd" -Force)
```

Recall that each property is preceded by a hyphen. For example, `-GivenName` is the given or first name, `-Surname` is the last name, and so on. `–Path` provides the location to place the user account. A secure password is created for `-AccountPassword` by the conversion code placed after the property.

The items that change for each user are: `Name`, `SamAccountName`, `GivenName`, `Surname`, and `DisplayName`.

Create an Input File with User Account Data

You might create a CSV file for these items with the variable names as column headings for the spreadsheet. Figure 10.17 shows a completed spreadsheet with user data.

Since a spreadsheet program is not available on the ADDS virtual machine, you create a CSV file in a text editor such as Notepad. Just press the , key after each column and press Enter at the end of each row. The data will not align vertically under the heading line, which is OK. You should enclose values with a space within quotes.

	A	B	C	D	E	F
1	Name	SamAccountName	GivenName	SurName	DisplayName	
2	MSmart	MSmart	Miles	Smart	Miles Smart	
3	FDunn	FDunn	Frank	Dunn	Frank Dunn	
4	REspinoza	REspinoza	Ruben	Espinoza	Ruben Espinoza	
5	DHawk	DHawk	Dave	Hawk	Dave Hawk	
6						

Figure 10.17
Spreadsheet used as input to script.
Source: Microsoft Excel 2013.

1. To open Notepad, press the Windows key, type Notepad, and click Notepad.

2. Type Name,SamAccountName,GivenName,SurName,DisplayName and press Enter.

3. Type MSmart,MSmart,Miles,Smart, 'Miles Smart' and press Enter.

4. Using this scheme, enter the remaining values in Figure 10.17.

5. To save the file, click File, and click Save As.

6. To navigate to the Administrator folder, click the Up arrow next to the address bar.

7. To eliminate the .txt extension, click the Save as type chevron and select All Files. Enter AppSelfService.csv and then click Save.

Creating New User Accounts

You will import the csv file and use the New-ADUser command to create the user accounts. This technique allows you to create hundreds of items quickly. The completed script is shown in Figure 10.18.

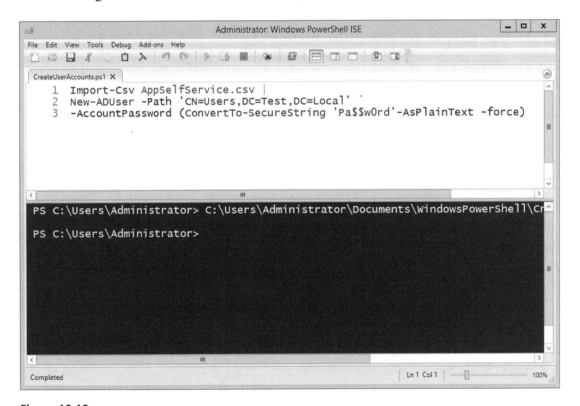

Figure 10.18

Script to create new users.

Source: Windows Server 2012 R2/Windows PowerShell 4.0 ISE.

1. Return to the ISE and the Command Console.

2. To verify that the data was entered properly, type `Import-`, scroll and double-click `Import-Csv`, type `AppSelfService.csv | Format-List`, and press Enter.

3. To correct the data, return to Notepad.

Combining Lines for a Long Cmdlet

The backtick, or grave character, is used to break lines for long cmdlets. The backtick key ` is located below the Esc key. To continue a cmdlet, press ` and Enter. The ` must be followed immediately by the Enter key.

4. To start a new script, click the New button.

5. Type the following command in the ISE Script pane and press Enter.

```
Import-Csv AppSelfService.csv |
```

6. Type the following command, type the `, and then press Enter.

```
New-ADUser –Path 'CN=Users,DC=Test,DC=Local'
```

7. Type the following command on one line and then press Enter.

```
-AccountPassword (ConvertTo-SecureString 'Pa$$w0rd' AsPlainText –force)
```

8. To save the script, click File, click Save As, enter CreateUserAccounts.ps1, and click Save.

9. To run the script, press F5.

10. Correct any errors and rerun the script.

Delete Users to Rerun the Script

To rerun the script, you may need to check to see if the user accounts were created. To do this, open Active Directory Users and Computers and delete these user accounts: MSmart,FDunn, REspinoza, and DHawk.

11. To verify that the users were added, type the following command in the Command Console and press Enter.

```
Get-ADUser –Identity dhawk
```

Adding Users to Groups

With the `Add-ADGroupMember` cmdlet, you can add your users to the `AppSelfService` and `Private Security` groups. `$u.Name` pulls the `Name` from the Users array, as shown in Figure 10.19.

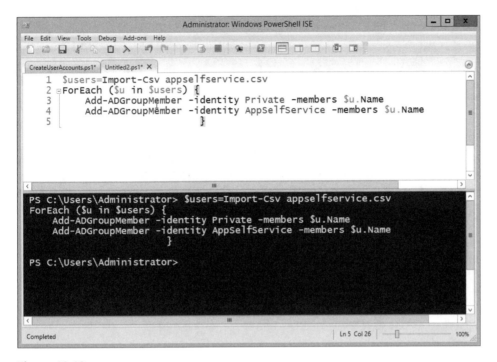

Figure 10.19
Script to add users to groups.
Source: Windows Server 2012 R2/ Windows PowerShell 4.0 ISE.

1. To start a new script, click the New button.

2. Type the following command and then press Enter.

   ```
   $users =Import-Csv AppSelfService.csv
   ```

3. Type the following command and then press Enter.

   ```
   ForEach ($u in $users)  {
   ```

4. Type the following command and then press Enter.

   ```
   Add-ADGroupMember –identity Private –members $u.Name
   ```

5. Type the following command and then press Enter.

   ```
   Add-ADGroupMember –identity AppSelfService –members $u.Name
   ```

6. Type a } and press Enter.

7. To run the script, press F5.

8. Correct any errors and rerun the script.

9. To verify that the users were added to Private, type the following command in the Command Console and press Enter.

   `Get-ADGroupMember –identity Private | Format-List –property name`

10. Press the Up arrow twice.

11. Edit the previous command, replacing `Private` with `AppSelfService` and press Enter.

WRITING SCRIPTS TO DEPLOY VIRTUAL MACHINES

In this section, you will prepare a script to provision virtual machines in the private cloud. You have seen scripts used by VMM to complete a number of tasks. Scripts that accompany wizards, such as the Create Virtual Machine Wizard, provide an opportunity to review the script in Notepad by clicking View Script. While the script creates a virtual machine, you use it as the basis for a script to deploy numerous virtual machines.

Obtain Sample Script

To provision virtual machines, you run the Create Virtual Machine Wizard to obtain the script that VMM uses to deploy a new virtual machine to the cloud. This is a script to create a specific virtual machine. Figure 10.20 shows the relevant portion of the script.

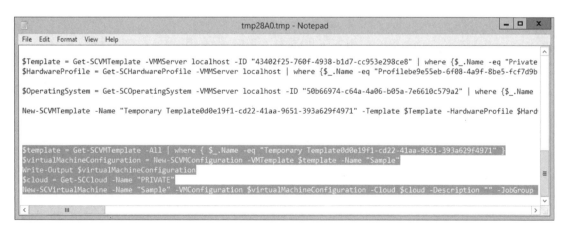

Figure 10.20
Relevant portion of the script.

Source: Windows Server 2012 R2/ Virtual Machine Manager 2012 R2.

1. Return to VMM and the VMM console.

2. To start the Create Virtual Machine Wizard, click VMs and Services, right-click on PRIVATE, and select Create Virtual Machine.

3. To select a template, click Browse, click Private VM Template, and then click OK. Click Next.

4. Enter Sample for the Virtual machine name and then click Next.

5. Review the Hardware profile and then click Next.

6. Review the destination and then click Next.

7. Review the cloud and then click Next twice.

8. Click View Script.

Wait to Run the Script

After making a few minor changes, you will be making a test execution from the ISE. If you run the script now, your new script will most likely fail.

9. Scroll to the last five lines in the script. Highlight these last five lines (scroll to the right on the last line), click Edit, and then click Copy.

10. Click Cancel. Click Yes.

Review Sample Script

Figure 10.21 shows the lines that you grabbed for the Create Virtual Machine Wizard. After you review the script, you can see that these changes need to be made:

■ "Private VM Template" for the generated template name

■ A GUID variable for the –JobGroup on the last line

■ An –Owner property to identify the owner of the virtual machine.

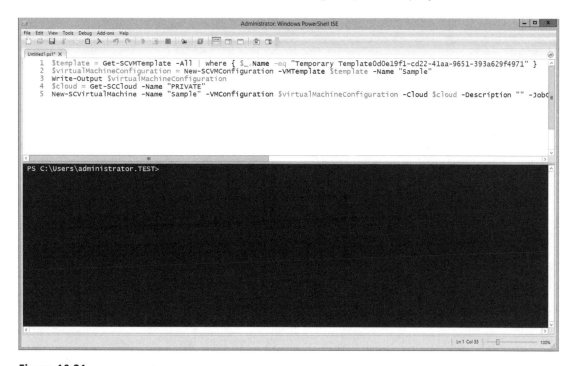

Figure 10.21
Relevant portion of the script in ISE.

Source: Windows Server 2012 R2/ Virtual Machine Manager 2012 R2.

1. Return to the ISE.

2. To paste the script, click Edit and then click Paste.

3. Scroll the content to the left.

Edit and Test Sample Script

You can make the changes that you have identified. Figure 10.22 shows the lines that you grabbed for the Create Virtual Machine Wizard and the necessary changes.

Figure 10.22
Edited script to rapidly deploy virtual machines.
Source: Windows Server 2012 R2/ Windows PowerShell 4.0 ISE.

1. Click File, click Save As, enter DeployVirtualstoPrivateCloud, and then click Save.

2. Replace the quoted text within the quotes in line 1 to "Private VM Template."

3. To create a new line, place the mouse pointer at the Home location for line 1 and press Enter.

4. Type the following command on line 1.

   ```
   $JobGuid = [System.Guid]::NewGuid().ToString()
   ```

Brackets around System.Guid.

There are brackets [ ] not parentheses around System.Guid. Type [System.Guid].

5. Scroll the last line to the right and replace the quoted text for the GUID within $JobQuid.

6. To create a new line, place the mouse pointer at the Home location for line 1 and press Enter.

7. Type the following command on line 1.

```
$Owner= "test\MSmart"
```

8. Scroll the last line to the right and add the following after −Cloud $cloud.

```
−Owner $Owner
```

9. Click the Save button.

10. To run the script, press F5.

11. Correct any errors and rerun the script.

12. To view the execution, return to VMM and the Jobs node.

Follow Execution in Jobs

To follow the progress of the submitted job, return to the Virtual Machine Manager window. The job progress is similar to Figure 10.23. Depending on processor speed, the new virtual machine will be created in three to five minutes. Since this sample virtual machine counts against Miles Smart's quota, you delete the sample virtual machine.

Figure 10.23
Follow execution of script.
Source: Windows Server 2012 R2/ Virtual Machine Manager 2012 R2.

1. Return to VMM and select the Jobs view.

2. Expand Create virtual machine in cloud.

3. Wait for the deployment to finish.

4. Return to the VMs and Services Node.

5. To delete the Sample virtual machine, right-click Sample and select Delete. Click Yes.

6. Wait for the deletion to finish.

Modify Script for Multiple Virtual Machines

With a few additional lines, you can create all two of Miles Smart's virtual machines. You need to make these changes:

- An array for the names of the two virtual machines.
- A ForEach code block to run the deployment for each of the two virtual machines.
- Replace each "Sample" with $VM.

These changes are shown in Figure 10.24.

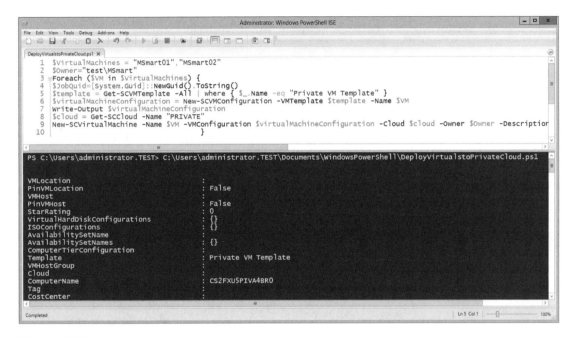

Figure 10.24
Modify script for multiple machines.
Source: Windows Server 2012 R2/ Windows PowerShell 4.0 ISE.

1. Return to the ISE.
2. Place the mouse pointer at the Home location for line 1 and press Enter.
3. Enter this at line 1.

    ```
    $VirtualMachines="MSmart01","MSmart02"
    ```

4. Place the mouse pointer at the Home location for line 3 and press Enter.
5. Enter this at line 3.

    ```
    ForEach ($VM in $VirtualMachines) {
    ```

6. Scroll to the end of line 9 and press Enter.

7. Type } on line 10.

8. On line 6, replace "Sample" with $VM.

9. On line 9, replace "Sample" with $VM.

10. To save the script, click the Save button.

11. To clear the Command Console, click the Clear Console Pane.

12. To run the script, press F5.

13. Correct any errors and rerun the script.

14. To view the execution, return to VMM and the Jobs node.

Follow Execution in Jobs

To follow the progress of the submitted jobs, return to the Virtual Machine Manager window. The job progress is similar to Figure 10.25. Depending on the processor speed, the new virtual machines will be deployed in 6 to 10 minutes.

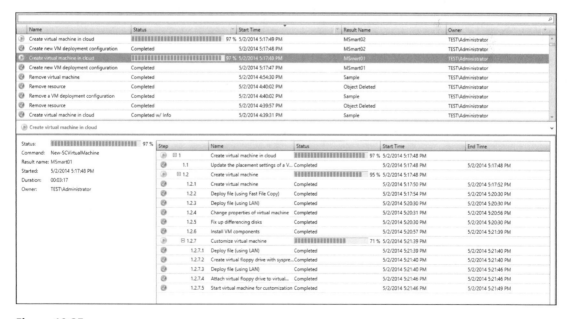

Figure 10.25
Follow execution of script.
Source: Windows Server 2012 R2/ Virtual Machine Manager 2012 R2.

1. Expand Create virtual machine in cloud.

2. Wait for the deployment to finish.

SUMMARY

This book prepared you to implement cloud computing solutions with their own network environments. You started with a conceptual foundation and by this chapter, you have learned to put in place a high-availability cluster to support a Microsoft private cloud.

Successive chapters helped you refine key skills you needed to implement private clouds using Microsoft technologies, including Windows Server 2012 R2, Hyper-V virtualization, System Center 2012 R2 Virtual Machine Manager, and System Center 2012 R2 App Controller. You learned to use the Virtual Machine Manager to work with library resources, to implement virtual networks, to configure storage, to create private clouds, and to deploy virtual machines. With the App Controller, you learned to deploy and access virtual machines in the private cloud. With PowerShell scripts, you learned to manage the private cloud.

Congratulations! You have acquired the private cloud computing skills you will need now and in the future.

In this chapter, you constructed scripts to simplify tasks using PowerShell 4.0. While you completed most activities to manage virtual machines, create user accounts, or deploy virtual machines with the GUI tools, you also gained efficiency by creating PowerShell scripts for repetitive tasks.

- Learned to use the Windows PowerShell Integrated Scripting Environment (ISE).
- Set up a user $profile for the ISE, which controls the ISE startup.
- Wrote scripts to view virtual properties and manage virtual machine states.
- Learned to use arrays and the ForEach construct.
- Wrote scripts for AD DS to create user accounts and place user accounts in security groups.
- Learned how to exploit VMM scripts to deploy multiple virtual machines.

CASE PROJECTS

Case 10-1: Add-on Tools Website

If you are interested in extending the features of the ISE, consider the Add-on Tools website. To go there, click the Add-ons menu and select Open Add-on Tools website.

Case 10-2: Free PowerShell Commands for Active Directory

Quest touts the ActiveRoles Management Shell for Active Directory as a set of free, predefined commands, which are designed to help administrators automate common, repetitive, and bulk management tasks for Active Directory, such as creating, removing, or updating objects in AD. Search for Quest PowerShell Commands for Active Directory.

Case 10-3: Sapien PowerShell Studio

When you are ready to make the next big step in PowerShell, you need to look at the Sapien PowerShell Studio. The quote "Work the way YOU want with PowerShell" says it all. They offer a free 45-day trial. The website is http://www.sapien.com/software/powershell_studio.

INDEX

433